The Chameleon Sings

Surviving and Healing

from

Childhood Sexual Abuse

a memoir

Ben Nuttall-Smith

Revised Edition 2007

Note for Librarians: A cataloguing record for this book is available from Library and Archives
Canada at www.collectionscanada.ca/amicus/index-e.html
ISBN 1-4120-6862-2

PUBLISHING™
Offices in Canada, USA, Ireland and UK

Book sales for North America and international:
Trafford Publishing, 6E–2333 Government St.,
Victoria, BC V8T 4P4 CANADA
phone 250 383 6864 (toll-free 1 888 232 4444)
fax 250 383 6804; email to orders@trafford.com
Book sales in Europe:
Trafford Publishing (UK) Limited, 9 Park End Street, 2nd Floor
Oxford, UK OX1 1HH UNITED KINGDOM
phone +44 (0)1865 722 113 (local rate 0845 230 9601)
facsimile +44 (0)1865 722 868; info.uk@trafford.com
Order online at:
trafford.com/05-1773

10 9 8 7 6 5 4

To write is to sit in judgement on oneself.
– Henrik Ibsen

In picture evoking language and dialogue, Ben Nuttall-Smith brings his life and era into sharp focus. Going beyond abuse survival, his life is a triumph about living fully.
— Bernice Lever, writer and editor.

This is a wonderful, evocative book about a very rough childhood and manhood – and surviving it.
— Margot Thomson, Retired Clinical Psychologist.

I have read your story cover to cover, could not put it down ... an amazing read, highlighting the uniqueness of each human being's life relating to God, neighbour, and self in their journey to wholeness.
— Father Tom Nicholson, Catholic priest.

Nuttall-Smith tells his story simply, thoroughly, and straight-forwardly and offers many useful insights. He manages to leaven the tragedy and pathos with humour.
For the hope that this offers, I recommend his book to all men. I especially recommend it to members of men's groups who are labouring with issues of personal recovery and fellowship.
— David C. Manning Professional Counsellor(retired)
and Leader of Men's Groups

Ben not only survives the misplaced guilt of childhood rape, he carries the weight of instilled Catholic guilt. Then members of the religious order to which he had dedicated thirteen years of his life are convicted for child sexual abuse. Guilt by association is added to an already overburdened conscience and the load becomes unbearable. Despite all this, the writer retains his faith conviction.
— Nora Sterling, Retired Counselling Psychologist

The Chameleon Sings tells the story of Ben Nuttall-Smith's survival and healing from Childhood abuse. Through this memoir, Ben offers help by example. And not just help. Hope – to those victims who still thrash about in the dark rooms of their childhood terror.

The chameleon takes on many identities, surviving to a ripe old age. He triumphs, but the journey is a precarious one filled with many dangers.

1

ACKNOWLEDGEMENTS

To my son who stood by me with support, and encouragement through some very tough times, keeping in constant touch, even when thousands of miles away. Without his love and understanding I might not have made it and this memoir might never have been written.

To David C. Manning, friend, mentor, teacher. I thank him for inspiration, advice, guidance, and painstaking editorial skill, and for hundreds of hours of dedicated help through the toughest phase of this work – sorting out feelings.

To my good friend, mentor and companion Margot Thomson for warmth , encouragement and understanding through months of editing and help in the crucial weeding process.

To Bernice Lever of The Canadian Authors' Association for editorial fine tuning and encouragement.

To the many friends who have loved me and supported me throughout my battle with this monstrous task. Special thanks to Chris, Carol, Nora, Ruth Kozak and Margaret Hume for dedicated reading and suggestions.

Thank you, thank you, thank you, and much love.

Ben Nuttall-Smith

INDEX

Foreward

One Saturday early in 1992, my wife and I went out for dinner and a movie. "The Prince of Tides" starred Nick Nolte as a trauma patient and Barbara Streisand as his psychiatrist. At the point where Tom [the protagonist as a boy], his mother, and his twin sister Savannah are violently raped by three armed ex-convicts, I experienced such a vivid flashback I sank down in my seat. I did not see, thus I did not recall, the remainder of the movie. I simply sat in shock and cried – audibly.

When I was seven and children were being evacuated from Nazi bombs, I was sent to live with an uncle in the heart of London. Night after night after night, while terror screamed down around us, my uncle raped me and made me his sex slave. I learned to keep the filthy secret, attempting to bury my guilt like soiled underwear beneath the compost heap. But that festering load kept popping up, more putrid than ever.

Mother married a French Canadian army major and I was given a new identity and a new country. I had crawled out of the ashes to live obsessed with the frantic search for an ever-elusive redemption and love.

At seventeen, I joined the Canadian Navy to be a hero in the Korean War. I was not hero material. I tried a stint as a Civil Rights volunteer when such activity was still a crime. Incompetent and unqualified, I had to be escorted back to Canada barely alive. Since I couldn't save my own soul, I would become a missionary and work "for the Lord" in deepest Africa. Bastards could not become priests! The Christian Brothers – a Catholic lay order – accepted me as a postulant and for thirteen years I studied and taught Music. I had found my niche and persevered until disillusionment set in and I could no longer keep my "Vow of Obedience".

4

Shortly after leaving the order, I met and married the love of my life, taught and lived happily for another twenty years until my demons resurfaced to destroy my marriage and end my teaching career.

I moved to a "handyman's delight" where I finally began to face my nightmares and conquer them. By writing, painting and performing with and for community groups, I gradually healed, found forgiveness for myself and for others who had hurt me. Then, having found love at last, I moved back to Vancouver where I met the wonderful person with whom I am able to share my life, my dreams and my grandchildren.

My life has been blessed. I could have become an alcoholic, drug-addict, male prostitute, abuser, criminal. There but for fortune ...

The Chameleon Sings is the story of that journey from childhood to healing with all its pains and joys, music, poetry, miracles, humour and immeasurable good fortune.

Ben Nuttall-Smith, March, 2007

Introduction:

There are other things I could tell you about my Uncle Siegvard. But not now. "... must never tell a soul."

Our Little Secret.

In 1941, the year I left my teddy bear behind
and would have learned to run,
you smothered all my faerie dreams
with Gold Leaf, London Dry, and flickering silver screen promises.
You oozed over me like the albuminous silver streak of a spotted slug.
You held me immersed in cobwebs and sour sweat.
Night after night after night,
you drove your poison dart deep, deep, deep –
and no one heard my sobs.

Outside your lair,
the Chelsea world screamed another agony.
Before the moaning sirens ceased, the shrieking metal fell;
it filled the crumbling streets with flames –
and running, running, running.

No place was safe
to hide away.

Chapter One
Fairies, Witches, and Birds In the Thatch   1937-1940

My mind goes way back
To that little room beneath the thatch
Where the wee folk came to play.

In 1937, Finchingfield was — in fact, it still is — a picture postcard village near Braintree in Essex, fifty-four miles northeast of London. At the centre of the village, a green rises from a duck pond with a foot bridge, a motor bridge and a war memorial. Up the hill toward Horsham stands the church of Saint John the Baptist dating to the 14th century.

We lived in Willets' Cottage, on the Causeway in Duck End. Though our roof was not thatched, many of the houses surrounding us were. Smoke curled from chimneys adding the delicious scent of woodsmoke to the perfume of open fields, farm horses, rabbit pie and Yorkshire pudding. From our bedroom window, my three-year-old sister Naomi and I, eleven months older, could stand on tiptoe and gaze down at pigs, cows and chickens.

We had a privy at the top of the garden. Close behind it stood an ancient wooden windmill. Because we had no fence or hedge to separate our garden from the field, my sister and I could jump in the hay, roll down the hill and play hide-and-seek right up to the top hedges behind the mill.

An old man in a raggedy coat was doing something behind the hedge. Naomi and I drew close but not too close.
"Hello children. Would you like to see my birdie? ... Don't be afraid."
We ran home. It wasn't a birdie.
"Don't be silly children", Mommy said, "that's only the farmer walking his dog. He wouldn't hurt you. He loves children. Now, go back out and play."

When Naomi heard the birds building nests beneath the eaves, I teased her. I told my sister the birds were coming to our bedroom to peck out her eyes 'cause she was "*sugar and spice and all things nice*". I'd be safe, "*Little boys are made of slugs and snails and puppy dogs' tails*". When my sister cried loud enough, Mommy spanked me with a hair brush.

Mother spanked me for climbing in the apple tree, too. The best thing about a spanking were the hugs I got after a long cry. Mother held me and rocked me until my sobbing subsided. Such moments of love and undivided attention felt wonderful, and I looked for them more and more.

Naomi was born in London. That made her more English than I, who had been born on safari near Tabora, Tanganyika. As my mother told it, because she had been frightened by a hyena, I was born African and forever laughing. I even smiled while being reprimanded, which was most annoying to those doing the scolding. Also, according to mother, since I was born in the bush, I had to be boiled in a pot for several days to make me blonde and fair skinned. Naomi, on the other hand, had been born fair.

> *"Never, never pet a rat. Rats bite."*
> *I petted a rat in the garden. Dettol stings like hot fire.*
> *Daddy killed the rat with the garden spade. Mommy*
> *poured Dettol on my finger. I cried. Naomi screamed.*
> *Mommy scolded. "A rat is not a pussy cat. a rat is a*
> *rat. Hold still."*

My father (Mother called him Fred, or Freddie or Darling) was "so terribly tall" – at least 5' 6" – and was forever bumping his head on the beam above the door into the kitchen. He was blonde like my sister and me and quite slim. My mother, Alice May, was fabulously beautiful (as all mothers no doubt are). Heads turned wherever we went. Of course, I always thought it was because she had such adorable children. Both parents smoked *Players Navy Cut* from the silver cigarette box on the living room table by the fireplace.

I can't remember my father working at anything in those early years. My mother had an allowance from Denmark, and my father probably received money from his father. Since my dad had been a reporter for the *London Times*, perhaps he submitted articles or stories about country life or bunny rabbits or the fairies that lived in our garden. Both parents certainly had time and the means to enjoy living in a village such as Finchingfield. Apart from cricket matches and tennis, I can never remember either of them being away, until the war would come to spoil everything. But not just yet. Everything was secure and we were safe ... for now.

When it was hot, my sister and I took off all our clothes and ran around in the garden naked. Once, when I was very small, I romped farther than the garden and was escorted home by a red-faced bobby.

Often we took turns giving each other rides in the wheelbarrow. Another favourite activity of ours involved lying on our backs and describing the animals in the clouds. Wherever Naomi and I went, our springer spaniel, Buller, accompanied us, chasing cats and rabbits and rolling in cow pies.

Grass snakes slithered. Worms wriggled. The big worm in my hand made me think of that man behind the hedge. I thought of chasing my sister with the worm but I threw it away instead. Worms weren't fun any more.

We played "babies" but not when Mommy or Daddy were watching. I could never be the baby, as anyone who ever saw a doll knew. Only girls could be babies. Boys just appeared in the gooseberry patch. They were never given a bottle and were never supposed to cry. Still, I wanted to be cuddled and loved, just like a girl baby. Why couldn't boys be babies, too?

Finchingfield, when grown'ups weren't looking, had a big fat bully. *Billy Bates [3] loved tormenting smaller boys – and girls too – who had the misfortune to cross his path. He chased us with stones or horse droppings or stinging nettles. When he caught us, he made us repeat the sort of swear words that, if our parents heard us use them, would get us sent to bed before tea time.

One day, he caught Naomi and told her, "Swear to Jesus, you're a shit-maid!" When I threw a rock at him, he released my sister to chase me. Naomi and I ran home. Luckily for us, it wasn't far away. Despite the fact that our legs were shorter than his, he was worn out when he reached our front gate.

In the middle of Finchingfield is a pond fed by the River Pant which is really a stream. Under the footbridge, Naomi and I caught "gollywogs" – tadpoles. There weren't any gollywogs in the pond because the swans ate them all. On sunny afternoons, we took a bag of bread crumbs to feed the swans. If we got too close, hissing swans chased after us. Then we dropped our bags of crumbs and ran home.

Punch and Judy bashed each other by the pond. All the children came to watch. Naomi and I were there. Punch whacked Judy, then threw the baby down on the ground. Everybody laughed and clapped.

> *Billy and another bully caught me all alone under the foot bridge. Billy took my fish net and twisted my arm behind my back while the other boy put his face right up to mine and growled, "Tell us what you know about the hairy cock."*
> *I didn't know the answer so both bullies pushed me down in the mud, and I wasn't allowed to go to the pond for a very long time.*

One day, crossing the foot bridge, I saw a gigantic big fish and ran home to tell my dad. The next morning, the fairies left a packet of fishing hooks in one of their circles in the garden.

My dad helped me dig for worms. Off I went to the bridge, pole and string and baited hook in hand, to catch the biggest fish in Finchingfield. Before long, a sudden tug pulled the rod from my hand. The enormous fish swam off, line and pole in tow, never to be seen again.

When our parents went to the village tennis courts a short way from home, Naomi and I were supposed to be asleep. But often we woke up, called for a drink of water and discovered we'd been left alone. We cried incessantly; at times like these, I felt alone and abandoned.

When the "little people" played with us, our parents caught us out of bed. I'm not sure about Daddy, but Mommy didn't believe us when we talked about the fairies. She smacked our behinds really hard for lying. When my sister and I contracted the German measles, the nurse, who came to look after us, kept the little people away. I still looked for them when we went for walks in the woods. I looked for them at the bottom of the garden. But they remained hidden. They never came back.

I can still picture the little people. They were smaller than my sister and I. Though they didn't look like the traditional depiction of fairies with wings, we knew they were fairies. Some were boys;

some were girls. They seemed older than we were, ageless in fact. Their clothing was ragged and colourful. They all wore tiny cloth shoes with pointed toes. Some wore hats with small feathers.

The fairies laughed and chatted with us in happy, bright voices. When they sang, it was always in a strange language, like nonsense songs. We tried to join in and invariably ended up falling down in fits of the giggles.

Their laughter was high pitched, like Christmas bells. Occasionally, they flew to the window, maybe to see if grownups were coming. When they danced around Naomi and me, we would join in. They would spin in a circle and disappear in a puff of sparkles. At other times, they shrank and slipped through the crack under the door. We wanted to go with them to see where they lived. But they never let us do this.

In later years, I saw other little people, mean, sharp teethed beings. In my nightmares, they tried to catch me and drag me into the coal cellar.

When I was small, we took faeries and elves and little people for granted. Of course they were true! My memories of them are still vivid. We were read stories about goblins and shown pictures in numerous books. Faeries and little people have always been part of the fabric of England and Ireland. Who am I to doubt they really exist?

Since Father Christmas left toys at the ends of our beds, Christmas was, for me, the most exciting time of the year. I remember one year, Naomi received a doll and tea set, and I a teddy bear and concertina. We weren't allowed downstairs until everything was ready. Then Daddy lit candles and sparklers on a gigantic tree, and we pulled crackers and wore paper hats all day.

On those winter mornings, when we woke up to snow, we went on long walks and got buried in enormous drifts. When the snow melted, we got stuck in the mud. In summer, we went with our parents to pick mushrooms in the cow fields. Or we went to pick blackberries and gooseberries

Also in summer, Daddy hitched the caravan to the family car, for our trip to the seaside.

Oh, how I remember my first view of the ocean, when we reached the top of a hill! I felt such wonder at the beauty of the blue sea, and the vision of miles and miles of long sandy beaches. With little spades and buckets, we dug in the sand. Our dad helped us build gigantic castles. When we got sunburns that blistered and peeled, Mom would rub our backs with Vaseline.

One time the fairies left money in a wishing well. Naomi and I bought ice cream and licorice all-sorts with it, and Daddy bought petrol for the drive home. I sensed, even then, that it was wrong to take pennies from a wishing well. Such a naughty act was bound to bring bad luck. Our lives would change because of it. Of course, Naomi and I never did tell.

But things did begin to change.

Across the road from Willets' Cottage, where Naomi and I peered over the garden fence to an exciting world of beggars, gypsies, milkmaids, umbrella menders, sheep herders, horseback riders, and urchins with runny noses, there lived a spinster who, in our childish eyes, was truly a witch with a big black cat named Satan. She was stooped over and very, very old. Her lips sucked into her mouth so that her nose and chin looked Punchlike. Her nose had a wart at one side, and her hair hung in stringy white strands halfway down her skinny body. She walked with a knobby cane and smelled of incense, sweat and pipe tobacco.

The witch lived in a wee house all alone. If ever she caught us, we knew she would eat us. It was a well known fact among the children in the village that she had a big pot in her kitchen where she boiled all the little ones she could catch. Holding a basket of apples or a jar of licorice all-sorts, she sometimes called my sister and me. In response, we ran shrieking into the back garden and hid behind the tool shed.

Our parents never asked us why we behaved the way we did. For our part, Naomi and I never spoke of the old woman, even when she held out an empty bucket to my dad on his daily trip to and from the village pump. Dad not only filled it, he'd bring a whole bucket for her, then return for more for us.

We had neither running water nor electricity at Willets'

Cottage. We went to bed by candlelight. In the morning, my father emptied chamber pots in a hole behind the privy.

Though I can't remember how we bathed, I'm sure we were kept clean at the big kitchen sink, where a drain pipe ran out to a deep, dark hole at the back of the house. A barrel caught rain water that flowed off the roof of the garden shed. My sister and I would stand up on bricks to see all sorts of wiggly creatures, swimming around and up and down, from the barrel's black bottom to its very top.

When it rained, Daddy taught us to read books and write letters, and Mommy taught us nursery songs and sang comical songs.

Singing and listening to music made us look forward to rainy days. My love of music came from those singsongs. We listened to songs too, on the crank-handled gramophone – songs sung by Paul Robeson, opera songs, and comic songs. After Naomi and I went to bed, my parents and their friends sang around the piano. It was wonderful to lie awake, all comfy and cozy, just listening.

Men with slobbering lips and giant worms chased me through the mud until I got stuck up to my waist.
"Mommy! Daddy!"
Nobody came to save me. It was ugly, horrible. I screamed awake. The moon shone through our bedroom window. My pillow was clammy cold.

Despite its small size, Willets' Cottage, in those days, was the center of many cheerful parties, with singers and artists coming up from London for weekends in the country. Mother had made numerous friends while at art school in London. With a generous allowance from her family in Denmark, there was always money for good times, and the house rang with music and laughter. Naomi and I, in our nightgowns, often sat at the top of the stairs listening to the happy sounds.

I remember when Paul Robeson came to visit. Mom painted his portrait in oils. In her picture, he held a clarinet. I sat on his knee, and he sang "Hushabie". [2]

My fascination with geography began when my father showed us how the world was formed. He peeled an orange, and we got to eat the fiery molten part beneath the earth's crust. When he lined up orange sections, we learned how to divide by two (with a leftover piece for the teacher). On a map, he showed us Africa, where I was born, and Australia, where kangaroos came from and where everyone walked upside down.

After the rain went away, we went for long walks with Mommy and Daddy. When our boots got stuck in the mud, we rode on their shoulders, singing silly songs we made up as we jogged along.

Among my most cherished memories are "horsey rides" on Mommy's knee. Naomi and I vied for our turn to mount the bucking bronco.

We seldom went alone into the village. When we did, it was to go to Mrs. Turner's greengrocer shop with a big woven basket, which Naomi and I carried between us.

We always dawdled. We stopped to see the pigs, to listen to the humming in the telegraph poles, and once in a while to watch the Gypsies. They camped in a field near the woods, not far from home. Their caravan wagons were brightly painted and pulled by shaggy horses; on the outside of them hung buckets, chairs, and pots and pans.

The Gypsy men mended pots and sharpened knives and scissors. They played concertinas and mandolins and violins and sang and laughed and spoke rapidly in Romany while little dogs barked and mothers called for their children.

Naomi and I fell asleep to the hubbub of their happiness, which echoed loudly until late into the evening. When the Gypsies set their bonfires at night, I was told the farmers locked up their chickens and pigs.

The colourful Gypsy caravans jangled as they rode through the village. Dark-skinned Gypsy children stared at Naomi and me – fair as lilies were we. We were never allowed to get as dirty as they seemed to be. Their mothers forever cooked over open fires, and their fathers did magic tricks with colourful flowers and puffs of smoke. Some village people went to the Gypsies to get their fortunes told. But we were warned not to get too close; the Gypsies might steal us away.

One of the Gypsies sang songs while playing a concertina.

Although I couldn't understand the man's language, I got caught up in the sheer joy of his music.

I wanted a concertina. My eighth Christmas, 1939, my parents gave me one, and I squeezed out my own happy and not-so-happy melodies. Despite the fact that my raucous noise got so annoying that I had to practice in the field or behind the tool shed, I nevertheless insisted that everyone – my parents and Naomi – attend my recitals.

In those days before the war, men other than the gypsies passed through our village. They lived off the land and carried their scant belongings in a large handkerchief slung over the shoulder, just like the North American hobos. They snared rabbits, skinned them, and cooked them over open fires. With branches and grass, they built shelters among the roots of a tree. In good weather, they slept in haystacks. They searched for berries, dug up turnips from farmers' fields, and liberated chickens and eggs from farmers' hen houses. They cooked everything in pots, with nettles and dandelions. The aroma was delicious. One of the men taught me how to blow my nose without benefit of handkerchief. Daddy laughed when I demonstrated but Mommy didn't think it was clever at all.

Other "adventurers" traveled in caravans, sometimes singing as they went. Many years later, I saw a film portrayal of these knights of the road – Lassie Come Home with Roddy McDowall and Elizabeth Taylor. I cried when I read the book and robbers killed the tinker's dog.[3]

I vividly recall the odd-job men with their barrows and carts. Some sharpened knives, others collected rags and bones, and still others sold merchandise. Naomi and I always ran out to greet the knife grinders and the traveling salesmen.

> Rags and bones. Rags and bones.
> Any old rags and bones.

Naomi and I picked mushrooms only when we were with our mother. She knew which ones were good and which ones were poisonous. The best ones grew in the cow pasture where the red-eyed bull stood guard. But with permission, we could go by ourselves to pick blackberries that grew along the closer edge of the cow field, on the other side of the stile.

One lovely day, with three buckets full of juicy blackberries, and our faces and fingers stained purple, our happy trip home was suddenly interrupted. As we approached the stile, the red-eyed bull charged across the field. Not wanting to spill the brimming pails of blackberries we were bringing home to our mother for a pie, we tried to help each other over the stile. I climbed over first. Before I helped her up and over, I told Naomi to hand me the buckets that now lay on the ground on her side of the stile.

I had not yet learned the "ladies first" chivalry. What is worse, it was my red cardigan that surely attracted the bull. By this time, my sister was crying. As I climbed back up to urge her on, she climbed up too and reached back for our buckets of berries. A short distance away, the bull stopped. His eyes blazed and his nostrils bellowed steam as he stood his ground, stomping and snorting, preparing to charge.

Naomi had just passed me the first full bucket when a rough voice from behind me bellowed, "Oi! W'at you two doin' stealing moi berries? 'and 'em over."

The bully!

Naomi stopped crying and picked up the other two buckets. "You can't have them!" she announced. Just like the bull, she stood her ground. Hoarsely whispering, "Here, take it," she passed the other bucket to me.

Suddenly, I felt stinging nettles on the backs of my legs. I dropped the buckets and turned around.

The bully fell on me, stinging me all over. Naomi climbed over the fence, screaming, "Leave my brother alone!" Distracted now, the bully chased my sister down the path with his nettles.

At this moment, the witch appeared! Shouting and waving her stick in the middle of the path, she looked like the witch from Hansel and Gretel. Naomi and I were in a sorry state. We burned from the nettles. Our buckets lay on their sides beneath the stile. Our berries had fallen into the mud. But the bully was gone. I saw him running across the field, as though his very life depended on his escape.

By the time we gathered our senses, the witch had already descended upon us. "That guttersnipe!" she rasped. "I shall be paying Mrs. Bates a visit, just you see. She'll give that Billy what for." Naomi and I wanted to run, but we couldn't. We were petrified.

"Here," the old lady said, "Let's rub some of this on those wee legs of yours and on your arms." The witch took what must have been dock leaves, which grew right by the stile, and rubbed Naomi's legs with them. I took some, too. Soon the sting went away. "You'd better get home now before your mother knows you're lost."

We took more dock leaves and rubbed our arms and legs with them. After a while, we made our way home, where our mother stripped us, washed us, and put us to bed.

The next morning, we found three buckets on our front door stoop. They brimmed with fresh blackberries.

"The fairies picked them," my dad said. I wasn't so sure.

That afternoon, Daddy took a fresh blackberry pie across the road. As for us, at tea time we ate big slices of blackberry pie, slathered with fresh, thick cream.

I never saw the old witch of Finchingfield again.

But I did learn more about her. I heard my mom and dad talking one night as I sat at the top of the stairs, wanting a drink of water. She had been engaged to marry when her fiancé went off to fight in the Great War. He didn't return.

Miss Timms lived the rest of her life alone.

My mind goes way back
To that little room beneath the thatch
Where the wee folk came to play
When we were shut up for the day,
With chicken pox or whooping cough.

You may laugh at what I say.
But I remember it well.

The wee folk danced and played at games
'Til Mommy came and called our names.
And smacked our bottoms into bed.
What was worse, she called a nurse
To come and stay,
Who kept the little folk away.

* * * * * * *

[1]   *Some names have been changed and first appear preceded by an asterisk. ***

[2]   *In 1939, Paul Robeson was in London filming Proud Valley, released at the beginning of 1940.*

[3]   **Knight**, Eric; *Lassie Come Home* (New York: Henry Holt & Company, 2003], [First published in 1940.)

Chapter Two
Parachutes, Spies, and Bogeymen.

"But war's a game, which, were their subjects wise,
Kings would not play at."
– William Cowper, (1731 - 1800), The Winter Morning Walk *1.*

One day, our dad came home in soldier's uniform. He had volunteered for the Home Guard. He looked smashing in khaki. I was so proud of him.

Once in a while, our Finchingfield bobby rode his bicycle through the village and up our way blowing his whistle. That told my father to throw on his uniform and get to the village on the double, where he caught a lift to his post at the antiaircraft battery on the hill.

Sometimes an airplane flew over low enough for us to see the red, white, and blue circles on the wings. When we saw the pilot, we waved. Sometimes the pilot waved back. Some airplanes had double wings and sputtered and banged.

When planes buzzed low over us, we had a lot of fun. The older soldiers shook their fists in the air and patted each other on their backs and laughed. In those days, no one thought of shooting at anyone. My father told us, "This is a silly war. It will all be over in a few weeks."

After a while, Dad went to the battery more often. He had to watch and listen for enemy planes. By that time, the lookout post had a big chart, showing the shapes of the different types of aircraft. My father spent hours studying it and keeping a lookout with his binoculars.

Since 1938, Naomi and I had been attending the Montessori Class at St. Christopher's Preparatory School in nearby Braintree. Now that he was in the home guard, whenever we weren't attending school, Daddy took us to his post on the hill. He even let us sit up behind the double gun called an "ack-ack". The place was exciting, with its trenches and sandbags to climb around and jump from. Some of the older men didn't want us there, because our dad reminded them to watch their language.

Then there was the day when, while Naomi and I enjoyed ourselves chasing around the sandbagged gun emplacement, an airplane flew over low. Amidst the usual shouting and scurry of activity, we heard a whistling sound, then, a loud "Whoomph!" Sand and rocks rained down on us.

As the ack-ack pounded out its "Pom! Pom! Pom!", Daddy shouted, "Children! Get down in the trench! Now!"

After that day, whenever the policeman came riding his bike and blowing his whistle through the village and up past Willets' Cottage, our dad went to his post alone. My sister and I stayed unhappily home.

We almost never went for walks any more with Mommy and Daddy. Instead, while Naomi and I spent time in our room under the gable, our parents played tennis or shouted at each other downstairs.

One night, we heard a crash, and my mother creaming, "There won't be any more money from Denmark. Get a job or join the bloody army!", She threw a plate at my father.[1]

My father shouted back, "You know the army won't take me. I have bad feet."

Another plate smashed against the wall. "Damn you! The least you can do is try." Then the front door slammed.

Naomi and I sat at the top of the stairs, shivering. "Get back to bed, you two!", Mother screamed at us, "before I come up there with the hair brush!"

Silently, we cried ourselves to sleep.

Next day, Daddy was gone.

He was gone for a very long time.

The next time we saw my dad, he wore a different uniform. As we ran to meet him, he got down on one knee, put down his pack sack, and lifted both of us into his arms.

Mom and Dad hugged and kissed, right there in the middle of the road. I tried to pick up my father's pack. I could barely move it. Yet he picked it up and slung it over his shoulder as easy as can be. My father was the strongest man in the world!

Soon Mom said, "Why don't you children go to Mrs. Turner's for me? I'll write out a list." I really wanted to stay and visit with my dad, but I also knew that he and Mommy wanted time alone. So, with the shopping bag between us, off we went to Mrs. Turner's.

This time we didn't dawdle. We ran through the village up to the greengrocer shop. When, out of breath, we told her the good news that our dad was home, Mrs. Turner gave us a big glass of sweet lemonade. She reminded us to drink slowly or we'd be sick. Returning home with a heavy basket took a long time. Fortunately, it was mostly downhill.

The next few days felt like old times. We went for long walks. Daddy took us up to visit his old buddies at the ack-ack station. One day, when he managed to buy some petrol, he took us for a ride in the car. ("Bessie" was a Morris Oxford 1928 model 14/28 'All Steel' Saloon.) But this time we had to stop at roadblocks and show papers. The next day, we left the car at a horse and carriage stable in the village.

Months later, when we next looked at Bessie, she was up on blocks in the buggy stall at Swan House, covered in cobwebs and straw. Her tires were gone as well as half her motor.

My father's visit was all too short. Just a few days later, in the morning, a soldier came to the door. A lorry waited outside. After admonishing us, "You children look after Mommy. I must go away for a while," Daddy hugged Mommy extra long, then someone offered him a hand to jump into the back of the lorry.

Everyone waved goodbye. "Don't you worry, sweetheart," one of the soldiers called out to Mommy. "Your soldier boy'll be back in no time." Then off they drove in a cloud of dust. My dad was gone.

Later, Mother told us that Dad had turned down a commission. He wanted to be an ordinary soldier and fight in the war in Africa.

I didn't think of deserts and tanks. In my imagination, I saw only jungles, savannahs and giraffes like those I'd seen in my baby pictures from Tanganyika.

I wanted to go with my dad.

In the weeks to come, hundreds of evacuees, fleeing bombing and Nazi occupation, passed through Finchingfield on their way north. They traveled in buses and in the backs of open lorries. They lined up to use our privy, and they sat on the hayfield next to our house and ate bag lunches.

Mom – we were getting too old to call her "Mommy" any more – took charge of the local first aid post as part of civil defense. In this job she busied herself with Red Cross nurses, changed bandages, and talked to evacuees, especially those from France and Denmark. Often she spoke in languages, we couldn't understand. (She spoke Danish, German, French, Swahili, Afrikaans, and smatterings of other languages picked up in her travels).

For the most part, the evacuees were mothers with small children, and elderly men and women. We heard one lady tell Mom that the Germans were coming.

Whenever we fell and scraped ourselves, Mom always used Dettol to kill "Germans". Naomi and I also contracted the German measles. We really didn't understand what kind of "Germans" could be coming to make people so afraid.

Most days, Naomi and I and several other children were bused by someone's mother or older sister to another school in Braintree. We no longer attended St. Christopher's Preparatory School and Montessori class. We also attended what the English would now call a "state school". In North America, this would be "public school."

Private or public, the teachers were often bad-tempered. The bigger children got caned on their hands, and the little ones got paddled on their bottoms. In adjoining classrooms, divided by a big, windowed partition, we all stood to sing "God Save the King". We also stood to recite the "Our Father – Thy kingdumcum, thy wilby-dun, ... deliver us from eagles. Amen".

Sometimes we sang a hymn such as "Onward Christian Soldiers" or "Gladly, the Cross-Eyed Bear"

And we prayed for the brave English soldiers, who got killed for us every day. We also knitted for the soldiers. I produced a khaki scarf for a midget.

The day finally came when Mom picked us up at the school bus and, instead of taking us home, she took us to Swan House, a small farm on the other side of the village pond where all our things had been moved. The house had its own well with a water pump. It had an indoor toilet, but its bucket had to be emptied every day by the gardener.

Floss Halls was a cleaning lady from the village who came to 'do' for my mother by cleaning and washing. She told funny stories, that made Naomi and me laugh. Sometime around that move, my birthday came. Finally I was big enough to get a red scooter! Now I could ride to and from Mrs. Turner's greengrocer shop and glide most of the way home with a basket hanging from the handlebar. Coming down that steep hill, I rode the brake. There were very few cars on the road.

Best of all were the barn and the two horses. Joyce was Mom's mare; Nellie the pony was Naomi's and mine. Now and then, the gardener hitched up the little surrey and Mom, Naomi, and I went riding down the country lanes. We fed our pony green apples from the big apple tree in the orchard, juicy carrots from the garden, and sugar lumps from the kitchen – which we took when Mom wasn't watching.

Late one afternoon, while we rode our horses, Joyce threw Mom. Because her leg was badly hurt, Mom rode Nellie, and led Joyce by her halter all the way home. Naomi and I walked.

A doctor bandaged Mom's leg; since the injured limb took a while to heal, a nurse had to look after all of us. She wasn't the nice young nurse we had when we were sick in bed at Willets' Cottage. This one was much older and grouchier. Because of her, my sister and I spent a lot of time in the barn, playing in the hay and brushing Nellie. When the gardener came around to empty the toilet bucket and clean out the horse stalls, we let him brush Joyce. When the nurse called us, we often hid in the hayloft and pretended not to hear.

One sunny afternoon, I climbed up the apple tree and tried to reach a big green apple that had grown just far out enough that I couldn't quite grasp it. Naomi called my attention to airplanes buzzing at each other in the sky. A German bomber and an RAF Spitfire were coming down with smoke trailing behind them. From my niche in the apple tree, I watched everything. As soon as white puffs appeared in the sky, I descended to firm ground. Close by, I could see one of the parachutes. Beneath its strands, at the other side of the house, a man slowly dropped, swinging back and forth. Before he landed, Naomi and I ran into the house to tell Mom. But she was already on her way to the village green.

Nurse ordered us to stay in the house. Then she ran off to call the Home Guard, screaming, "The invasion! The Germans are coming! The Germans are coming!"

As soon as she disappeared, my sister and I ran out to have a closer look at all the fuss. While the parachutist held his arm, Mom looked at his leg. He must have banged into the war memorial when he landed. He was very close to it; in fact, his parachute was tangled on the monument.

Mom said something to one of the other ladies. Next thing, we were all going home for tea. The pilot came along, supported between two men. Mom offered him a chair at the kitchen table.

"These little blonde angels must be yours." he said to Mom as he ruffled my hair. " For a moment, I thought I'd landed in heaven." While Mom busied herself with cotton wool, Dettol, and bandages, villagers gathered in our kitchen. They must have been surprised to hear the visitor speaking such good English.

The stranger smiled at my sister and me. "I say, I haven't had a proper cup of tea in ages."

"I'll put the kettle on", Mom replied. She limped over to the sink pump and filled the kettle.

"What the devil happened to your leg?" the man asked.

"Ach! Herunterfallen." (I fell.) Mom's answer surprised everyone.

"Sie sprechen Deutch!"

"Da ich ein Kind war." (Since I was a child.)

Smiling, the parachutist returned to English. "I read at Cambridge before joining the Luftwaffe."

Just then the nurse returned, followed by a rather out-of-breath policeman. "We're just about to have some tea. Would you care to join us? It won't take long." Mom invited the bobby and nurse to sit down.

"I suppose I could", replied the constable.

The nurse just stood and glared at my mother. "I'd rather not." She turned and walked out. A moment later, she came back, only to say, "I'll be back for my wages, if you don't mind, when he's not here."

With that, she was gone.

After the German left with the bobby and a couple of the Home Guard, we all went off to the first aid post in Spring Mead

24

where Mom was the person in charge. Flo Hardy was there attending to some other Germans. Then Mom, along with Cecilia Ruggles-Brice and the Reverend Paul Walde, tried to interview the other three Germans. I say "tried" because one of them had bitten off part of his tongue and couldn't talk.

Shortly after the parachute incident, the neighbours in our village snubbed us. When we went out for walks - which wasn't often - people moved to the other side of the road or turned away their heads and whispered to each other in small groups.

One day, part of a German airplane crashed in a field just behind our home. When the curious villagers came to look at it, one of the children walked over to Naomi and me and said, "Your mother's a bloody German spy." Angrily, her mother told her, "You stay away from them!"

It wasn't long before I asked Mom about this. "Mom, what's a spy? Are you a German spy?"

"Of course, not. Sometimes we sing little songs I've taught you in Danish or German or French. Or that little African song we used to sing. Some people don't like anyone who is different or does things differently. Never mind them."

After this experience, I promised myself I'd never speak any language but English.

At school in Braintree, we learned Scottish dancing and to sing "God Save the King" and "Rule Britannia". And we discovered that the world belonged to the English, who had "civilized the savage nations." Also we heard stories about good King John and Oliver Cromwell and found out that Napoleon was a madman, like Hitler and Mussolini.

Some of the older children dressed up and sang songs by Sir Arthur Sullivan. I was six or seven when I first was exposed to "For He Is an Englishman" from HMS Pinafore and to a shortened version of The Mikado.

We were fortunate indeed that we had "chosen" to be English.

Swan House had a cellar that contained a large coal box and several old wooden tea crates. It was full of cobwebs. Naomi and I were terrified of that place. One night I woke up screaming. I had walked into the dreaded cellar! German spies, little men with sharp teeth, reached out at me from the coal box.

Frequently, we saw Mom crying. As for Naomi and me, we often said, "If only Daddy were here." Finally, Mom grew exasperated when we asked, for the umpteenth time, "When's Daddy coming home?" and replied, "Your daddy's dead!" Her tone felt so cold we didn't ask again.

Together, Naomi and I walked to the far end of the orchard – and cried. Mom came out to find us. She hugged us both and cried with us.

The next day, the gardener made a hutch. Soon we each had a rabbit to look after. We fed our bunnies dandelions and grass and watched them get fat. Sometimes we took them out and let them run around on the grass. One morning, we noticed that the hutch was empty. We called all over - until the gardener walked out of the barn with two freshly skinned rabbits and brought them to Mom at the kitchen door.

We had often seen skinned rabbits hanging outside the butcher shop, but we hadn't expected to see our own bunnies dead like that. Too much had happened too fast. The gardener had been our friend. Now we stayed out of his way and hid when we saw him coming. Mom's involvement in the killing made me less trustful of her, too.

I don't remember eating rabbit pie or rabbit stew. Then again, Mom may not have told us what we were eating. I just don't remember.

One night an incendiary bomb dropped on the barn. The horses screamed. When Mom ran outside, the air raid warden sent her back into the house. Flames shot up everywhere. One of the horses was killed outright; the other was taken by the Home Guard.

Next day, some of the village children ran past our house and sang, "Serves you right. Your horse is dead."

"Daddy too", I thought. I climbed as high as I could into the apple tree. When Naomi called me, I pretended I couldn't hear her.

"If I were dead, you'd sometimes say, Poor Child!"
- Coventry Patmore (1823 - 1896) [2]

Indeed, I wished I were dead. I even fantasized my own funeral. If I were dead, I knew, the day would be rainy and cold as they lowered my coffin into the deep earth. Mother would cry and cry. But there would be nobody to hold her and comfort her. Then she would know how lonely I had been and how I had suffered. No one would be able to stop her constant sobbing. She would beg me to come back. But I wouldn't. I would go off to be with my dad and the angels. Mother would be all alone, and it would serve her right. Of course, Naomi would be dead too – of a broken heart.

Eventually, Mom came and called me down. I knew I was in for a good spanking. Instead, she just hugged both of us – for a long time.

Not long after that, while we played in the school yard – at recess or lunch time – an airplane came out of the clouds and dove at us. Everyone screamed; there was a lot of noise. Somebody knocked me down. My leg hurt. I don't remember what happened next, except that cars and ambulances arrived and Mom came to pick us up. My knee had been grazed by a bullet from a Nazi strafe plane. I was lucky I hadn't been killed. [3]

Naomi and I didn't go back to school for quite awhile after that. I had to get stitches in my knee. The doctor said I was a brave wounded soldier. I felt very proud to be a wounded English soldier.

After awhile, we went to the two-room school in Finchingfield. Though a glass partition divided the classes, we all assembled for singing and Highland dancing – jig and reel – point-toe-heel-skip-turn. Arms flung high.

* * * * * * * *

[1] *Following their return from Africa in 1934, until 1940, my parents were supported by inheritance from Denmark and by the occasional gift from Grandpa Nuttall-Smith. The Danish funds were cut off following the Nazi occupation.*

[2] **Patmore**, Coventry; "If I Were Dead", in *The Oxford book of English verse;* Quiller-Couch, A.T, ed. [Oxford: Clarendon, 1919, [c1901]], p. 761

[3] *The strafing incident was confirmed by Flo Hardy (in her nineties), in the company of Ron Hawkins – village historian, during a visit to Finchingfield in May 2006. The remembrance was unsolicited .*

Chapter Three
The Headmaster's Parrot.

I am going to boarding school. Going to prison to be taught good behaviour.
– E. Cobham Brewer 1810–1897. [1]

Soon after the incendiary bomb, Mom got a job in a sausage works, then in a munitions factory. Naomi and I were sent off to a Catholic boarding school.

The other workers called our mother "Mrs. Lah-de-Dah". She, who had been brought up with everything fine – with maids and a gardener and cleaning women and a trust account from Denmark to pay for it all. Now she had to work with the class of people she so often despised.

At boarding school, we were given castor oil regularly, whether we needed it or not. This gave me bad stomach aches.

We had regular bath nights, but more than five inches of water was unpatriotic. We younger children lined up for our three-minute bath in the same water that ten before us used. The water was often cold and filthy. Usually one matron washed us; another rubbed us vigourously with a soggy towel, inspecting our bums to make sure we had rid ourselves of all newsprint ink. (Toilet paper was a luxury I only discovered when we came to Canada.) One word of complaint and we got whacked on our bare bums by a matron with a bamboo cane. Even babies got whacked. Being naked invited whacks. I learned to associate nakedness with badness. If you talked while naked, you must have said something bad, something dirty.

Mother wasn't happy when she came to see us. Naomi and I received terrible school reports. We were homesick. We weren't making new friends. And the headmaster and his wife took an early dislike to us. Perhaps we lacked the rough edges possessed by so many other boarders. Often we lined up to get caned on our hands for all sorts of things we did wrong or didn't do at all. Despite our age difference, my sister and I were placed in the same form; as a result, we were way ahead for some subjects and behind in others.

While our form prepared for First Holy Communion, Naomi and I weren't to participate. The school didn't have our baptismal certificates. We'd been christened by Grandpa, a priest in the Church of England. But that didn't count. While the other children attended catechism, Naomi and I were sent to scrub pots and sweep and dust and set tables.

I wanted to learn what the other children were being taught. So I borrowed the little Catholic Truth Society booklets from the back of the church, where we went regularly for Mass and Benediction. I read the booklets sitting on the toilet and faithfully returned each one when I finished reading it. I read all about purgatory and popes and Protestants and the English Catholic martyrs and how God loved me.

One day we were taken on a field trip to visit one of the old mansions, where Jesuits hid from Queen Elizabeth's soldiers, in their "priest's holes". This made me think I could be a martyr some day. Everyone would love me, then, and say nice things about me.

In the middle of a daydream, I was called from class to go to the headmaster's study. Those of us who had never before entered the headmaster's "sanctum sanctorum" regarded the place with awe and dread. Strange voices emanated from its sacrosanct precincts at all hours of day and night.

As I approached the door, I heard a raucous fuss. I knocked, my knees shaking; I could barely stand.

"Come."

I opened the door a crack. There, in a huge cage, a macaw climbed about, beak and claw, screaming obscenities at a large orange cat which sat grinning like Alice's Cheshire on the back of a green chesterfield.

From behind a huge desk, the headmaster scowled down upon me. He was thin as a string. His face, blanched like a plant grown in deepest shade, framed his bushy white eyebrows. His mutton chop sideburns flared out beneath a mop of unruly white hair.

His voice sounded hoarse, like he had cobwebs in his throat. "Nuttall-Smith, empty your pockets." Wondering why, I obeyed — and surrendered a couple of Catholic Truth Society booklets.

Whatever else I possessed proved inconsequential. The headmaster called in one of the teachers, a miserable old woman with teeth like tumbling tombstones. Her hair was all wrapped up in a tight bun and stuck through with huge knitting needles. While she glared at me, her hands pinched at one another like quarrelsome crayfish.

The headmaster extracted a light bamboo cane from the umbrella stand behind the door and swished it a couple of times through the air. He enjoyed my terror. The woman sniffed loudly. At a signal from her boss, she grabbed me by the hair, pulled my pants down, and forced me, struggling, over the arm of the chesterfield.

"The more you struggle, the worse it's going to be, Master Smith," she hissed. The moment of stark terror while I waited for the caning to begin seemed like forever.

Then it began. I screamed.

My scream nearly drowned out the parrot's screech.

Others who had been "whacked" had warned me not to make a sound. That meant more licks. But I wasn't able to follow that advice. Nor was I able to sit down, for a long time. Naomi was also implicated. She got caned too, along with a couple of others. But I was considered the ringleader of this band of thieves. So I stood for my meals at a table by myself, hating that cursed parrot and dreaming of its demise.

The headmaster said we had stolen many books, at great loss to Holy Mother Church. The school had been so good to us heathens, and we'd dishonoured its trust. I was branded a thief forever. I'd end up in the fires of hell. This was a foretaste. "As your backside stings, think of hell."

Soon after, my very displeased mother came to remove us from the school. It was then I lost my concertina; I didn't have it in my belongings when we were ready to leave. Since Mother was in such a big hurry, I didn't get a chance to grab it.

Our next school was a convent for girls. (Mother was nominally Catholic.) We were supposed to stay there only until another school could be found.

I developed running sores all over my body. The old sister who supervised our baths said I was disgusting. Everybody had to stay away from me.

An ambulance came and drove me to the hospital. I was put in isolation with scarlet fever. I couldn't read books; they'd have to be destroyed after I handled them.

At first, no one came to visit me. I nearly died of loneliness. God, I knew, had punished me for being a thief and a heathen.

Eventually, a young nurse came in. She sat there, talking to me, cheering me up. She even tickled me. She was wonderful! Then an older nurse in charge called her out of my room. I waited for her to come back. She never did. I lay there in isolation while the long fingers of the setting sun reached in through the solitary window, casting grotesque shadows on the green wall.

Only once my mother came to visit. But she wasn't allowed to come close. After just a few moments, she left. I cried so hard my pillow had to be changed.

When I got better, some men in white sealed up my room with tape and disinfected it. My clothes had to be burned. I remained in a hospital gown until Mom brought more.   We all went to live with Uncle Sigvard. It was at about this time that Naomi and I were told we were now too grown up to call Mother Mom. "No more Mommy or Mom, you're too big for that! Call me Mother". For me at that time, "Mother" wasn't nearly as comforting a name as "Mom" or "Mommy".

* * * * * * *

[1]   **Brewer**, E. Cobham; *Dictionary of Phrase and Fable* (New York: Bartleby, 2000),
(First published by Henry Altemus in Philadelphia in 1898.], p. 154

Chapter Four
Farting Through Gas Masks.

Roll me over, in the clover,
Roll me over, lay me down and do it again.

When we first moved to London, we were sent to a local school. Boys played warplane "dog fights" in the school yard. We were all Spitfires; no one wanted to be a Messerschmitt. Aiaooow! Pta! Pta! Pta! Pta!

The school was bombed so we went to live with our Uncle Siegvard at Ealing in the heart of West London. Because of the war, Mother could no longer look after us, nor could she afford to send us to any more boarding schools.

Uncle Sigvard was Mother's half-brother and a Doctor of Science. Sometimes, he lived like a millionaire, despite the war; other times, he was poor. At one time before the war, he had headed his own film studio in Hollywood, California. Apart from working on a variety of inventions to do with film and x-rays, he was a cameraman for Ealing Studios. My uncle was pudgy but not fat. He had very wavy hair and a cigarette forever dangling from moist lips which had bubbles of spittle at the corners. His sky blue eyes could see right through me, and his hands forever pulled me to his smoky tweed jacket. The pockets had sweets which he slipped to me one at a time with a wink.

Mother asked her brother to get her a job. She was sure she could be a movie star. But Uncle Sigvard didn't get her what she wanted.

Living with my uncle was a whole new adventure. Not only did he take me with him to shoot film, he put me into some movie "co-op spots". I once got to sit on a barrel eating a banana made of a sugary paste. There weren't any real bananas during the war. Uncle Sigvard also took me to movies and bought me sweets to eat during the film while he smoked his cigarettes.

While living with my uncle, I got to be a cub. Uncle Sigvard knew Lord Baden-Powell personally and had been a scout leader himself. At that time, Boy Scouts acted as air raid wardens and as organizers for recycling drives. We collected newspapers, string, and foil from cigarette packages for the war effort. I remember a cub outing where we camped overnight in a farmer's barn and played parachutes, jumping in the hay.

My Uncle Sigvard was one of the few people anywhere who still owned a car. Driving for pleasure was not allowed. One day, he had to make one of those "necessary" trips – to film for the War Department, or something like that. He returned home by bus. The government had labeled his car "unnecessary", put it up on blocks, and removed the tires and rotor arm. If the Germans had invaded at that time, they would have had a hard time finding ground transportation.

For people living in London, a full moon meant a restless night. Thick cloud, once so depressing, meant probable relief and a night's sleep.

For us kids, air raids offered welcome breaks from boring lessons. In boarding school, with the first wail of the siren, we walked to the cellar, in single file and in silence. Once there and checked off against the register, our teachers led us in rousing choruses of "One Man Went to Mow" and "Hitler Has a Bunion..." We drowned out the violent sounds above us.

When I attended day school in London, we all marched behind our teachers to the civic air raid shelter close by. I'll never forget the old, old man who sat in the dark, hardly able to muster the breath necessary to whisper, "Don't forget your gas mask."

We carried our gas masks everywhere we went. We found out that, if we blew hard enough during a gas drill, we could "fart" through our gas masks. Since so many of us did this, the teachers couldn't sort out anyone in particular for punishment. Soon we all farted – until finally we were ordered to "Take those bloody things off!"

In the shelters, people often sang. In places where there were plugs to plug them in, some regulars brought a wireless. Then we listened to Radio America playing "Roll Me Over..." People complained, "Bloody Yanks! Overpaid, over sexed, and over 'ere."

During long raids, we listened to George Formby, Gracie Fields, Vera Lynn, "It's That Man Again" (ITMA), Tommy Handley,

Henry Hall, Tessie O'Shea, Mrs. Mop, and Claud and Cecil. As counterpoint to this, we kids noisily ran about and got underfoot, while the bossy grown-ups yelled at us to settle down or to blow our noses.

This is number one and the fun has just begun
Roll me over, lay me down and do it again.

Whoever went out at night walked in the dark. White lines on curbs, trees, lampposts, and even on the mud guards of buses helped us to find our way without bumping into things. Just a tiny crack in people's curtains often provoked the air raid warden to shout, "Put that bloody light out!"

There were sandbags all over London, trenches in the parks, and sticky paper strips on all the windows. (Sandbags and trenches were to provide shelter and protection from blasts and bullets. Sticky paper was to lessen the danger of flying shards of glass.) When we lived in the country and didn't have a cellar, we had a shelter in the back garden instead. Measuring about 5' by 8', the pit was covered with corrugated tin and sandbags and heaped up with earth. It contained bunk beds, some items of food, and other supplies to keep us through long raids.

As often as not, garden shelters held only muddy water and, perhaps, a floating doll or teddy bear or bits of soggy clothing. Reminders that children had spent drier days playing house or doctor.

When we did live in the country, I don't think we ever used our garden shelter except for keeping vegetables. Very few people had refrigeration. We certainly didn't. Some people lived in partially bombed out houses with blankets and sheets hung for privacy. We visited friends of my uncle who lived with dust, dust, dust and moldy, cracked ceilings. And, oh, in the shelters when we did have to go to them, I remember the smell of sweat! And the stale reek of fish and chips in old newspapers!

We children got warned a lot, about a lot of things. "Don't pick up lost toys, packets of sweets, and model airplanes." The Germans had dropped – or so we were told – innocent looking, explosive materials into parks, fields and city streets. As soon as unsuspecting children picked them up – bam!

About this time, Mother absented herself more and more, sometimes for two or more consecutive weeks. Instead of attending school then, Naomi and I spent many happy hours reading. Because Uncle Sigvard had no faith in the shelters, he refused to go to them. According to him, many Londoners had been trapped in the tube stations. Some had even drowned in the sewage. So, we sat up during the air raids and talked. Sometimes we opened the curtains and observed the fires around us. Also, I accompanied Uncle Sigvard and Trevor onto the roof while they did their filming. (Trevor, in his late teens, lived and worked with my uncle until he joined the RAF as a fighter pilot.)

We saw German bombers in their daylight raids and in the beams of searchlights generated from parks all over London. We watched dogfights between Spitfires and Messerschmidts high above the barrage balloons. I remember German bombers trying to destroy the King's Cross railway station nearby.

During the times of the bombing, dogfights, crumbling buildings and great loss of life, I felt safe with Uncle Sigvard. Not only that, I felt truly, gloriously alive. It all was "bang on", "smashing" even.

I was unaware of the pun.

One night, during a particularly heavy raid, part of the flat was blown away. Trevor grabbed me by an arm and pulled me from my bed. Just a few feet away, the floor had ceased to exist. Perhaps this was one basis for my developing fear of heights – but at the time, I think I was in a state of shock, and felt little about it.

As well as my uncle, Trevor sometimes gave my sister and me money and ration tickets to buy sweets. Instead of sweets, I often bought Boys Own magazines (a popular magazine full of stories and pictures for boys my age).

From the fireplace mantle - where Trevor left piles of change - I once took half a crown. When questioned about my newly found wealth, I said I found it on the street. Trevor knew I stole his money. But my uncle took my side and let me keep the silver piece.

I was jealous of the attention Trevor received when he was with my uncle. I vied both with him and with my sister for all the love and attention I could get.

A mother and her daughter, who had escaped to England from one of the Nazi-occupied countries, once came to spend a couple of days with us. The little girl spoke no English. She slept in the same room with Naomi and me, and cried all night. I hated the intrusion. Here was someone else demanding my uncle's attention. I felt unsympathetic towards the little "crybaby". I shushed her. Fortunately, I couldn't say mean things to her; she couldn't understand a word I said. I just wanted her to stop crying.

After the loss of our flat in Chelsea, my uncle moved to "digs" near Croydon. Our new home was really an unused shop with rooms in the back. There Uncle Sigvard and Trevor mixed huge vats of molten lipstick, which they then poured into molds. (My uncle had invented a new smear-proof lipstick and was producing it to sell to cosmetics shops.)

Trevor drew cartoons in lipstick all over the walls. Eventually he joined the RAF and was shot down over the North Sea. The first time I saw a grown man cry was when my Uncle Sigvard wept for Trevor. Perversely, I was glad my competition was gone.

For a while, Uncle wanted to be alone. Naomi (now seven) and I (eight) took long walks and spent a lot of time watching the planes take off and land. Some aircraft arrived with wings all shot up or on fire. One day a Spitfire almost touched our heads as it came in for a crash landing. It burst into flames against a big old tree in a park.

We always avoided the local boys and girls who ran ragged through the ruins, picking out souvenirs and pieces of shrapnel. When I found a bullet casing that made a super whistle, a big boy knocked me over and took it from me. A workman accosted Naomi and me and ordered us to stay out of bomb sites.

Bomb sites weren't the only dangerous places. Barrage balloons, weighing fifty to sixty pounds, were flown all over London to protect against dive bombing and low level attacks. Each was moored to a wagon by a thick steel cable, strong enough to destroy aircraft that collided with them. In a wind, balloons could break away, dragging thousands of feet of steel cable with them. Sometimes Messerschmitt 109s flew in ahead of bombing raids to shoot down the barrage balloons. I remember seeing helium filled balloons in flames. Firemen rushed all about trying to save the houses in their fiery paths.

Soon we all moved to a flat near Hampstead Heath in Northwest London. I don't remember going to school there, only that Naomi and I spent hours every day exploring the area.

After she finished at the munitions factory, Mother got a job riding motorcycle dispatch in London. Following that, she worked as an ambulance driver, on call for air raids. As soon as a siren sounded, off she went. Before the "all clear" and for some time after, she dodged bomb craters, raced past burning buildings, falling debris and smashed buses, picked up wounded firemen and civilians, and rushed them to emergency wards.

After that, when she went to work as an examiner for the British Censorship Office, she absented herself for great lengths of time.

During several long treks through London, Naomi and I got lost and returned home late. This caused my uncle all sorts of worry. On one occasion, a couple of men followed us for a long way. Convinced that they wanted to kidnap us, we took a circuitous route and didn't arrive home until long after dark. Nobody believed our "kidnapper" story. We both got spanked and sent to bed without supper.

As a punishment, going without supper became more and more frequent.

My ninth Christmas – Naomi's eighth – went by with barely a mention. We had little money and food. We seldom got milk; what there was of it, often went sour. When Mother was home, she put the sour milk in cups on the window ledge until it turned into custard. Then we ate it with sugar. The best part of getting fresh milk was taking the cream from the top. This we put it into a jar and shook until it turned into real butter. We drank the buttermilk that remained, sweetened with vanilla and sugar.

For a while at least, we enjoyed life. People laughed a lot. Uncle Sigvard owned a wireless. Every night after supper, we sat close and listened to the BBC news. When the Yanks came, we quickly learned the songs they played on the wireless. "Roll me over in the clover ..." Mother sang them louder than anyone. She and

Uncle Sigvard outdid each other with limericks and dirty jokes. What an education!

Since we weren't going to school, Mother gave us poems to memorize and recite in front of company. My earliest introduction to Robert Service was <u>Bessie's Boil</u>. Mother had a delicious sense of humour. Some of the poems she encouraged me to memorize were not the sort a child would normally learn in school. But they were fun. She used to tell jokes using accents and dialects. For example: "A missionary approached a doctor in South Africa. 'Do you love Jesus?' The doctor replied, 'Ach, no. Hate the cheezes. But ah! Ze leetle Camembert, zat I like."

Mother gave me a fondness for language, and an ear for accents and dialects. She taught me the beauty of speech and gave me the capacity to remember good jokes as well as the fearlessness to tell them even if they shocked the listeners. Language became my private gem collection. Tact, I had to learn on my own, the hard way.

When I think of Mother fondly, I remember her perfume and licorice all-sorts on a rainy day. I remember jam sandwiches, and strawberries and cream. Those are the happy memories.

When Mother and Uncle Sigvard went to a pub in the evening, Naomi and I sat up reading until we heard them come in, singing at the tops of their voices and shushing each other not to "wake the children". Quickly, we snapped out the light. We were "sound asleep" when they came in to check on us. In those days, my sister and I shared a bedroom.

After lights out, we read by the light of a candle on the floor between our beds. One night a candle tipped over and made a small burn on the floor. When I tried to fix it with shoe polish, it only looked worse. Luckily for me, the flat was bombed before the landlord or anyone else discovered it.

We were never happy when we spent a weekend at a faraway flat back in Chelsea with Aunt Robbie, an old lady who wasn't really our aunt. Uncle Sigvard always wrote down our bus travel instructions to ensure we didn't get lost in transit. Aunt Robbie was a widow from the Great War; worse, her only son had been killed in a jungle, fighting another enemy, the Japanese.

The woman was terribly lonely. She wore her hair tightly bound under a net, never smiled, and heaved sighs at every move. Her skin tone looked grey, her varicose veins showed big and deep purple, like a road map on her legs, and she snored like an old horse. Worst of all, she smelled of stale pee. Naomi and I had to sleep crammed into the same bed with her.

One day, when we arrived to keep her overnight company, her building was gone; in fact, the whole street was gone. With mixed horror and relief, we made our way back to Wimbledon, very late.

There are other things I could tell you about my Uncle Siegvard. But not now. "... must never tell a soul." [1]

* * * * * * * *

[1]   *I hid the continuing terror of abuse for much of my lifetime, refusing to admit the truth to myself or to anyone else. This and other sexual abuse is dealt with in detail in a later chapter. Meanwhile, I struggled to survive in a very unreal world.*

Chapter Five
For What We Are About to Receive.

> *"If you are bad and break the rules,*
> *you will be shut up forever and ever in a deep black hole*
> *full of rats and snakes."*

One afternoon, Naomi and I returned home from an extra long exploration through bomb craters and ruins. Mother met us. She had packed our few belongings into two small cardboard suitcases. "Give Uncle Sigvard a hug. I've managed to find a good school for you both. I'm sure you're going to love Holly Hall." [1]

Uncle Sigvard gave us both a bear hug. He gave me an extra squeeze and a wink as he slipped a guinea into each of my trouser pockets. I was rich indeed, but sad at the prospect of another boarding school.

Holly Hall School was divided, according to forms, into boys' and girls' sides. At meals, Naomi and I sat at opposite ends of the hall. When I could, I caught Naomi's eye during grace and wiggled my fingers in her direction. The headmaster droned out the grace in Latin. I don't think any of us ever knew the meaning of the words.

> *"Benedicite."*
> *"Benedicite"*
> *"Benedic Domine nobis et donis tuis quae ex largitate sua sumus sumpturi et concedi ut abiis salubriter enutriti tibi debitum obsequium praestare valeamus, per Jesum Christum Dominum nostrum mensae caelestis nos participes facias rex aeternae gloriae. Amen"*

We all responded *"Amen"* and sat down. Those whose turn it was to serve, served. We passed each plate of sausage meat and mash until all were served. Sometimes we chewed our way through twice slaughtered mutton. (The meat in boarding school was killed once by the butcher, then again by the cook.) After the headmaster rang a little table bell, we dug in like hounds on the scullery floor. During many meals, someone read to us while we ate in silence. There was to be no talking during meals. We listened to such classics as "Tale of Two Cities" and "Little Women", a chapter at a time. Some of the readings were taken from the lives of the saints. After the main course came dessert which was often tapioca. I associated tapioca with the saint who ate maggots as a form of heroic penance.

I was miserably lonely. Once again, my sister and I were behind in everything. We didn't know "Ackbay Langsay" (Pig Latin). For a variety of misdemeanors, such as trying to make contact with each other, Naomi and I were sent to "Coventry", which meant that nobody was permitted to speak to us.

"Smith!" (They never called Naomi and me by our full names.) I jumped from a refectory hall daydream with a start. Had I been discovered waving at my sister during grace? "Smith! Come get it or you'll lose it."

"Psst! That's you. You've got a parcel." I started up to the head table and beckoned to Naomi to join me. I was handed a parcel, said "Oh, thank you", and turned to open it with my sister.

"You may open it right here, Smith."

Between us, Naomi and I opened the parcel: socks we had needed but somehow felt cheated receiving, several chocolate bars (an unheard-of luxury), and a letter. We were allowed to keep the socks which had our names sewn in on tags. The letter was checked by the headmaster for spending money, which would be held for safekeeping. The chocolate was to be shared with everyone (at a later date). We never saw it again.

The letter came from Mother. The chocolate was a gift from our "new father". We were told to work hard at school. Nothing else. After being given "sufficient time" with it, Naomi and I had to yield up the letter – for safekeeping.

We were dismissed to our separate tables. From there, we went to recreation. Later, we proceeded to study hall until bed time.

I just had to find out about this "new father". Who was he? What had happened to the father I'd known so long ago? Days turned into weeks. Still, there was no word.

Every Sunday afternoon we had to write letters to our mums. We also could write to our dads, provided we had their army addresses. We were allowed to write to other relatives only under special circumstances, such as when both parents were dead. Never were we to correspond with anyone else. The cost of paper,

41

envelopes, and stamps was taken out of the pocket money that was held for us. Every week, Naomi and I faithfully wrote to Mother.

Our letters were returned to us with spelling and syntax errors circled in red. If we mentioned we were not well - or anything else negative - the sentences got crossed out until there was little left. Sometimes, when we had to rewrite a letter several times, we couldn't submit it on time for the post. Or we ran out of our share of writing paper. Staff supplied envelopes and addressed them.

Mother never sent us another letter. I liked to think she too had her paper rationed.

I still had the money from Uncle Sigvard tucked away under my clothes beside my bed. I knew his address, so I decided to write a secret letter, find a way to buy an envelope and stamp and post the letter from the pillbox near the school.

That night, letter written, I lay awake working up the courage to get out of bed. Eventually, I put on my clothes. Then, ever so quietly, opened my drawer and felt around for the two guineas so carefully hidden weeks and weeks before.

I couldn't find them. I took everything out of the drawer and put each item of clothing carefully back. The money was gone. Then I heard footsteps. I leapt into bed and pulled the blanket up over my clothes. For a long time I lay there, waiting for the bed check and dorm inspection. I fell asleep fully dressed.

One Sunday afternoon, Naomi and I were called down to the grand hall. We had a visitor. Uncle Sigvard greeted us with a whispered "How would you two like to come to a pantomime?" we must have burst with excitement as we both forgot the rule against running in the school and tore off to fetch our coats.

On that glorious Sunday with Uncle Sigvard, we sat in a huge auditorium, where "Buttons" introduced us to an actor who, with a flash of magic smoke, changed before our very eyes into the evil giant. The production of Jack and the Beanstalk was enthralling. I never discovered how such magic was done.[2]

After the performance we walked and talked about magic beans and golden eggs. I forgot about the one issue I wanted so desperately to talk about. While we traveled by taxi to have tea with a friend of Uncle Sigvard, I remembered the letter still tucked in my pocket. I took it out and showed it to my uncle. He read it with a laugh. "Why do you think I came for you?" he asked, mysteriously. "I have telepathic powers. I knew all about your letter. When did you write it?"

"Several weeks ago."

"Of course! I've planned this outing for weeks now. As for your mother, she'll be contacting you very soon; you mark my words."

The day was perfect.

After tea, Uncle's friend packaged up sandwiches and cake. Into a bag he popped corked bottles of ginger beer, some apples, and some sweets. These were all for us to take back with us to ...

"Don't you worry about a thing," he said, winking to Uncle Sigvard. "We know all about boarding schools."

We said our goodbyes and happily went with our uncle to catch the bus to return to school. He came with us. Two stops before we would have expected to disembark, we got off the bus and began walking.

At the bottom of the school grounds, a gate led into a wooded area. It was strictly out of bounds, but a wonderful place for hiding away when solitude was needed. Uncle Sigvard opened the gate. We found a hollow in an old tree where we secured our bag of goodies. Then we turned back to the gate.

"We'll say cheerio here," he said. He gave Naomi a hug, then put his arms around me and squeezed very hard.

"I miss you very much, my Benny" he said.

"I miss you, too."

I meant it.

Just about every boarder at Holly Hall School - once a school for boys, now co-ed because of the war - knew that the scullery door, which led to the back of the building where the ashes and slops were kept, was never locked. The kitchen staff went out at night and frequently returned in the wee hours. Then they banged into pots and pans as they crept in long after blackout, slightly the worse for wear. Towards the end of term, certain seniors put up fancy barricades to ensnare the unwary returnees in a tangle of noisy utensils.

To be sure, we ate the following day's meals with great care.

Some form of terrible revenge might be taken out on us by an angry cook or embarrassed scullery maid. Those unfortunates, usually intermediates, whose turn it was to help out with kitchen cleanup, were always given an extra mountain of greasy pots to scrub. It didn't matter that intermediates were far too young to have participated in the previous night's trickery.

As soon as possible after lights out, Naomi and I planned to meet outside the scullery door. It was simple to bunch up our blankets to make it look as if we were in bed. Then too, people did occasionally slip off to the bathroom.

We each had a torch; this was common fare for reading under covers after lights out. For every torch that was ever confiscated, another was found and hidden. The huge freestanding bedding closet in the hallway outside each dormitory provided a common hiding place for contraband items. These were stashed on top and as far back as one could possibly reach, with a boost from a chum or with the aid of a chair. Objects placed there by peers were generally respected as private property. Everyone took turns boosting others up to reach for snacks, torches, and, of course, cigarettes and matches that had been pilfered on weekend visits home.

Even the monitors respected our right to a safe hiding place, which they had enjoyed as intermediates, even as juniors.

Monitors were the senior boys and girls who had survived the years of hazing and initiations, detentions and caning, and who were now only too ready to help ensure that such traditions continued. Anyway, seniors were not in the habit of boosting one another up to search in high places. They had much better things to do with their time. They left us lesser creatures at peace once we learned the rules and showed them the respect due to their position in the institution's hierarchy, within which we all had our proper places.

I crouched shivering behind a dustbin as one of the seniors stood just outside the door having a lengthy smoke. In a while, he was joined by a peer who pulled a large bottle of beer from his dressing gown pocket. The two stood in the shadows sharing beer and cigarette. Finally they went inside. Naomi nearly bumped into them in the hallway. She was giggling with excitement when she reached me.

Just as the two of us started off, we were stopped in our tracks by a light shining right at us. To our relief, we were joined by two girls from my sister's dorm.

"Put out that bloody light!" The voice came from the boy who occupied the bed next to mine.

The next thing we knew, there were nine or ten of us, boys and girls from both dorms. We all made a dash for it, careful not to step in puddles or bump into wooden posts or trip over rope.[3]

The moonlight washed the grass with silver as we streaked toward the copse at the bottom of the hill. Out of breath and with much giggling and hushing, we all arrived at the hiding place where Naomi and I retrieved our prize. This was to be the price for some short-lived popularity within our own groups.

We sat on stumps or stood against the tree and shared our feast. One of the boys passed around a cigarette – a dog's end. We competed to see who could muster the mightiest drag and hold it down the longest. This sent one or two first time smokers into fits of coughing and slaps on the back, accompanied by much laughter. Someone farted. More laughter. This started a barrage of farting and meowing noises. One of the girls imitated the voice of the matron, who was reported to have said, "Give me the instruments with which you are making those rude noises." More fits of laughter.

Our hilarity was brought short by the wail of the air raid siren. Since everyone had to be ushered into the lower hallway under the stairs, our absence surely would be discovered. On the other hand, we conjectured, maybe we wouldn't be missed. Fat chance of that. Since it was too late, we might just as well stay and sneak back at the "all clear".

We watched the searchlights combing the night sky, heard the "room-room-room" of German bombers, and saw lines of tracer bullets from the antiaircraft battery nearby. Shells spattered about us like fireworks. When we heard the shrieks from the fluted fins of falling bombs, we instinctively dropped to the ground.

With each explosion, the earth shook; my fingers dug into the dirt. I heard the high pitched scream of a large, oil-filled incendiary device – and held my breath. It slammed into a rise, much too close for comfort. A furnace burst open; smoke and flames leapt into the night sky.

I wet my pajamas, swallowed hard to lessen the lump in my throat, and fought back my tears.

Nearby Naomi cried. "Won't do. Won't do."

Then – silence.

Eventually, I heard an "all clear". Once more, silence reigned. Someone cried. Another said, "Oh, shut it, will you?" Still another giggled, "Oh, shit! I'm shot!" We all snickered nervously at the alliterative joke. Most people, however, kept quiet. My hand bled where I'd scraped it while grappling with the ground.

Then someone pointed. "Look! The bloody school's on fire!" Sure enough, flames leapt from the upper story.

"We'd better get back."

"We're for it now."

"Oh, bloody hell."

We made our way to the back courtyard. Already, a bucket brigade was in full progress as fire engines clanged their way up the driveway.

"What the devil are you doing here? Get around to the front of the school with the rest of your form." It was one of the teachers. The drizzle became a downpour. We moved quickly. Before long, we realized that it wasn't rain descending on us but water from the fire-hoses.

"Where have you lot been? The whole staff's been looking for you."

Eventually, we all assembled in the chapel in pajamas and dressing gowns and blankets. In a daze, I heard the headmaster addressing the raggle-taggle student body. He muttered a few words about some of the unfortunate victims who'd been caught by the suddenness of the attack.

One dormitory had not managed to evacuate on time. A number of children and one staff member had been sent to hospital. Fortunately, they were expected to be up and about within a few days. Several dormitories were gone as were some staff sitting rooms, classrooms, and part of the refectory. But the library and chapel had been saved.

Teachers, head staff, and a number of seniors were black with grime from helping to put out the blaze. Several had bandaged hands and arms. They received congratulations for their excellent effort in saving most of the school from utter destruction and stood for a round of applause.

Then the hammer fell. "A number of you will be going home. Some will be transferred to other schools. As for the truants..."

"Those of you who spent part of the evening having a jolly old time at our expense will kindly step forward."

Slowly, shamefully, we made our way to the front of the chapel. We stood in silence. "You may all stand here, so the rest of the school might see you in your shame and disgrace."

Time ticked painfully.

At the appointed time, bamboo struck flesh. As each teary-eyed face reentered the hall and met mine, my stomach sank another foot. I felt like throwing up. "All your fault," a former "best friend" muttered as he passed me. Then Naomi went in. Stroke after stroke descended on her. She cried, in agony.

"You!" the headmaster bellowed at me. "Do you realize we had people looking for you in that blaze? I'm going to make you wish ... Take down your bottoms." I backed away, shaking my head in refusal. The matron stepped forward and grabbed me by an ear. She threw me onto the table and grabbed me by both wrists, holding me firmly so that my entire upper body was face down. I kicked wildly as the headmaster yanked my pajama bottoms to the floor. Someone else had to come in and hold my feet, before the caning could begin.[4]

* * * * * * * *

[1]   *"Holly Hall" is a pseudonym. The events are real. Some names and places are clear; others are hidden by the trauma associated with them.*

I recall the uric stench of unwashed bodies, especially mine; yet I don't recall the uniforms we wore.

Vaguely, I recall a monitors' earliest instructions: "If you are bad and break the rules, you will be shut up forever and ever in a deep black hole full of rats and snakes." After hearing this, no one complained. In any event, boarding school complaints usually got chalked up to homesickness and the usual friction involving masters, monitors, and pupils.

[2]   *Childhood moments of stage and film are sheer magic. We had been to the Hippodrome one Christmas to see* Peter Pan, *where the children had flown out over the audience. We all had wished and believed so very hard for Tinkerbell to live "I believe in fairies. I believe in fairies."*

At times when sadness seems overwhelming, they remain to soothe and comfort. Even today, upon hearing the refrain from Walt Disney's Bambi, *which Naomi and I saw with Mother soon after the "loss" of our dad, my tears give me relief. When I hear Benjamin Godard's* Berceuse de Jocelyn, *I feel overwhelmed with emotion. I shed tears when I hear Paul Robeson sing a lullaby, as he did for me when I was so very young and, as yet, untouched by sadness.*

Memory can be an ocean, in which people, places, and events plunge deep. Often, when I hear a scrap of music, I receive a dive chart to a long forgotten – and most welcome – memory.

[3]   *Iron railings that once enclosed the back courtyard had been removed to be melted down for use in the war effort. At that very moment, they may have sailed as parts of corvettes somewhere on the North Atlantic. Or have been fired out of guns in some jungle or desert. Or, saddest of all fates, they could lie rusting in heaps next to a factory in England, never to be used for anything as useful as killing .*

[4]   *I cannot remember when it stopped or when I ended up at Uncle Sigvard's, in bed with a fever. Naomi and I suffered such serious welts, they oozed for days.*

Chapter Six
Qui, Moi? (1943)

"Speak roughly to your little boy,
And beat him when he sneezes:
He only does it to annoy,
Because he knows it teases."
– Lewis Carroll, Alice's Adventures in Wonderland [1]

One day, a pimply faced Canadian soldier came to take us to our new home in Sussex. Too young to shave, but filled with his own importance, he declined to answer any of our excited questions. He was terribly short to be a soldier but we were smaller.

Through a countryside of pillboxes, checkpoints, and barricades, he flew the jeep over bumpy roads as if we weren't there. Maybe he was late. We hung on, wind and dust blowing in our faces. Our two small suitcases slid and banged from side to side as we swerved around corners. This was fun!

The kid spoke up only when he delivered us to Mother. "Voilà Madame, vos deux enfants." Then he squealed off in a cloud of dust.

Naomi and I suddenly had to get used to new names. My first name was to be Benoit – French for Bendt – and our new surname was Boucher. Benwa Booshay.[2]

It was September, 1943. We were taken into Horsham and registered in the Catholic school. Transportation was not provided to Catholic school students. Furthermore, we weren't allowed to accept rides from servicemen, be they British, Canadian, or American. We were to walk the two miles to school and the two miles home, without dawdling. Broadbridge Heath was a small village, an hour's walk from Horsham, within easy reach of Aldershot.[3]

On the road, we passed khaki lorries filled with khaki soldiers singing khaki songs. When it rained, which it did often, Naomi and I got soaked by passing, splashing lorries and jeeps. Our only reward for this came when Canadian and American soldiers drove by in convoys and tossed us sticks of gum. But Mother always made us spit out the gum. "Get that disgusting wad out of your mouth!" Then she'd make us empty our pockets.

We often saw tanks on the road. I loved tanks and dreamed of being taken for a ride in one, though I never was. Housewives hated the tanks, especially the American ones. They drove over lawns and flower beds and knocked down fences.

"Are you coming in for tea?"

When it wasn't raining, we walked through fields where blackberries grew in hedgerows. We stumbled upon soldiers and village girls "doing it" behind the bushes as we walked through the fields. "You wanna come watch?" While the girls yelled at us to "Get lost!" or "Fuck off!", we giggled and ran.

We witnessed mock battles. Soldiers ran through hedgerows and in and out of clumps of trees, throwing small bags of flour at each other. As we walked home from church one Sunday morning, planes swooped low over us. Instinctively, my sister and I dove into a ditch. Covered in smelly mud, we had to undress at the back door before entering the house. The smell of manure made Mother sick.

Mother got sick a great deal of the time. As a result, my sister and I had more and more to do in and around the house. Before long, it became obvious Mother was going to have a baby.

Naomi and I weren't allowed to play with the neighborhood "guttersnipes". So, we spent our spare moments in and around the back garden shelter. I found the nose cap of a bomb in a crater near our house. Many of the kids collected bits of shrapnel, incendiary bomb fins, and spent bullet casings. So the nose cap was a real treasure. With a large iron ring on its conical tip, it was at least eight inches in diameter and weighed several pounds. I could have traded it for gum and sweets. Mother confiscated the souvenir.

Food was severely rationed but we made do. I don't remember complaining much.

Mother sent us to the butcher with money, a note, and ration tickets. Sometimes, the butcher slipped a small packet of liver in with the salty sausage meat. Mother told us we'd learn to love liver "whether you like it or not".

People got together in groups to raise a community pig and share the benefits of saving scraps. We deposited our kitchen slops and food scraps in a bucket, and a woman came around with horse and cart to collect. Sheep grazed on the commons and in the parks. I remember rabbits and chickens in many back garden pens. People fed their pets dandelion leaves until cuddly bunnies got big and fat. Then the bunnies disappeared.

Every home had a victory garden. After the milkman came by, we raced out to pick up the horse dung steaming in the morning air. Since everything was valued, nothing got wasted. At school, we grew carrots and radishes and beet root and potatoes. Our teachers took us on outings to pick berries for jam. We also picked crab apples for jelly and rose hips for the syrup that mothers gave to babies.

At night, soldiers walked through Broadbridge Heath singing at the tops of their voices. They stopped to relieve themselves against bushes and fences and to deposit empty bottles. Warnings were posted by military police: "Drive with care; the child you hit may be your own".

Christmas, 1943, brought parcels from Canada, with clothes and food and knitted booties and baby gowns. Naomi and I were invited to meet Santa Claus at the Canadian Forces base. We sat on wooden chairs in a huge quonset hut and sang carols and received bags of sweets. Santa Claus appeared with an obviously false beard that kept slipping, and a continuous "Ho! Ho! Ho! Merry Christmas!" that we had never heard before. Our concept of Father Christmas was an elfin character who resided mainly in our imaginations.

Some children were invited up to receive presents from Santa's sack. Naomi and I weren't called, despite the fact that our new father was Canadian. We felt left out.

March 23, 1944, just as an air raid siren sounded, Mother determined it was time for her twins to be born. "Put on the kettle, get out clean towels and cotton wool, and scrub those hands."

Since the midwife wouldn't come during an air raid, Mother sent Naomi next door to get help. Nobody came.

At just under eleven years of age, terrified, I helped bring twins into the world. I'm not sure what I did, but I fetched hot water and towels and mopped up. There was blood and yelling. The house shook, maybe from what was going on within, maybe from a V-1 exploding outside. I can't say. Finally a nurse arrived from the village. I was sent off to bed. Next day our back garden air raid shelter, which we never used and which always had ankle-deep water in it, lay in ruins.[4]

I told my friends at school about the miracle of the birth. They sang in my honor:

"Tra, la, la boom-ty-ay,
Ben's mum had twins today.
They sucked her tits away.
Tra, la, la, boom-ty-ay."

In the weeks and months to come, I learned to change babies, wash diapers, and prepare bottles. Naomi and I did everything but cook. We sang duets and exchanged silly jokes while we washed and dried dishes and played with the babies on a blanket on the back lawn.

Mairzy doats and dozy doats and little lamzitivy.

We splashed one another or flicked the tea towel at each other's bare legs. The sound of our fun exasperated Mother, who needed peace and quiet. When she told us off, we'd burst into uncontrollable fits of giggles.

When doodle-bugs flew over, we stopped everything and watched them until their "put-put-put" suddenly stopped. Then we all lay flat, covering the babies, and waited for the explosion.[5]

On April 25th, 1944, Louise, Nicole, Naomi and Benoit, all declared to be the "children of Francis and Alice Boucher", were baptized according to the rite of the Roman Catholic Church at the Church of St. John the Evangelist in Horsham. Naomi and I had already been baptized privately in the Church of England, by our grandfather, the Reverend J.N. Nuttall-Smith, on July 6th, 1934. Now we were to be confirmed by the Bishop of Pella, in Horsham, on the 28th of September, 1944. I can't remember when we made our First Communion.

Who could ever forget that memorable June 6th, 1944, when the sky was blackened with the hundreds and hundreds of aircraft heading south towards France? For some days before that, there had been more movement than usual of tanks and "ducks" and lorries. All moved in the same direction. But the hustle and bustle didn't last long. One morning, we awoke to sudden quiet.

No more rumbling of military machinery. Even the soldiers were mostly gone; the camps seemed deserted. Some girls wept in the streets. Mothers cheered. People looked toward the sky, which gradually filled with aircraft of all sorts, including towed gliders. All headed for the French coast.

The invasion of Europe had finally begun. The war soon would be over.

On Tuesday, June 6th, we stayed home from school. We listened to the wireless for news from the beaches and from the small towns along the Normandy coast. The Fifth Symphony blared its V for Victory over the airwaves as BBC announcers proclaimed the people of Europe soon would be free once more.

We'll meet again, don't know where, don't know when...

In the days and weeks to come, we tried to continue normal existence. "Doodle-bugs" flew overhead more frequently. Once in a while, Spitfires and Hurricanes flew alongside them and touched their wings to redirect the bombs to explode over fields to the south of us rather than over London. In horror, we watched one brave RAF pilot touch the wing of a V-1. As it exploded, it reduced his plane to a shower of flaming shrapnel.[6]

Eventually, we moved back to London to await word from Canada House concerning transportation to Canada. This time, Uncle Sigvard lived on Grays Inn Road near King's Cross Station. That is where we went to stay.

While on standby notice, we couldn't leave the flat for more than short walks. The living room was always strung with washed nappies and baby clothes, which got soaked and wrung out in the kitchen sink. The flat was so crowded my sister and I had once more to share a room. This was far better than having to sleep with my uncle. Mother slept in uncle's room with the babies. Uncle Sigvard slept in the living room on a cot. Sometimes, he visited friends.

Again, Naomi and I stayed out of school. In our rediscovered freedom, we explored Wimbledon Common. The V-2 rockets terrorized Londoners. At home, when a flash of light was followed by an explosion, we stood in the dark with the curtains open and gazed at the glowing skyline.

One morning, after much begging, my uncle gave Naomi and me money for our first ice cream cone ever. We arrived just as the blast from a rocket destroyed a queue of over a hundred people. We saw a flash. Then we heard a whoosh and a thunderous explosion that echoed on and on. At one slap of a giant hand, the long line of men, women, and children flattened like a wall of playing cards. (Naomi and I had been protected from the blast by the walls of buildings that stood between us and the catastrophe.) There were screams and shouts and whistles and racing ambulances.

A woman ran towards us. "Oh, thank God you're all right!" She grabbed my sister. Neither of us knew who she was. Eventually a policeman came to lead the confused woman to an ambulance.

The money still in our perspiring palms, we ran back to Uncle Sigvard's. Throughout that night, people's screams rang in my ears.

The next day, ambulances still picked up the pieces. Glass and debris had flown outwards in all directions. A huge building had been wiped out, leaving behind just one enormous crater.

THE BOMB

where were you when the bomb dropped
when feet and fingers flew
when bits and pieces
lay about
I'm asking
where
were
you
?
that was so very long ago
but just the other night
and every night
the glazed eyes stare
to scream my sleep
and drown my
tears tears
tears
!

It was during that period that I began to wet the bed. The

more I tried to hide the fact, the more I sensed a smell about me like an old dead fish. When my uncle discovered my secret, he got me up every evening to go to the bathroom. Soon the problem was solved. But only for the time being.

One night we were picked up by a Canadian Navy Wren to start our journey to Canada. We had to sit in the back of a blacked-out lorry with several other families. Children were allowed one small suitcase apiece. Mother was allowed two, one for her and one for the two babies; these had been packed since shortly after our arrival in London. We weren't allowed to bring anything else but the clothes on our backs and our gas masks, which we had carried with us forever. Gramophone records, books, toys, paintings, all had to be left behind, to be sent on, maybe, at some later date.

At Canada House, we sat in a large room as more and more people arrived. When night turned to day, we were served sandwiches and tea. Night fell once more and people sprawled out on their luggage. Babies cried and cried. People lined up for the washrooms. "Hey! Wait your turn." "But I gotta go." The air was filled with cigarette smoke. Some were ragged and thin, thinner even than we were. Many just sat and stared at nothing, as though blind. Some chatted away in strange languages.

In the middle of our second full night, we were led out single file and loaded into buses with windows blacked out. Someone said we were heading to Portsmouth. Someone else said we would be going by train to Liverpool. Another reminded us that no one knew how or where we were going; word might get out and we'd all be sunk before we sailed past the south coast of Ireland, where the entire fleet of German U-boats sat waiting to blow us into the frigid March waters. Relieved at such cheerful news, we enjoyed the dark bumpy roads. Someone sang:

> *Old Hitler has a bunion,*
> *A face like a pickled onion,*
> *A nose like a squashed tomato,*
> *two legs like broomsticks.*

Someone else chimed in:

Hitler has only got one ball;
Goering has two but very small;
Himler has rather sim'lar
But poor old Goebells has no balls at all.

Another favourite was the song that the Yanks sang as they marched through the villages before D- Day:

This is number nine and the baby's doing fine
Roll me over, lay me down and do it again.

As more people joined in, we felt cheerful for the first time in days. But when the driver passed along word that we should be as quiet as possible and not bring attention to ourselves, we hushed up for a long time. Babies stopped crying.

At last we were led off the buses and into a large empty shed awash with puddles and reeking of oil. In pouring rain, we went in small groups up a gangplank to be welcomed aboard the RMV Rangitata (a New Zealand (Kiwi) name) – a converted oil tanker.

As the wife of a major with four children, Mother was awarded the privileges of an upper cabin and service at the captain's table. Most of the other passengers had to spend their time seasick in cramped quarters.

As soon as we sailed out of sight of land, we were summoned to lifeboat drill. Each of us was assigned a spot in a lifeboat. There we were instructed to sit, wearing our life jackets and carrying our ever-present gas masks. We were ordered away from our lifeboats and back to them several times, until deemed speedy enough to be seaworthy. Then we went for steaming mugs of hot cocoa and biscuits ("cookies").

While many on board ship were seasick, Naomi and I enjoyed our adventure. We hid behind the stacks and smoked Pall Mall cigarettes with a Canadian boy, sailing with his mother. He taught us the Canadian saying: "Aw, gee whiz, ma!" This we tried out just once on our mother.

We heard stories of the Canadian prairies from sailors who had been brought up on farms where it took all day to ride on horseback from the front gate to the house. We were told how in winter it grew so cold that people spoke, then had to go inside for words to thaw out before they could be heard. We heard how in summer the mosquitoes grew so big they could pick up a cow and fly off with it - if someone didn't shoot the mosquito first, that is.

Sometimes we hid in the lifeboats where we could observe without being seen. When caught, we'd be pulled out and sent running. Then we'd find somewhere else to play, away from bossy grown-ups.

One black night, about five days out, Noami and I and our friend from Canada sat in a lifeboat watching explosion after explosion as corvettes fired depth charges into the ocean. We should have been with our mothers below decks, but our mothers were too busy looking after babies so we weren't missed when the call to "action stations" came.

I saw ships on fire and heard men screaming in the water below our cutter. Sailors and lifeboats floated about on the icy sea amidst the flotsam and jetsam. They had struggled to the choppy surface through oil slick, debris, and frantic companions. People cried. Some were burned. Some were broken and bleeding. Nearly all were encased in thick, viscous oil.

In all this agony, our ship picked up no survivors. She couldn't. In doing so, she would have endangered her own passengers and cargo.

As we raced along at full speed, I heard the distant thuds of bursting depth charges. The u-boats were the wolf pack; we were sheep for the slaughter. In such tight quarters, gunnery could do little. The Royal Air Force could no longer help us out; we were probably too far beyond their reach, in that part of the North Atlantic World War II sailors called "The Black Pit".

The rescue ship had to be close by. But she couldn't come in all the way without an escort. Worse, Grand Admiral Dönitz had instructed his U-boat captains to take no prisoners. The Nazis were in a death struggle as the Allies closed in to end the war.

On the deck below, a sailor remarked, "It's the graveyard watch!" Another replied, "Yeah. Rightly named!" I gazed out at the eerily glowing horizon. The sea stared back, cruel, heartless, and threatening. My stomach churned.

We had sailed from Liverpool on March 13th. We would not reach Halifax until March 24th. [7]

Following "stand easy", we three rejoined our mums for supper. Naomi and I had our ears boxed. "Where were you two? I was worried sick." We didn't tell what we'd seen.

Eventually, we docked in Halifax. For all the secrecy of our voyage, a newspaper reporter greeted us when we boarded the train in Halifax. Our picture appeared in Le Soleil, with a story in French, on the day we arrived in Quebec City (March 24th, 1945). The headlines in other Canadian papers, just a few days previously, read:

> *Convoy ships returning to Canada sunk by German U-boats, including the HMCS GUYSBOROUGH, LOST with 51 hands, March l7th, l945.* [8]

* * * * * * * *

[1]   **Carroll**, Lewis; *The Annotated Alice* [New   York: New American Library, 1960.], p. 85

[2]   *This was so sudden. I didn't know it then, but we were going into hiding. We would disappear from the Nuttall-Smith family. No one would ever find us.*
The house, "Fircroft" on Guildford Road in Broadbridge Heath, doesn't stand very firmly in my memory. Nor does our first meeting with "Papa", the major.

[3]   *The home of the Canadian Army Overseas was at Aldershot, in Hampshire. The entire area of Hampshire and West Sussex was a practice ground for D-Day.*

[4]   *I don't remember if the air raid was German planes trying to bomb the army barracks nearby or a doodle-bug on its way to London.*

5   To escape the terrifying V1 rockets, a million children were evacuated during June and July 1944 from all over the south of England.

The V-1, "buzz bomb", doodle-bug" was more terrifying than the bombers. It "put-putted" slowly overhead. We had fifteen seconds from the time the droning noise stopped until the powerful blast that followed.

Some large chunks would flatten houses. Mostly, those that didn't reach London left sizeable holes in farmers' fields.

About 8,000 V-1 rockets were launched at Britain; over 2,000 of these hit London, killing over 6,000 people and destroying about 500,000 homes.

The terrifying V-2s proved even more destructive than the V-1s. They flew very fast and high, much too high and fast to be shot down by antiaircraft guns or fighter aircraft.

Five hundred V-2s hit London, killing 2,855 civilians.

6   In a letter to my stepfather, Mother tells him what a problem I 've become. "I was very foolish even to let him go with Sigvard for this week – for it seems to me he is now more difficult than ever! .... Sigvard even tried to influence the boy against religion." How different my life might have been could I have revealed my terrible secret.

Nobody knew then, nobody was ever to know, the incredible sexual abuse I had been suffering at the hands of my uncle ever since I first went to live with him during the blitz. I hid the unbearable memories like dirty laundry under my bed and lived much of my life running from the guilt of "my sin".

7   For years afterwards, the silent, disembodied screams, signaled by oil-coated hands reaching out of the water, disturbed my sleep. My nightmares even awakened my wife. It was partly out of a sense of debt to those tortured sailors that both Naomi and I joined the Canadian Navy as soon as we were old enough.

I have been asked why people were willing to ship and be shipped across the Atlantic while times were still so dangerous. Thousands of children were sent to Canada, the United States, Australia, and New Zealand. Anything was better than sitting night after night as the sky screamed down on us.

8   see World Wide Web:
http://uboat.net/allies/warships/ship/2666.html

Chapter Seven (1945/46)
Canada

> Well-loved land of mighty rivers,
> Bark canoes and beaver dams,
> Indian warriors on their ponies,
> French in snowshoes, giant logjams,
> Forests tall and endless prairie,
> Rocky mountains, hills of snow,
> Redcoats riding, singing cowboys,
> Fields of wheat, and buffalo.

We came ashore in the dim light of early morning to be ushered into a large drafty shed in Halifax Harbour. The adults stood in long queues to have documents checked while the Canadian Red Cross doled out hot cocoa and buns.

Then we were taken on buses to board a blacked-out train, cramped among crying babies and bossy mothers we didn't know.

"Stop picking your nose, you little guttersnipe."

I doubt anyone had managed a bath since leaving lodgings in London two weeks earlier. The air, blue with cigarette smoke, reeked of sweat and urine.

When we left the train in Quebec City, the day was already over. On the dimly lit platform, fresh air and light snow signaled our arrival in Paradise. Relatives greeted many with hand printed signs. Other passengers remained on the train to shuttle on to Montreal and points west.

Aunties Patricia and Madeleine and Uncles Louis and Emilien took us by taxis to the family home – the upper level of a large house in Limoilou. With half a house for five adults, two children and two babies, this was more room than we had ever known. We were given towels and face cloths and invited to wash up. Then we were shown to our rooms. Naomi got a bed in our Aunties' room; I had my stepfather's bed across from my two uncles in another huge bedroom. Mother and the babies were given the grandparents' room. Biggest of all, this had been kept for special guests. I had never seen such high ceilings.

Both Pat and Madeleine were short and slim. Madeleine smoked a perpetual cigarette. Their voices were high pitched but gentle. Emilien, hunched over with a limp, sported a perpetual smile.

His eyes twinkled. He loved to tease. Louis was more silent and businesslike. Tall and slim, he was as kind as his brother. All four talked among themselves in a rapid French. How they heard one another remains a mystery.

Despite Mother's persistent refusal, Naomi and I were given clean clothes that had belonged to our uncles and aunts when they were our ages. Mother insisted Naomi and I go to bed immediately but Auntie Madeleine asked when we had last sat down to a proper meal. Mother was gently overruled. I went to the dinner table in knee britches and a warm pullover. Naomi wore a full length dress, the babies wore new dresses, and Mother looked more beautiful than I'd seen her in a very long time.

The table was set with lace cloth and candles and we all had wine with our meal. The two sisters ran back and forth carrying heaped dishes, each outdoing the other in kindness. Naomi and I ate as if we had never eaten before, and we drank far too much wine. With all the excitement, we babbled constantly, forgetting the English rule – "children are to be seen and not heard".

Mother was embarrassed. Everyone else was delighted. We talked and talked about the boat trip and asked hundreds of questions about Canada. Can we ski? Can we paddle up to Montreal and the Great Lakes in a canoe? Where do the Indians live?

Aunties Pat and Madeleine included Naomi and me in their conversations. They listened to each of us with great interest and quiet respect. Even when I wasn't talking and joining in, I felt included.

Following dinner, Aunties wrapped Naomi and me in woolen scarves, and mitts, coats, and overshoes – surprisingly they fit – and uncles Louis and Emilien took us for a walk in the cool night air. We could see first hand the high snow banks that lined the streets. On the way, my sister and I lost our supper. We had to be taken home and helped into bed.

The next day, feeling much better, Aunties fed us a breakfast of porridge, toast, butter, marmalade, big glasses of real milk, and oranges. Aunty Pat reminded us both to eat slowly and to enjoy.

We were not used to such food and so much loving attention.

That day was devoted to sightseeing with Uncle Emilien and

Auntie Pat. Uncle Louis went to work at the bank; Auntie Madeleine stayed home with Mother and the babies to help them get settled. Uncle Emilien and both aunties had taken the day off.

We went first by bus to see the Chateau Frontenac, where my stepfather had worked as a boy, and to the Ramparts with the huge sled run, where Uncle Emilien had been hit in the back and crippled for life.

The sled run had just ceased operation because of warmer weather. Despite that, I saw more snow than I ever had imagined. We explored the Plains of Abraham and the old city by horse-drawn calèche. After that, we visited the shop on Rue St. Jean where the aunts sold lingerie.

At the end of the day, we ate – and enjoyed a small glass of wine – in a beautiful restaurant. The bus ride back to Limoilou had people turning to see "les deux jeunes émigrés de L'Angleterre". We didn`t stop our excited chatter for an instant until we climbed the stairs, when Mother reminded us that the babies were sleeping.

More sightseeing was to come. We took memorable trips to the shrine at Ste. Anne de Beaupré, with its huge, panoramic, scale model. We visited Les Laurentides, where people went to ski, and Les Chutes Montmorency. On L'Isle d'Orléans, we ate bread, fresh baked in an outdoor oven. We went to the Quebec Zoo.

One of the best experiences of all was a visit to "la Cabane à Sucre" where we ate "taffée d'éràble" (maple toffee) and pancakes, smothered in real butter and maple syrup. There was so much to see and do that Mother had to remind us that our holiday couldn't last forever. Adults had to work and children had to attend school.

Auntie Madeleine took us first to St. Patrick's, taught by the De La Salle Christian Brothers. I was to enter grade five for the balance of the term, then repeat the grade starting in September.[21] Auntie gave me a bag lunch, a bus ticket, and a slip of paper with directions for getting home. Naomi enrolled at St. Monica's just down the hill from St. Pat's. She would be in the fourth grade which she would repeat the following year.

The grade five teacher, Mr. Sheehe, was about to begin reading Tom Sawyer to the class.

The boy in the desk next to mine was James *Simpson, who became my best friend at St. Pat's. Jimmy Simpson: champion high pisser, at school and at camp.

In the days to come, I joined the boys' choir. I also had a lot of fun exploring the Plains of Abraham with Jim and his younger brother Peter. They lived with their mother in an apartment on Grande Allée, overlooking the Plains. Their dad was still overseas, as was my new father. Since their mother was out much of the time, we had lots of time to get into mischief.

We took a couple of shotgun shells apart and rammed the powder into a model cannon with a wick. We put pellets down the barrel and fired the gun from the window. The explosion was terrific, and the apartment filled with smoke. Another day we dropped a water-filled balloon from the window onto some people on the street below. Jim also owned a chemistry set. We experimented with hydrogen sulfide and had to leave the door and windows open to get rid of the rotten egg smell before his mother got home.

It wasn't long before Mother made me dress again in the clothes we brought with us from England. I looked more like a British schoolboy than a Canadian. Naomi was lucky. Her school required a uniform; even if she didn't sound the same, at least she looked like everyone else. In my short pants, knee socks [which never stayed up], and oversized sweater [which came from some grab box] I was as English as any English kid could be. In comparison, every other boy my age wore knee breeches, parka, and toque.

The boys teased me, mercilessly. I was "Skinny", "Slim", and "Bloke". I shied away from rough-and-tumble. I couldn't catch a ball; I didn't know how to hold a baseball bat. I knew nothing about hockey; hadn't even heard of "the Rocket", Maurice Richard.

The violence of my past caught up with me in small ways. Whenever I was called to the principal's office, no matter what the reason, I hat the terrible feeling I was about to be strapped, caned, or spanked.

I tried making up for my weaknesses by asking and answering a lot of questions in class. That was not the tradition at St. Pat's; I had to be reminded to give other people a chance. Teachers were kind. Better yet, good food and loving care from aunts and uncles began to put meat on my bones.

Transportation home each day required a transfer at the bottom of Boulevard St. Jean to the Limoilou bus. As I headed home on my own, a group of boys near the transfer stop called to me: "Eh! 'ti gar." I answered: "I'm awfully sorry, I don't speak French."

That was a mistake. "Un maudit bloke!"

One of the boys pushed me until I fell backward over another boy crouched down behind me. Then they pounced. Blow after blow bloodied my nose and blackened my eye. A man came and pulled the bullies off me and asked questions in French. A bigger boy answered and pointed to me. The man cuffed me across the back of my head, and said, "Va t'en!". This I had no difficulty understanding: Get out of here.

I got out. Never mind the bus. I'd lost my transfer in the scuffle.

I ran the best I could in the direction of l8th Street and arrived home late. Despite my pleas and tears, I had to go without supper. Mother was insistent: I had to fight my own battles. If I lost a fight, I deserved what I got.

Later, Uncle Louis brought me up a sandwich and a glass of milk. Then he went back to the kitchen to chip some ice from the big block in the icebox. This he wrapped in a towel for my swollen eye. Though he understood my dilemma, nobody wanted to interfere in my discipline.

That night I had a terrible dream. I hid from Germans under my bed. I screamed and thrashed. Uncle Emilien shook me awake rescuing me from flames and mass murder. The next day, both uncles joked about my antics; nevertheless, they were concerned.

When Naomi and I left together for school, I had a "shiner". We caught the same buses as always and planned to meet at dismissal to return home together.

After school, I ran down the hill and waited at the gate to St. Monica's for my sister. I waited and waited but Naomi did not show up. I thought she had left without me but she had been kept in to get caught up on school work. The Sisters were very strict.

I boarded the next bus and got off at the same transfer point at the foot of St. Jean. The same gang of boys pushed and shoved one another at the bus stop. While everybody disembarked, I hid behind the last adults. The boys saw me and I made a run for it.

Though I arrived home late again, I was in better condition than the day before.

That evening, Uncle Louis gave me a present. From now on I could use his bicycle to ride to and from school, and wherever I pleased. It was mine to keep. Auntie Pat gave Naomi her bicycle. We had never owned bicycles before, but it didn't take us long to learn to keep our balance.

Naomi still preferred to take the bus to and from school. But I decided it would be far healthier and less expensive if I used the bicycle. That convinced Mother to let me keep the gift, at least, for the time being.

A great many of the boys who attended St. Pat's were from the Cove. The Cove was home to the Irish who landed at that point during the Great Potato Famine. The Irish had long been persecuted by the British. Even the Brothers told tales of how the "Black and Tans" would break into Catholic homes and beat and smash in the pretext of looking for hidden arms.

We all learned about "Black Friday", when British soldiers recruited from the prisons of England and "the North", massacred the Irish. Not only that, they carried out house-to-house searches and imprisoned those Irish who refused to belong to the Protestant Church of Ireland.[2]

It was Ireland's troubles with the British that got me into trouble. Since I spoke with an English accent, I was the enemy.

One weekend, Naomi and I rode our bicycles along the waterfront near the Lévis ferry terminal. Someone shouted "Hey, Limey!" I recognized one or two scruffy faces from St. Pat's.

Naomi and I pedaled as fast as we could to the big hill that wound its way up to the far end of the Plains of Abraham. There we got off our bicycles to push our way up the hill. Halfway up, having taken some shortcut unknown to us, the Cove boys waited. Naomi and I turned our bicycles around and sped down the hill. At the bottom, I misjudged the turn and crashed into a monument. The bicycle got the better of the deal.

A kind passerby had to drive me home. I was in a terrible mess. The result was that Mother made us return the bicycles.

When the school term finally ended, we all headed to a

65

cottage on Lac Sergeant. Aunties stayed with us while someone took over their shop for the summer. Uncles Louis and Emilien stayed in Limoilou during the week and came up weekends.

Meanwhile, Naomi and I rowed a "shaloupe" out on the lake and caught frogs and sunfish. We picked blueberries on the hill near an orphanage. The nuns at the orphanage seemed kind. But the flies and the smells from the kitchen brought back memories of boarding school.

Because Louise and Nicole were just babies, Mother let them play naked on the sandy shore by the wharf. This invited a visit from Monsieur le Curé (the parish priest) and several women. All were shocked by Mother's "loose" moral standards. She told them all, including Monsieur le Curé, what she thought of them.

Shortly after, the local Chef de Police visited her. In French, which she knew well, Mother tossed about a few choice words that shocked our aunties but brought delighted laughter from Mon Oncle Emilien.

Still, the authorities won out. The babies wore little dresses while playing in the water. When we went to Mass on Sunday mornings at the local parish, Mother stayed home. "Renégat damnée."

All too soon, the summer holidays were over, and the terrors of returning to school had to be faced once more. Though the war was over, many soldiers would not return for quite a while.

Worse, battles still raged in my mind. Often, while we played in the school yard, planes from the Air Force base at Valcartier flew over our heads. This inspired a terror in me worse than I felt in England. Instinctively, I crouched down and covered my head. Of course, no one understood delayed emotional response. So I got scolded for "play acting".

The more nervous I became, the more I got picked on. Boys flew past me in mock raids and batted my head with their "wings". To their delight, I responded by covering my face with my arms. To add to my woe, the bed wetting returned.[3]

In September 1945, I was still in grade five but with a different teacher. The Brother who taught me didn't show the same sympathy and protection that I'd received from Mr. Sheehe. More and more, I was openly laughed at in class, especially for using

British rather than Canadian terminology and pronunciation.

The Brother constantly corrected me. He strapped me for poorly done homework and for failing to memorize my Catechism answers. "How does God love you?" Whack!

I asked questions a boy my age had no business asking. The brother told us about the terrible sufferings that awaited in purgatory, even eternal damnation, if we touched ourselves in an "impure" way or if we allowed ourselves to have "impure" thoughts. "There are more souls in hell from sins of impurity than for any other sin".

I was sure the Brother could gaze right through to my soul. My bed wetting and the constant smell that went with me were a direct result of sins of impurity.

Soon we had to move. My enuresis was part of the problem, as was Mother's row with my aunties. The babies teethed on the dining room chair legs.

We moved to Sillery. Despite the upset at losing our aunts and uncles for the time being, I was delighted to discover that we were within walking distance of school.

As my aunties no longer were close by to baby-sit, Mother's patience with Naomi and me grew shorter. I was sent to school stinking of pee. I had to put my mattress over the front railing every day. I was no longer given a bottom sheet.

In the winter months, after getting draped over the railing most of the day, my mattress got caked with ice. I had to turn it over many times. It got covered, not just with pee stains, but with rust.

I can't remember why or when I stopped my bed wetting. Having nothing to drink after supper, then waking myself up with terrible nightmares and going to the bathroom may have helped.

Eventually, Mother gave me a cover for my smelly mattress. Life improved.[4]

We lived on Cremazie Street, in rooms above a store run by two elderly matrons. One day, Mother decided to get rid of a full length fur coat. Maybe she suspected it would attract moths. She ordered me to put it in the garbage; instead, Naomi and I took it downstairs to the shopkeepers. They were so delighted that, for quite some time, they supplied us with all sorts of candies and "junk". Pixy Stix: straws full of tart sugar you sprinkled on your tongue. Tiny wax Coke bottles with colored sugar water inside. Wax lips and wax buck teeth you could both wear and chew. Jawbreakers - also known as gob stoppers; as you sucked them, they turned different colours. And candy cigarettes, the mint ones with pink tips. And chocolate cigarettes. And licorice pipes.

They also supplied me with comic books, which I read in secret and traded with my friends. If Mother found comic books, she destroyed them, whether they were ours or belonged to friends. I especially enjoyed Classic Comics, as well as Beano, Rover, and Hotspur. These were the glorious absurdities. Though I was less interested in Superman and other Marvel Comics, I read and traded them anyway.

We kept our loot hidden from Mother. Though we still fought over dishes and diapers and other housework, Naomi and I drew closer.

Since I didn't have any friends during that school year, apart from Jimmy Simpson, I welcomed the school choir. Some Sundays, we sang at St. Patrick's Church.

Naomi and I walked to church every Sunday. One sunny day, my sister forgot to wear the obligatory hat or scarf. To make up for this, she put a handkerchief on her head. The result was that we were both seized by fits of the giggles, during which I pretended to sneeze, grabbed the hanky from her head, and loudly blew my nose.

On Monday morning, we paid for our impertinence and disrespect. We each got called to the principal's office at our respective schools. I got the strap. As long as Mother didn't find out, we took everything in our stride and faced the world's inconsistencies together.

On weekends in the winter, we went to the Plains of Abraham and tobogganed down hills on pieces of cardboard. On one hill, an excellent bump sent the kids sprawling. Then someone discovered a hand sticking up out of the snow. Our "bump" was an old man who had frozen on the hill and got covered by snow. Even though I'd seen dead people before, I dreamt of that hand coming out of the snow to grab me by the penis.

My nightmares became a nuisance. My screams got loud enough to awaken the babies. Mother told me that, if I didn't stop trying to "get attention" in this way, I would have to sleep in the back shed. This didn't stop me. So Mother walked in and slapped my face when I screamed. That didn't help either. I also walked in my sleep. On one occasion, I strolled into my sister's room and tried to make Naomi "get out of my bed".

Always I got punished for my "foolish" antics. Once, when she got really furious with me, Mother gave me a black eye. I had to tell teachers and friends at school that I had bumped into a door.

Naomi had her share of grief. Once she was thrown into an icy bath for not washing properly.

If we tried to defend ourselves when she slapped us, or if our hands rose as an automatic response to being swung at, Mother struck us with anything that lay handy. As most of her blows occurred when we washed and dried dishes, we frequently got hit with wooden spoons, but sometimes with pots and pans.

Though Naomi and I each found separate friends as time went on, we still went for long, exploratory walks together. Sometimes in the winter, when we returned home late and freezing cold, Mother locked us out. So I found a way to climb over the roof of a shed at the back of the shop; if my window wasn't also locked, I managed to get us in. Otherwise, we had to wait around until Mother unlocked the door. Either way, we were in for it, no matter our reason.

After the school year passed, Mother decided I would spend a couple of weeks at YMCA summer camp. Maybe this was a gift from the Boucher family or from my stepfather. One of my uncles gave me a sleeping bag. I can't recall if Naomi went to a girls' camp. Camp in the Laurentians was a tonic. Not only were Jim and Peter there, I made new friends, too.

We all whispered and farted and snored and giggled during the first night. "Pipe down in there before I come in and smack the lot of you." Silence for two, maybe three minutes. Then we whispered and farted and snored and giggled some more, until early morning light. After that, we just carried on – until time to get up.

I started to wet the bed again. But I wasn't the only one. Some days, quite a few sleeping bags were hung out to dry. One of the counsellors began getting us up at night, and we all felt better.

There were no girls within miles, apart from adult kitchen staff, so we boys swam in the buff. One day, during general swim, a group of us were playing "Tarzan" from a rope which swung out over the water. We were unaware of a hornets' nest until someone threw a stick into the bush. Large stinging wasps swarmed the waterfront. I had to be taken to the infirmary, placed on a rubber sheet, and bathed down in milk of magnesia.

The camp scheduled a rest period after lunch, which we spent in our tents. This was a time for writing letters home or reading comics or telling stories. Though it was supposed to be a quiet time, it never was. On one occasion, our counselor, a boy in his teens, had us all laughing by jumping up and down on his bunk bare naked. He asked someone to pull his finger and emitted a loud fart. We all laughed.

On Sunday, Jimmy's mother was deeply offended when Jimmy told her about the counsellor, and how we had all laughed and joined in. On Monday morning, the camp director called us, one by one, into his office.

The counselor had been sent home in disgrace. The rest of us – all but Jimmy – were spanked.

When I was ushered in before the camp director and saw him sitting there with the miniature canoe paddle, known by most campers as "the board of education", I trembled and felt as though I was going to throw up. Nothing in what others had already told me gave me cause for such a reaction. I just stood there and cried.

I couldn't explain myself. I knew I had to get it over with. Surprisingly, the spanking itself didn't hurt much. What hurt more was when the director remarked on the smell of pee from my underwear and asked if I wet the bed. I tried to hide the fact that, despite being gotten up at night, I still had the occasional accident.

Later that morning, my sleeping bag was opened and hung out to dry while others from my tent were present. After that, Jimmy and I no longer were friends.

* * * * * * * *

[1]   *I had already completed beyond this level in England. But, because of missed time during bombing and moves, the principal at St. Pat's insisted I repeat grade five. Some school administrators did not know, or chose not to acknowledge, that education in England was often far more demanding than in Canada.*

[2]   *The Brothers talked a great deal about the British savagery of 1916 in Ireland. But they said very little about the I.R.A., nor about the Irish Civil War in which Irish killed Irish.*

[3]   *A flaw exists in human nature that makes men and women reject the weak and wounded in their midst. Children are often attracted to a school yard fight. They cheer the victor and scorn the weeping loser.*

We need scapegoats so we may purge our own inadequacies. We feel superior in seeing others lose. Birds peck the weakling to death.

In the survival of the species, we kill off the "undesirables". The abuser acts out his anger at his own unacknowledged pain by picking on the struggling victim.

[4]   *Child psychologists now know that bedwetting can be an indication of sexual abuse amongst other things. When parents finally face the fact that their child might have been abused – quite possibly by a family member – they must pursue therapy for the child, and supportive counselling for themselves. In Canada, this is often funded by the province.*

Chapter Eight (1946/50)
Heading For the Ice.

> Waters that deep below
> The stubborn ice can go
> With quiet underflow,
> Contented to be dumb
> Till spring herself shall come
> To listen to your song!
> – Robert Kelley Weeks, Man and Nature [1]

While I was at camp, my stepfather, Papa François returned from Europe. Soon we moved to "L'Ecole d'Hotèlerie" – Canadian Vocational Training School for Veterans, at St. Paul l'Hermite, just east of Montreal. Major François Boucher had been commissioned to start the school having learned his trade at the Chateau Frontenac before the war. The place was a huge barracks, and most everyone spoke French. Meals were served by waiters in training. We had the best food and the best service because the major was big man on campus. My step father was shorter than I, much plumper but not fat. He was handsome with small moustache. His English was impeccable. His men respected him.

Naomi and I spent time exploring. I won't say we didn't get into trouble. Apart from that, I have nothing to relate at this time. We moved to little house in Strathmore, thirteen miles to the west of Montreal and a stone's throw from Lac St. Louis.

Naomi was registered to attend the English class at L'Ecole Ste. Jeanne de Chantalle. I enrolled for grade six at St. Ignatius of Loyola in Montreal West. We both received bicycles for our birthdays so we could ride to school.

On weekends, we cycled up Sources Road on the far side of the railroad tracks, until the road ended at an old quarry. There we saw used safes dancing on the bushes – French letters, loaded and tied, trophies waving in the wind.

Other times we cycled along the lakeshore, to Pointe Claire and Lachine. In the fields surrounding Dorval Airport, we spent many contented hours playing in the ruins of air force planes. Immediately, I became an RAF pilot defending London from Messerschmitts and heavy bombers. Reliving dogfights, my imagination laboured overtime.

In those days, the new highway had not been constructed; we lived practically in farm country. Grown tall and lanky by now, I dressed like other boys my age. Though my English accent was fast disappearing, Mother didn't permit sloppy speech; she made sure my sister and I spoke clearly and distinctly, often making us repeat our phrases until she was satisfied with our enunciation.

I enjoyed my two years at St. Ignatius and made friends, both at school and in Strathmore. When the heavy snows came, I found it increasingly difficult to ride my bicycle the thirteen miles each way, to and from school. Papa François gave me a train pass for the coldest months.

At Christmas, my sister and I received skates. At the hockey rink in the park behind our house, I spent a lot of time keeping out of the way of the local hockey players and holding on to the boards. Gradually I strengthened my ankles enough to propel myself without mishap. But one thing didn't change: my scapegoat status. The local ruffians enjoyed butting me over the boards into mounds of snow.

Naomi learned to skate a lot faster than I. Soon she had a group of friends to skate and spend time with. My best friend was Ian *Cavalier, whose father was our Scout Master. Ian could figure skate better than any of the girls, who tried copying his pirouettes and jumps.

François Boucher determined I would become the son fate denied him. "Do not associate with that "fifi" fancy-skater, at least not on the skating rink. Play hockey like a Canadian for Christ sake."

Fat chance! As soon as I skated onto the ice with a hockey stick, I ended up in a snow bank or flat on the ice against the boards.

One day, a gang of rough kids chased me home. The front door was locked. The bullies beat me up right there on my front steps. My stepfather was furious that I didn't put up a fight. Definitely, something was wrong with me. He wanted a son to be proud of.

God knows, I tried my best to please him.

Ian Cavalier did as well on roller skates in the summer as he did on the ice in the winter. Once, he let me try his roller skates. I attached the clamps to my shoes, tightened them with his skate key, and then stood. I moved slightly, my feet flew from under me, and I

73

landed with a thump. Painfully, I removed the skates.

My one escape came through books. Throughout my school years, in fact, since I first learned to read, I devoured every book I could get my hands on. I read the Greek heroes and the Classics. I cried over Charles Dickens, Charlotte Brontë, and Jane Austen, explored with Mark Twain, Jack London, Robert Louis Stevenson, Jules Verne, Rudyard Kipling, and Sir Walter Scott. I curled up in corners at school, even stood in the school yard absorbing every Hardy Boy adventure I could borrow from friends or acquire as Christmas and birthday presents. At night, I read by flashlight under the bedcovers. I read until my eyes ached.

Grade Seven turned out to be the year for discovering girls. According to boyhood boasting, every boy except me had "done it", gone all the way, with one of the girls near St. Ignatius. In an apple orchard some distance from the school was a pup tent where rites of passage were supposedly played out.

I asked the girl who had the most promising reputation if she would go into the pup tent with me. She refused. Not only did she say no, she told me I was sick, queer, and "wouldn't know what to do anyway."

Once, after early dismissal from school, we sat around in a circle. We, boys and girls alike, lounged, sprawled, wrestled, watched, and pissed ourselves with laughter.

The girl opposite me hiked her skirt up around her knees. She wasn't wearing panties! I looked around, hoping, praying that no one else saw what was happening to me. I laid my arms over my boner.

Little booklets of pornographic cartoons, depicting men with gigantic penises, penetrating girls tied to trees and demonstrating every perversity imaginable, were sold from under the counter in a corner store near the school. These books set my imagination awhirl. After masturbating in the school washroom and in the bathroom at home, I destroyed my booklets in dread that I might die and go to hell before getting the chance to go to confession.

How many times did I repeat the same confession? How many little booklets did I rip up and flush down the toilet? My life was a torture of shame and desire, imaginings and guilt.

I remember a high school kid who peddled porn. He hung around St. Ignatius' playground at lunch time, his pockets jingling coin. To get our interest, he gave us all quick glances at his flicker cards. It cost a nickel to see a woman pull up her skirt while a man ran at her with a tool as long and thick as a baseball bat. When someone paid him, he held tight to his deck with his grubby left paw and rippled through his cards with his right thumb.

"Hey! Not so fast. I missed it."

"Bring your nickel and see a show. Step right up, me boys."

The porn kid offered bargains, too. "Three flicks for a dime. For a quarter, you get to hold the cards yourself."

"Sins of desire are as bad as sins actually committed." If you think about it, you've committed a mortal sin.

Maybe it was just as well that I was usually penniless on those occasions. Although Naomi and I both earned money baby-sitting, we were expected to turn our earnings over to Mother for safekeeping. Mother would then give us what we needed for the occasional movie in Pointe Claire or at the Parish Hall, and for other special expenses as needed. We were seldom permitted the luxury of spending foolishly.

The Paroisse Ste. Jeanne de Chantale showed movies on Saturday afternoons. Dimes clutched in sweaty fists, we chaotically crammed the ticket table and paid our admission just as soon as the doors opened. After that, we scrambled to claim seats as close as possible to the screen.

The only trouble with the movies was that, every now and then, the projectionist turned off the sound and gave tedious explanations in French while the kids threw paper airplanes or shot spit balls with elastic bands; no one really listened.

We often watched series to be continued the following week. If we weren't allowed to attend, we missed part of the story. Once someone got the bright idea of bringing in several French safes and blowing them up. The Brother in charge caught one as it flew through the line of projection. He stopped the movie, and we were sent home.

Some people are good with animals. I've always been good with children and babies. As one of the best baby-sitters on the

Lakeshore, I made fair money looking after other people's kids. I changed and fed babies, read bedtime stories to toddlers, and wrote down telephone messages for partying parents. I was a natural. I also spent countless weekend hours pulling my baby sister, Jackie, through the snow on long toboggan rides.

Jackie was born November 20, 1947, a year and a half after our move to Strathmore. The twins, almost four years older now, hated getting stuck with their baby sister. Sometimes, to get rid of her, they initiated a game of hide-and-seek. Jackie covered her eyes, pressed her face against the wall, and shouted the few numbers she knew at two years of age. As soon as she ended with a breathless "Cent!" (one hundred), she ran off in all directions to find her older sisters. Louise and Nicole were not to be found; they had disappeared down the street to Majoleine's house. I took my sobbing sister to the park and pushed her tears away on the swing.

One rainy day, I was having a rough-and-tumble on the floor with the three babies when my stepfather barged into the room, jerked me to my feet, and checked my fly. Every button was done up. But I felt as ashamed as if I had done some terrible act. Sent outside to find companions my own age, I felt judged for what I might have done.

It's not that I was oh-so-innocent either. Ian and I had played "rudies" in the woods. We would try to get a hard-on and compare sizes. Then we'd see who could piss the highest up a tree.

This otherwise innocent childhood experience of exploration and discovery shrouded me in shame, and I had to tell my "sin" in confession. "Father, I played with myself ... and my friend was with me." This was the worst kind of sin, very hard to tell a priest. Especially the part about being with someone else. Any thought of homosexuality or being "gay" had not entered my mind. Indeed, I had not even heard the term "gay" as a sexual term.

Naomi and I often rode our bicycles up and down the Lakeshore. We explored way up Sources Road to a gravel pit, where the road ended. After one long hot ride to the gravel pit, I offered to switch bikes for the ride back if she'd show me her pussy. I don't remember what we called it at that time. Certainly, I had heard the words "cunt", "box", and "vagina". Since "Pussy" sounded nice and safe to me, likely I used that. Because her bike was harder to peddle than mine, Naomi obliged. There was no way she'd let me touch it, even if I wanted to.

I had my peek, and we rode silently back to Strathmore. We never mentioned the "pussy" incident again. Perhaps, to Naomi, it was like showing a knee scab or a wart. To me, it was not a monumental discovery; in fact, I was disappointed. Pictures in books proved far more exciting.

Papa François and I were never close. He never administered physical punishment, except on one occasion, when Mother insisted that he spank me with his belt. I cried out for effect. He didn't hurt me as my mother had so often done; in fact, he looked uncomfortable throughout the experience. Maybe he'd witnessed too much suffering in Europe. I don't remember ever having felt love for my stepfather. I remember no intimate "father-son" talks. I did not have fun with him. But I did respect him.

I will always remember Papa's great devotion at Mass every Sunday. He knelt, with his head bowed low, and prayed fervently. Mother stayed home with the "babies". She appeared religious only at times. Sometimes, she seemed irreligious.

In September, 1948, I had one of three choices: Loyola High School taught by the Jesuits, a French school in Montreal taught by Les Frères des Ecoles Chretiennes (which had a great reputation but charged a fee), and L'Ecole St. Louis de Strathmore taught by les Frères de l'Instruction Chretien. I made my choice mainly to please my parents. Attending high school in Strathmore would save transportation costs and fees. I would also have to become fluently bilingual. Maybe then I'd no longer be the phony English kid with the French name who didn't belong in either world. I knew I was going to have a tough battle, but I was determined.

Grades Eight and Nine were taught together by one Brother. This was total immersion. A couple of boys, who also spoke English, helped me give my answers en français. But "J'aime fourir ma mère!" (I like to fuck my mother) did not go over very well. I got the strap while my classmates split their sides laughing.

In our history lessons, we learned about the cruel outcome of the Battle of the Plains of Abraham and the torture of the French and

Hurons by the savage Iroquois and "les maudits Anglais". Frequently, we reenacted these battles on the playground - until I found excuses to remain in class, cleaning blackboards and brushes or catching up on corrected assignments. But this, by making me "le petit pet", only aggravated matters.

Despite difficulties, I gradually succeeded. By age sixteen, I knew as much French as a boy needed to use, at least for a place like Strathmore.

School learning proved to be simple – and simple-minded – rote memory: names and dates, countries and capitols, cities and towns, rivers and seas, times tables and rules of arithmetic, and Catechism and Missal passages. Endlessly, mind-numbingly, we recited everything. Serious thought seldom required.

In singsong fashion, we repeated phrases from lengthy lists, mathematical tables, and prayers in French and Latin. I became trilingual, by rote.

For me, the lessons dragged on. And on. My Math got muddled, my geography parched, my history became heinous, and my French grammar turned frustrating.

Still, at the end of that first year at L'Ecole St. Louis de Strathmore, I rose to the top of the class. Mind you, the more affluent sent their sons to l'Academie Piché in Lachine, taught by les Frères de la Salle, or to one of the better Ecoles Sécondaire in Montreal. So my competition was weak to begin with.

My memory was excellent. I could recite all the major prayers in English, French and Latin. I served Mass, with all the correct Latin responses. I even took part in a school play in French, which neither of my parents attended. Of course I was disappointed!

Grade Nine proved more of a struggle for me. I had such a terrible time with geometry that I knew I'd fail. When I asked for extra help, no one gave it to me.

I sensed unfairness. Mother had argued with Monsieur le Curé over his decision to tell the Town of Dorval to pour rocks along the sandy beach in front of the parish church. (This would discourage the "indecent sunbathers" from flaunting themselves there on Sunday afternoons.) Also, at a meeting of the Legion of Mary, she disagreed with Monsieur le Curé when he informed the ladies that it was their duty to encourage their husbands to vote for Maurice

Duplessis. According to him, a vote in any other direction would be "un péché mortel" (a mortal sin). Naomi and I, as children of "that sinful woman", were treated accordingly.

Then there was the issue of fifteen cents – the amount each of us took to Mass. Ten cents was for a seat tax and the other nickel was for the collection. Sometimes we shrugged when the men came to collect "le dime". If we also didn't put our nickel in the collection basket, we had a dime for the movie matinée at l'école St. Louis and a nickel for a packet of fizz. One of the ushers informed Papa that his children were not paying "le dime". In short order, he brought us to account. Not only did we have to bring the missing money to Monsieur le Curé and receive a stern lecture, we had to go without pocket money for many weeks, to make up for our dishonesty. God needed those dimes and nickels.

I could always scrape up spare cash by shoveling driveways or mowing lawns or baby-sitting. And I always found people ready to take my hard-earned pennies, dimes, and quarters.

Alongside the chocolate bars and spearmint gum, Legault's store sold packaged "magic" tricks that guaranteed instant fame: "Fool your friends." "Be the first on your block." I bought chattering false teeth and a small round membrane that was supposed to enable me to throw my voice like a ventriloquist. But that wasn't all. I found itching powder, a ring that buzzed when I shook someone's hand, a bar of soap that turned the user's hands black, chewing gum that did the same to a person's mouth, and a chewing gum pack that snapped like a mousetrap when I offered someone a stick of gum. Two of the best tricks though, were a sugar cube that melted and left a spider floating in Mother's coffee and realistic doggy poo made out of plaster.

Naomi and I pooled our pennies to buy a whoopee cushion. Mother thought it was an amusing trick. When one of the parish ladies visited, we hid the inflated "fart maker" under a cushion. It sounded off appropriately when the visitor sat down. The cost for our joke at the woman's expense was to be sent to our rooms for our "outrageous" behaviour. Later, when the woman left, Mother called us downstairs, and we all had a good laugh. This same lady had announced at a function at our house that she couldn't understand why her fingernails got so dirty when she came to visit. "Perhaps, my dear, it's because you scratch yourself" was Mother's reply. Mother always had a wonderfully wicked sense of humour - except when she was exasperated with her teenage children.

Another amusing incident involved our parish priest in Strathmore. A dozen or so men regularly ducked outside for a smoke during his overlong sermons. At those times when Monsieur le Curé listed forbidden books and films or ranted on about mothers who prevented "God's gifts" – children – from entering the world, the number of men swelled to a crowd.

One Sunday, I heard a commotion of laughter at the front of the church. Monsieur le Curé left the pulpit and marched to the front door. Two dogs were copulating on the front steps. The parish priest was furious – with the men and dogs both. In short order, town council posted notices that all pet dogs were to be kept on leash or at home. All strays would be impounded. From that moment on, we had to walk our Great Dane on a leash.

That winter, Mother got more frustrated with Naomi and me. As a result, we found more excuses to avoid her. One freezing cold day, we went off with our tie-on skis and with newspaper wrapped inside our pants to keep our legs warm. We skied on the Grove Hill golf course and came home freezing cold, only to find ourselves locked out, unable to get warm and needing badly to pee. I undid my buttons and widdled against the wall, as high up as I could. Some of it splashed back and froze on my clothes. Naomi laughed so hard she almost wet her pants. But she held on until we finally entered the house, in spite of my attempts to make her wet herself. For several days after that, I had to be extra nice to her, so she wouldn't tell.

The local merchants refused to let us warm up in their shops, unless we bought soft drinks and chips or played the pinball machines. Older boys typically hung out in Legault's store. They smoked and spent their newspaper money on bottles of Pepsi and games of pinball. We younger kids only made puddles on the floor from the melting snow all over us. When it became obvious we had no money to spend, we were told to get out.

Eventually, I became seriously depressed. I felt I had nowhere left to go and that nobody loved me. I walked down to my friend Ian Cavalier's house. I wanted to talk to his father, our scout master and one of the few adults I knew who cared enough to listen.

No one answered the door. Blinded with tears, I walked to the church. But it was locked. I was so cold I didn't want to carry on any more. Then, painfully, I walked onto the ice of Lac St. Louis. The river, I knew, ran under thin ice just past the lighthouse. I wanted to fall into the water and die. "Maybe then," I thought, "somebody will love me."

It was at this moment that I cried out in desperation for God to help me. My experience of religion had been one of cold shame and fear. I had been taught to "fear God". Never had I imagined a loving God. The Crucifix portrayed for me man's terrible cruelty. Why would a loving God require or even permit His own Son to die such an ignominious death? I didn't know or understand the concept of Christ offering Himself out of love for us, let alone for me. Not having experienced love except in my earliest childhood, I found little meaning in the word. Like Oliver Twist, I wondered where love was or if I'd ever find it.[2]

Nevertheless, I begged God to love me. At that moment, a very kind man came and walked with me back to the shore. Blinded by tears, I hardly looked at him. I vaguely remember a ragged brown robe. And sandals. I was too filled with my own misery to wonder if his feet were cold. I do remember his warm, soothing voice.

We sat on a snow-covered bench and talked. While my feet and hands warmed, I talked out my troubles to the gentle listener.

Then, he vanished.

I didn't see him leave. I stood and looked back at the bench where we had sat together. The sun, slanted low across the ice, fell on just one set of footprints. Mine.

No second set.

I looked all around. I looked up at the sky. The scalloped moon floated, cirrus-white, in the deep blue of the frigid expanse. On the bank up to the road, the chattering squirrels searched the snow for scraps of food and found little.

After a while, I walked home. Warm, happy, and light of foot.

I told no one of my experience. It was too incredible.[3]

* * * * * * *

[1]   **Weeks**, Robert Kelley; "Man and Nature", in *An American Anthology;* Stedman, Edmund Clarence, ed. [Boston: Houghton Mifflin, 1900], p. 767

[2]   *Why do we call bad things "acts of God" yet we seldom recognize daily miracles like the blossoming of flowers or the birth of babies as "acts of God"? Why do we teach children to "fear God"? Is our God the god of catastrophe?*

A great many Christians misinterpret the Biblical "fear". Etymologically, the word means "to treat with wonder and awe". For the early Israelites, God (Yahweh) was two-sided. He was a figure of love and a figure of great power and majesty (fear). The New Testament God is a God of love. Jesus taught love.

[3]   *Today, my rational mind tells me this didn't really happen. Yet, for all these years the vision remains, and I've held on by blind faith. This was a turning point in my life.*

I wanted to live. I was worth saving. In the midst of unhappiness, here was love. The stranger radiated the kind of love my aunties had provided when we first came to Canada. It was the kind of love I knew as a small child. It wasn't something I felt entitled to, now.

Give me a psychological explanation for my "invisible friend" if you like. I believe in miracles. I certainly believe in a spiritual world. What happened was real for me. It saved me from suicide.

Chapter Nine
Bell Bottom Trousers (1950/53)

> *"Theirs not to make reply,*
> *Theirs not to reason why,*
> *Theirs but to do & die."*
> – Alfred Lord Tennyson, *Charge of the Light Brigade.*

One day, Mother went out and left a sum of money on a ledge by the front door to pay for an item to be delivered. Then, a boy came to visit with Naomi. When he emptied his pockets, ostensibly to be more comfortable, he placed his money and keys on the same ledge by the door. Then he sat with Naomi on the stairs, talking. When he left, he picked up his belongings and put them back in his pocket.

When Mother returned home, all hell broke loose. The delivery person had not arrived, but the money was gone. Naomi went up to her room. I tried to explain what I thought must have happened. Mother got so angry that she pushed me down the cellar stairs and told me to stay there until I could come up with a better explanation.

Next day, my stepfather told me I could go to work until I repaid all the money. Though they didn't accuse me of stealing it, he and Mother held me responsible.

The school year wasn't finished, but Papa discharged me and took me to a farmer in what is now Montreal West. There I went to work hoeing between rows of spring vegetables.[1]

In the spring of 1950, at sixteen years of age, I hadn't completed Grade Nine and I had no prospects. The farmer was foul-mouthed and cruel. I became intolerant of my employer, and he of me. So I quit and got a job at a sign-painting shop in Montreal. I made telephone signs on glass by spray painting over stencils. Then, I cleaned up the edges around the letters as each sign dried.

I painted hundreds of signs this way, in the company of a Jehovah's Witness who daily harangued me on the evils of Catholicism. I fared poorly in religious argumentation.

My parents didn't mind that I quit the job on the farm, as long as I brought money home each week. Now that I no longer attended school, I was also required to pay room and board.

On June 25th 1950, the North Koreans invaded South Korea. The resulting "police action" provided my rescue. About a month after my seventeenth birthday, I went to the Royal Canadian Navy Recruiting Station at HMCS Donnacona on Drummond Street in Montreal to sign up.

At seventeen, I had to get signed permission from a parent or guardian. Happily, I marched home, forms in hand. Papa François gladly signed. But Mother insisted that a monthly amount had to be deducted from my pay and sent home by allotment, "so that I would not spend my money foolishly".[2] While waiting for my call-up, I scrubbed pots in the kitchen at Grove Hill Golf Course.

The weeks dragged by until September 1st when the call came to report to HMCS Donnacona. My prospective shipmates and I boarded HMCS LaHulloise and were issued micks - hammocks - for our first cruise down the St. Lawrence to Halifax.

We were "salts", for sure, boisterous, loud. Several recruits already had served during the war. Most of us were pimple-faced teenagers.

After docking at HMC Shipyards, we were bused to HMCS Cornwallis, our basic training base. Upon arrival, we stripped to the waist and nurses stabbed us with a series of needles. Then a medical officer made us lower our drawers for "short arm inspection", wincing at each proffered penis as if the sight alone would infect him.

A medical orderly "sickbay tiffy" ordered me to open my mouth. Before I could utter a single smart-ass remark, he sent me down the hall to the dental surgeon and into the torturer's chair. No waiting required. The all-too-gleeful fang farrier jabbed me twice with a blunt needle. Then, forceps in hand, he went about the excruciating business of plucking a protruding canine and a couple of molars from my overcrowded mouth.

The rest of the preliminaries included a haircut "bean shave". Then the navy issued numbers (mine was 8921H) and stacks of supplies, including Canada flashes and colour flashes. The latter indicated our division; we sewed them on our coats and uniforms.

First, we were to stencil our numbers with black India ink onto every bit of equipment provided for our personal use by His Majesty's Canadian Government. Second, they told us to polish our boots until we could clearly see our faces in their mirror-like toes and heels.

Recruits, who had gone through the ropes before, taught us the secret of "bulling" our boots. With much elbow grease, we smoothed the leather grain on the toes and heels with a spoon handle preheated in candle flame. After we made the leather sufficiently smooth, we applied a thick layer of boot polish through the infamous "spit and polish" method.

"Spit and polish" worked like this. We took a piece of cloth over our forefingers and dipped it into black polish. [Kiwi polish was considered best.] After that, we spat on the polish and worked it into the boot with small, circular motions. We endlessly repeated this procedure until the whole area had a smooth coating of polish, which we then brought to high gloss through the judicious use of water and a strip of silk scarf.

We did all this kit preparation during our spare time, in what was known as "make and mend". All the while, Frenchy, our petty officer, shouted orders at us "on the double", and let us know we were the sorriest bunch of mothers' babies he'd ever seen.

Since we were happy to have escaped home, school, and parental discipline, we were a cocky bunch. Little did we know we were to be seized forcibly out of boyhood and dumped helter-skelter into a state of neither boy nor man.

Old enough to die. Too young to vote.

Early next morning – much too early for most of us – our Division Petty Officer introduced us to our first brutal awakening. He was to repeat this every day, month in, month out.

The day began with reveille, played on a bugle. Then came a mad dash for the "heads" (washrooms) as the Division Petty Officer marched through the block with "Wakey, wakey, rise and shine; the sun is up, the morning's fine." To make life more interesting, he employed endless variations of these refrains, such as "Wakey wakey, hands off snakey" or "Let go yer cocks 'n' on wif yer socks!"

These expressions – and others – gave new meaning to the term "rude awakening". Slackers caught stealing a few extra winks had their blanket yanked off. When this didn't work, their buddies upended their bunks.

The first morning was the worst. After about twenty minutes, we assembled, a full division of raw, shivering recruits, on the parade square. All of us had sore arms from needle jabs. Some of us had sore jaws from dental delvings. None of this mattered.

Time for basic calisthenics.

The muscular P.E. instructor glared at us. "If you miss your mommies, better leave now. When we're done with you, you won't need your poor mothers to wipe your snotty noses. We'll have you beaten and kicked into shape and you'll be ready to give your all for George."

Did yer mother come from Newfie?
If she did you must be goofy...

Some there were who preferred to keep their individuality throughout. One fellow in our division we nicknamed "Radar" because of the enormity of his auditory appendages. From the start, he refused stubbornly to conform. He was a likeable fellow. Sorry to say, he ended his life on the west coast as a human helicopter. Fueled by infusions of ditto fluid, he took off from the roof of one of the navy's administration buildings.

His arms proved to be no replacements for rotors.

I don't give a damn for any old man;
I'm from P.E.I.

Many of my fellow recruits were greedy, cruel, noisy, and prosaic. For the most part, their language consisted of short, colourless phrases, punctuated with profanity. But, like my shipmates, I was happy, despite – and maybe because of – the roughness.

In the following weeks, floors became "decks", ceilings "deckheads", and walls "bulkheads". And the biffy became the "heads" (because, so we were told, sailors shouted "heads!" when they did their business over the sides of ships during the days when ships were ships and men were men).

We marched "like dogs trying to shag a pack of razor blades".

If any one of us yearned for the comforts of home, we were instructed to notify the petty officer who, from now on, was to be called "Sir!" When we moved, we were to fly! Everything in Cornwallis was on the double. Some sorry souls cracked within days. Listed AWOL, they quickly were caught and put on punishment detail – which made them wish they had never been born.

Very soon we were permitted to enter the gymnasium. "I want two volunteers for the ring; you and YOU!" One was a big black fellow from Montreal and the other was me, the skinny bloke with the French name. Everyone laughed as I stood in the ring with boxing gloves on my hands and pee running down my legs. I was a flyweight, pitted against the heavyweight champion of the world.

Looking almost sorry for me, the black fellow said, "Close your eyes; you're going for a ride."

I went for a ride. To the hospital.

I later surmised that Commander Budge had received instructions from a certain ex-major of the Canadian Army that his stepson was to be transformed, by some unexplained miracle, into a man.

After a couple of days in the hospital, I returned to my division, only to encounter the fate of many new recruits: I was charged with a minor infraction, of the "insubordination" kind, and ended up with seven days of "number eleven". This punishment detail involved extra drills, complete with heavy packs and many hours of K. P.

K. P. (kitchen patrol), as with all assignments of cleanup duty, involved scrubbing and polishing miles and miles of wooden decks, cement pathways, stone steps, and, of course, greasy pots and pans.

Possibly the most bizarre eccentricity of scraping, scrubbing, and polishing in basic training concerned the "fire point" just inside the entrance to every building. This was a red-painted wooden stand, on which two or four red buckets, bearing the legend "FIRE" in black paint, stood. Half of these contained sand and the other half water. Before inspection, the water in the buckets had to be changed to remove the dust that had settled on it, and the sand had to be raked to show a clean surface.

One morning, running around the parade square with my heavy pack and holding my rifle at arms length above my head, I tripped over my own feet and fell face down. Unwilling to yield to the fatigue that overwhelmed me as well as to the screaming petty officer, I got up – only to fall down again. Several others from the detail stopped beside me. In a spirit of support, they urged me to stay down. But I was angry and stubborn and got up again anyway. This time I lost consciousness and ended up back in the hospital.

Following several days of bed rest, I was transferred to Fraser Division where I remained until graduation five months later. I was happy in Fraser Division. I sent regular letters and postcards home. Although my letters were not answered, I wrote faithfully every week. I sent home photographs of myself taken in a booth in Digby with my cap placed jauntily above my curly blond forelock. I was proud to be in uniform. Looking at the photos in later years, I would have passed for a fourteen or fifteen year-old sea cadet.

On a chilly morning in November, we were taken to the outdoor pool to pass our basic swimming test. Wearing white ducks (heavy cotton summer uniforms), we had to tread water for five minutes. Then we removed our pants and tied the bottoms, filled the legs with air, and used our navy whites as water wings. The weather was blustery. As the cold wind blew across the icy water, I couldn't help but shudder at the thought of spending the last moments of my life fighting to survive in North Atlantic waters. I had seen sailors drown.

Here I was, five and a half years after that voyage on the the RMV Rangitata, feeling the same panic. It's hard to put into words how relieved I was when we finally made that mad dash for hot showers and a steaming mugs of cocoa.

On another occasion, we ran the assault course in pouring rain. We crawled through pipes and under barbed wire in freezing mud, while live ammunition, we were told, was fired just above our heads. The more we accomplished, the prouder we became as a division.

Shenanigans and hazing occurred, too. One of the rituals was to shave a recruit's pubic hair, then apply a good coat of shoe polish. Though I didn't yet have pubic hair, I still got "blackballed".

Every Sunday we lined up for church parade – no one was excused – and we had just one choice: Protestants or Dogans. The Protestant service was Church of England. Our Commanding Officer officiated with the Protestant chaplain. Brownie points could be earned there, but not in the Dogan or Mick – epithets for the Irish [thus Roman Catholic] – parade. Jews and atheists had to choose one or the other service.

On December 24th, 1950, Midnight Mass was celebrated for all the "Micks". The following morning, we arose to a beautiful white Christmas. Since we already had our church service, we Catholics were issued snow shovels and spent a couple of hours clearing the parade square and various pathways. We grumbled. Still, I enjoyed the fresh air amidst crystal sparkles, while joyful carols floated all maple syrupy from the Anglican service. The sounds and feelings of the morning brought back Christmases in Finchingfield.

Almost everyone was given leave between Christmas and New Year's Day. On Christmas afternoon, I packed my small bag and set out to hitchhike home to Strathmore. Everything was fine through Truro and on to Moncton. Outside Moncton, I stood in the freezing rain as car after car sped past. Some threw bottles at me; some tried running me off the road. Finally, in the wee hours of the morning, feet frozen and soaked through, I flagged a car heading back towards Moncton. I felt cheated and angry that my allotment home left me no money for a proper trip home, especially at Christmas.

From Moncton to Halifax I got a series of short rides. One ride took me to a house in Windsor, Nova Scotia, where a family of black people were having a party. Here I slept the night through in a chair. The people were kind and I did have fun. The house was a shambles.

The next morning, one of the men drove me to Halifax. At Stadacona I was given a bunk, a hot breakfast, and a ride back to Cornwallis. I spent the rest of my Christmas leave reading and attending movies on base.

Before any periods of leave, we all were given lectures and shown movies, warning of venereal disease and other dangers. The young salts were handed packages of condoms and antibacterial creams. Many made the bus ride to Digby and the beautiful Annapolis Valley, dreaming of sexual conquests. Too young to drink and too scared and out-of-pocket to take part in lustful activities, I nevertheless followed everyone into town and played the role of sightseer.

I attended a dance in Digby. Many of the sailors had mickeys, purchased from the local bootlegger. They passed brown paper bags around outside the dance hall. Some of the girls joined them. A few took off, young salts in tow. One girl asked me if I knew how to "poontang". Not knowing what the word meant, I said "no". That got around and remained with me for the balance of my time at Cornwallis! "Hey! Slim doesn't poon tang. He doesn't have a poon tanger."

Boasting about sex was almost the only subject of conversation for many, as virile experts compared seduction techniques.

Digby had a tattoo parlour, too. Here the "real" men had their "pigs" (girl friends) inscribed on hearts or anchors. Some even had sailing ships tattooed on their backs. They were covered in scabs for weeks and had to be extra careful when they showered. Others had an actual pig tattooed on one knee and a rooster on the other. If a girl put her hand on the left knee, or better still, sat there, he could always say, "You have your hand on my cock" or "You're sitting on my cock." If proof were needed, the sailor rolled up his bell bottom and showed the tattoo. Everyone then had a good laugh at the girl's expense. By the end of five months, some sailors became walking art galleries.

Despite the frantic rush of navy life, I made new friends and felt part of something greater than I ever had imagined. Our learning of seamanship, Morse code, semaphore, and a new vocabulary made us members of an elite group.

We marched and ran with heavy packs and daily became stronger. Finally, ready to join the ranks of men, we moved on to further training in our chosen - or allotted - fields of specialization. During our training stint on the Pacific Coast, Joe, the black recruit who knocked me out at the beginning of basic training, became one of my best friends.

The night before our graduation parade, a group of the more daring from our division planned a fire-hose raid on one of the petty officers who had been more zealous than most. With pillowcases over their heads, they knocked at his door in the early hours. The very sleepy PO was greeted with a torrent of icy water. Before he even managed to recover, we all were "sound asleep" in our bunks. He aroused us from our "slumber" with bright lights and blowing whistles and ordered us to stand barefoot in front of the Division hut until the culprits stepped forward. Though we stood for what seemed like hours, no one confessed.

I can't leave this section on Cornwallis without saying more about our commanding officer, Commander Patrick Budge. I came to know him later as Captain of the Quebec, a cruiser. He was later promoted to Admiral of the Pacific Fleet. Having risen through the ranks from boy seaman in the Royal Navy, he knew his spit and polish. His residence at Cornwallis became "Seamanlike Manor". Budge was reported to have declared, "This navy has been going to the dogs ever since they began letting civilians in."

One of my favourite stories of Commander Budge concerned his crossing the parade square at Cornwallis to address a "snotty", a brand new sub-lieutenant, who was being saluted over and over by a much older chief petty officer.

"What's going on here?" Commander Budge asked.

"This rating passed without saluting, sir."

"Very well. Carry on!"

After several more salutes, Commander Budge inquired of the sub-lieutenant, "Do you not return a salute when you receive one?"

"Oh! Of course sir."

"Very well, begin again, one hundred times. And let me see each salute smartly returned."

"Thou wilt scarce be a man before thy mother."
– Francis Beaumont and John Fletcher, Love's Cure
(act II, sc. 2) [3]

Early in February, 1951, I arrived home in Strathmore, for my first thirty days' leave, before moving on to courses at HMCS Naden, in Esquimalt, British Columbia. I was a man at last, a hero, ready to face the enemy in Korea. I marched home smartly, kit bag and high expectations at the ready.

The major did not return my salute. He ran his finger behind my ear, looked at Mother and shook his head. "Still wet!"

"It's salt water, sir", I retorted.

"Smart ass!" He smiled.

The four girls were happy to see me. Naomi looked at me with envy. I was free at last.

Following an ordinary supper, (Did I not expect a hero's banquet?) I was ready to show myself off to whomever I could find.

But home was back to normal. Dishes had to be washed. Naomi was not happy at school nor at home. We talked little. Time had lengthened the gap.

The next day, I marched over to L'Ecole St. Louis and proudly presented myself to the Brothers. But the boys who I thought would now look up to me, didn't. In the school yard, someone grabbed the sailor hat from my head. The hat flew from one to another through snow and slush. I retrieved it without the tally and its carefully tied bow and retreated home. I changed into "civvies".

With almost no spending money and former friends tied up with school, I soon regretted being home. I sat sullenly and read. Papa François wanted to see my "spit and polish" and handed me three pairs of shoes. Mother gave me the children's shoes. I sat at the bottom of the cellar stairs, Cinderfella polishing shoes. Louise and Nicole had started school so I looked after the youngest of my little sisters. I took Jackie on endless toboggan rides, then skied alone on the Grove Hill Golf Course.

I decided to hitchhike to Quebec City and visit my aunts and uncles. Arriving in Limoilou late and tired, I felt welcomed and loved. I had much to tell about Cornwallis and about my hopes and aspirations. The aunties took me out to a restaurant for a scrumptious dinner, complete with wine.

We reminisced about my family's arrival in Quebec and of how excited Naomi and I were to be in Canada. Now, here I was "bien grandi, mais toujours le petit Benoit" (all grown-up but still little Benoit). I spent time in "Lingerie Boucher" (Aunties' shop). I was introduced proudly to customers and friends. And I explored parts of the old city I'd never seen before. Everywhere I went, people smiled at "le jeune matelot" (the young sailor). I felt proud.

All too soon, it was time to return to spend a few last days at home before taking the train to the Pacific coast. Everyone wanted to make sure I had spending money before they put me on a bus back to Montreal. They refused to let me hitchhike. I was glad. The weather had turned bitterly cold.

Back home, when I tried bringing up the money situation, Mother made it clear the topic was not open to debate. With mixed emotions, I said my goodbyes, walked to the Strathmore railway station, and took the train to Central Station in Montreal.

The railway car westward was filled with Army, Navy, and Air Force personnel. Bottles in brown bags were passed around. Card games started up. The air hung thick with smoke. Meals, first class railway style, were served in exchange for meal tickets issued before we left Cornwallis.

At night, the porters transformed the day cars into bunked sleeping quarters. Here we dozed to the rhythm of the "clickety-clack", and awoke, too many times, when the train stopped or when the revelers got too noisy. Throughout the long nights, I was frequently awakened to the sounds of stumbling and cursing as some inebriate staggered back to his berth or tried climbing into the wrong compartment. The washrooms smelled of liquor and vomit. Now and then drunken fights broke out. Fortunately, these ceased as soon as they began. Often, the fights were caused by alleged cheating at cards. The few military police who accompanied us spent most of their time in an adjacent car, accompanied by females they'd met on the train.

When we moved onto the prairies, sailors disembarked at the water stops for the mad dash to the nearest bootlegger. They returned out of breath, carrying armfuls of fresh supplies. I was witness to the edge of a mad dream, fortunate I had neither the desire nor the funds for booze. I did join in when singsongs got underway.

Ship ahoy, sailor boy, don't you get so springy.
The admiral's daughter is down by the water,
Waiting to grab you by the dinghy.
He's got the cutest little dinghy in the navy;
Heave Ho! Heave Ho!

He's got the cutest little dinghy in the navy
And you aught'a see the little bugger go.
It isn't very long, it isn't very short,
But it's the thing that gets him in and out of every port.
He's got the cutest little dinghy in the navy;
Heave Ho! Heave Ho!

And, of course, there were rousing choruses of *The North Atlantic Squadron*:

Away, away with fife and drum,
Here we come, full of rum ...

After days of snow-covered forests, frozen lakes, and endless frozen prairie, we came to our first view of the Rocky Mountains. I had never seen anything so majestic! From then on, even from my bunk at night, I gazed transfixed through the window. As the train wound its way through tunnels and along stretches overlooking vast ravines, I forgot the commotion around me. Throughout the train, all hands settled down.

When we left our boots out, we found them shiny clean in the morning. The porters were wonderful. Always smiling and polite, to the rudest amongst us, they kept the cars clean, too!

At last, we passed through the portals of Paradise! The descent from snowy peaks into lush green valleys made me wonder if we'd entered a different country. It was only when we made our final dash through the Fraser Valley that we were ordered to get our kits together. Next stop: Vancouver.

Supply School in Esquimalt, near Victoria, provided a mixture of Typing, Shorthand, and Office Procedure courses, a good balance of drill and physical exercise, and the opportunity to live for a year in one of the world's most favourable climates.

We ran miles every morning before breakfast. Though our route often varied, it always led over moss-covered rocks and along trails bordered by the ubiquitous arbutus of the Pacific Coast. The roughness of basic training was gone. At last, I felt at peace.

My experience as a Boy Scout in Strathmore inspired me to volunteer as an assistant cub leader for the First Fairfield Pack near Oak Bay in Victoria. After several days of instruction and practice at the Courtenay Swimming School, I passed my RCN Royal Life Saving test in early March, 1951. Soon after that, I volunteered to teach swimming at the Victoria YMCA.

I had insufficient funds for wet canteen. But then, I was too young anyway. So I spent my spare time hiking with Cubs and upgrading my basic Math qualifications. I had passed my Basic English Test at Cornwallis. But I didn't pass the Mathematics test until April, 1953. I failed the test several times, despite intensive study.

One Friday evening, a group of zoot-suiters came over from Vancouver.[4] Fights broke out, and several naval personnel landed in hospital. We were rounded up by the Shore Patrol, from locations in downtown Victoria, and loaded into trucks. Back on base, we mustered on the parade square to be informed by the Commanding Officer that all further leave would be canceled if one zoot-suiter remained on the Island by Saturday midnight.

There's courage in numbers. Though I didn't get physically involved, I was a member of the base which reported that, by the time the ferry left Victoria Harbour for Vancouver, not one pair of strides remained on city streets. They all hung from the telephone wires of downtown Victoria. As for the "invaders", they were ushered into paddy wagons by the Victoria Police and returned by special boat to Vancouver.

Since there was nothing to do in Victoria the following Sunday – or any Sunday, for that matter – we removed the offending garments, to maintain rapport with the locals. The Monday was proclaimed "make and mend" until midnight.[5]

It was a tradition with a number of people in Victoria to invite sailors to their homes for Christmas and Thanksgiving. Personnel who could not be with their own families were selected at random and sent out in pairs. Thus it was that I was invited for Thanksgiving dinner with Joe, my boxing friend from Cornwallis.

When we arrived at the address assigned, the lady informed us a mistake had been made. I was welcome but not my black friend. The sidewalks of Victoria were "rolled up" for the holiday, so we both reported back to Naden. But, we were too late for Thanksgiving dinner. Joe had a buddy in Cooking School. His friend served us a fantastic meal, complete with a bottle of officers' wine and extra plum duff.

Navy cooks were able to dig up goodies that no one else could obtain. Pilfered items were called "rabbits". That term originated when a cook at <u>Naden</u>, who lived off base, decided to take a bunny home for his daughter. (Rabbits ran wild on the base.) He was stopped at the main gate and ordered to show what he had in the bucket. When he lifted the lid, the bunny jumped out and hopped away. The next day, the same thing happened again. On the third day, the cook passed through the main gate, unchecked, with his "rabbit". The custom spread as other ratings began taking "rabbits" home.

Somebody "rabbited" some clothes-washing soap from the Supply School. Clothes washing in the Navy was called "dobying". The rabbited dobey soap turned out to be extra strength detergent for sails and other canvas. The culprit and his buddies limped bowlegged to sick bay with a severe case of "dobey itch".

One day, a fellow at Supply School suggested a double date. His girl had a sister "built like a brick shit house". We were to meet for a movie. I paid for two and my buddy paid for his girl and himself and we sat down, popcorn in hand, to enjoy the show. A third fellow came and sat on the other side of the girl I was with. We were a "five-some"! She held our popcorn and he helped himself. Then I noticed the two holding hands. After the movie, I returned to base alone. I'd been had!

In general, I was shy in the company of girls and couldn't afford expensive dates. So I spent much of my spare time reading and working with the Cubs. I was unaware of the reputation this gave me. After I spent several months as "Balloo" for the First Fairfield Cub Pack, my parents succumbed to my repeated requests and sent my Scout uniform. The Cub Parents' Committee complemented that with a neckerchief and a few badges. At first, I carried the uniform with me and changed at the Cubs and Scouts Hall. But soon, feeling proud of my contribution to the community, I began to wear my uniform on Cub nights, both leaving and returning to base.

One nippy night, when I returned to base, a group of bare-knuckled boozing bullies surrounded me. One of them yelled, "We don't like Boy Scouts on naval property." Then they pounced. They head butted me on the nose and kneed me in the groin. When I fell, they stomped me all over. Then, they stuffed me head first into a garbage can.

I landed again in the base hospital. This time, for several weeks. Part of the reason for my longer stay was "emotional fatigue", brought on in part by my parents' refusal to answer my letters or even discuss my need for spending money. In the one letter, I did receive from her, Mother described me as "a yapping puppy, barking from a safe distance". That letter arrived with my Scout uniform. [6]

On November 9th, 1951, I graduated from Supply School as an Administrative Writer, with instructions to report to HMCS Stadacona in Halifax. En route, I had thirty days leave plus two weekends. I intended to make the best of my free time. I solved the problem of lack of funds by selling my travel voucher and embarked on a hitchhiking holiday.

> *For my part, I travel not to go anywhere, but to go.*
> *I travel for travel's sake. The great affair is to move.*
> – Robert Louis Stevenson, *Travels with a Donkey*
> *in the Cévennes* [7]

The ferry ride from Victoria to Vancouver was an overnight trip with a group of progressively drunken sailors and a "female companion" with an overnight cabin. I enthusiastically took part in some of the singsongs, but had no wish to drink from the bottles being passed in brown bags. And I had no wish to visit the overnight cabin. I was certain the woman would turn me down, anyway.

After depositing my kit bag at the railway station on West Hastings in Vancouver, to have it shipped to Stadacona, I took a trolley to the Pacific Highway and headed towards New Westminster, the Patullo Bridge, and the Peace Arch Crossing into the United States.

Intermittent lifts took me past Seattle, Tacoma, Portland,

Oregon, and a very snowy Grant's Pass. Then I caught a ride in a logging truck. As the sun rose between the ridges and peaks of mountains to the East, I sat high in the cab and observed, with awe, the giant redwoods surrounding us – until we came to the Pacific Ocean at Crescent City, California.

The coast was shrouded in fog. We stopped at a café where loggers sat drinking strong black coffee and eating huge plates of flapjacks and eggs. My driver, a small man compared to the other men in the café, pointed in the direction of a lighthouse, way off the coast, built on the site where more than two hundred had drowned when their ship hit a reef in a fog such as this, almost one hundred years before. Despite his own short stature, this trucker was proud of his fellow countrymen. "Some of these men will soon be cutting into trees that have stood along this coast long before Columbus rediscovered America. This here's Paul Bunyan country."

I looked around at the lumberjacks, some standing tall with arms the size of tree limbs. These men were certainly giants. Their conversation and laughter matched their statures.

I managed to polish off a huge breakfast of flapjacks, sausage and eggs, offered free of charge to the young Canadian sailor. Then, my host driver and I continued towards his destination, Eureka. We drove on narrow Route 1, hugging the Pacific Coast. Here and there wide enough for only one-way traffic, the road perilously embraced oceanside cliffs, at the bottom of which were needlepoint rocks. At some points, the loudest horn got the right-of-way. And the yielding traffic had to tuck itself into wayside pull-offs. Every bend took my breath away until Eureka where the rotten-egg smell of pulp mills blew in at us with the ocean breeze. The houses, all built of redwood were pretty. And the people were loud and cheery. I was treated to a delicious crab supper and a pitcher of beer. Once again, for the sailor from "way up north", the meal was "on the house".

Following lunch, I headed back to the highway, with many warm wishes for a safe and happy journey ringing in my ears. Soon I was picked up by a travelling salesman. I failed to notice the man was drunk, in spite of his slurred speech and boozy breath. When I finally did pay attention, I couldn't muster the courage to ask him to stop and let me out. Worse, since I didn't know how to drive, I couldn't offer to take the wheel. I just held on tight to the side handle and fretted.

When I pleaded with the inebriate to please slow down, he stepped on the juice. Terrified now that we'd careen over a cliff or smash head-on into a northbound semitrailer truck heading north, I held on tighter than ever to the side handle. And felt sick.

At last! We stopped for coffee. But he wanted me to continue travelling with him, so he grabbed my travel bag as we exited the car. Weaving, he locked the door and lurched into the café. I followed.

An American Marine sat at the café counter. He told us he had a couple of pals in the Canadian Navy stationed in Halifax and that he was thumbing his way south to Ft. Bragg. When I suggested he ride with us and take over the driving, he jumped at the offer. I was off the hook!

While the soldier drove, the car's owner snored loudly in the back seat.

At Fort Bragg, an American sailor returning from furlough offered a ride to San Francisco. I felt overjoyed – and secure. The sailor regaled me with anecdotes about a trip to Hawaii and a journey up the Amazon with missionary friends.

We crossed the Golden Gate Bridge well past midnight. I wondered where I'd find a place to sleep at such a late hour.

As my driver did not have to report to his ship until the following day, he took me to an "excellent place" where we could "spend the night". I paid for my lodging and was handed a towel and a key and taken by an attendant down a long corridor to a small, cubicle-like room. I received many admiring glances. In this land so proud of its servicemen, I must have looked dashing and heroic in my naval uniform. Then, a heavyset man groped my behind. Another man came up to me, told me that I was cute, and asked about my friend.

I had paid to spend the night at a gay steam bath! In one room, a sweaty mass of naked bodies writhed about like snakes in a pit.

In a state of panic, I left the American sailor to do his own thing and fled to the front desk. The clerk laughingly – and kindly – returned my money and told me how to get to a USO that was open all night. Despite the late hour, they could direct me to reasonable lodgings.

That night, I slept in a San Francisco USO/YMCA. By noon the next day, I was back on Route 1, headed to Los Angeles.[8]

As palm trees appeared in greater abundance, I saw beautiful sandy beaches. My excitement grew. Then I discovered Santa Barbara, swam in the ocean, and visited the old Franciscan Mission Church.

In the sunshine and clean air, I shook off the feeling of despair I'd felt in San Francisco. I shoved that nightmare into a closet, along with old ghosts.

In 1951, there wasn't the pollution and bumper-to-bumper traffic in Los Angeles that we know today. There was no Disneyland. Hollywood and Vine was still the centre of the movie world.

At the USO, I was given a pass to a "Meet the Stars" party. I checked in at the YMCA and decided to take a nap before going out. I must have been exhausted; I didn't wake up until the next day. So I missed the party. I did, however, meet several graying film stars at the Brown Derby and got their autographs "for my sister". But I went on no tours of the studios; entrance wasn't permitted without prearranged permission. Before long, I headed out of town once more.

In San Diego, I stayed at the naval base and was invited to another cocktail party. Edgar Bergen was there. His puppets, Charley McCarthy and Mortimer Snerd made rude remarks about various guests, especially the ladies. Charley asked me what I had in my pocket. The audience laughed. I patted my pockets and shrugged. This elicited more laughter.

Boy, was I dumb.

The next day, I walked in sunshine in the second best climate in the world (#1 is in the Canary Islands). I thought San Diego was one of the most inviting towns I had ever visited. Mexican fan palms, giant cacti, ficus trees, and monarch butterflies informed me that I was finally in the tropics. I saw adobe houses, some of the oldest buildings in California, as well as Spanish Colonial buildings. I regret to this day that I didn't visit the zoo, famous throughout the world.

On November 19th, I decided to visit Tijuana, simply

because I wanted to say I had visited Mexico. Fortunately, I left my travel bag at the base. In warning me to be careful, people told me it was easy to get into trouble south of the border. Since I intended only to see the sights, I was sure I'd be safe.[9]

In the Tijuana bars, everyone drank and talked to the señoritas. One of the fellows – or was it one of the bar girls? – talked me into trying a small glass of tequila. "If you haven't tasted tequila, you haven't been to Mexico".

In a matter of minutes, all became a blur. The room spun about. I couldn't hold myself steady. I began vomiting on my way to the washroom.

Vaguely, I recall a dirty sink in a filthy bathroom. Miraculously, I managed to remove my shoes and uniform, wash my shorts, and clean myself up as well as I could – before passing out.

The U.S. Naval Shore Patrol picked me up, sans uniform, sans wallet, sans camera. I was way luckier than I ever imagined at the time. I'm sure the Shore Patrol brought me back to San Diego with the usual assortment of rowdies and drunks. Where I spent the night I can only imagine. The hours between passing out in Tijuana and being handed a towel and shown to a shower on the Naval base are a total loss. How I got away without being charged I'll never know. Not only was I treated with the utmost kindness by the Naval authorities, a Good Samaritan at the San Diego Naval Base had helped me out even further. My uniform was returned to me clean; even my shoes had been freshly polished.

Though base officials told me, "Don't ever travel on your own", I stubbornly held to the belief that my only error was that I drank with people I didn't know. Why was I so well treated when I really deserved some sort of military punishment? Both the Yanks and Canucks knew they were both fighting the same "police action" in Korea. But I was no hero. I was just a kid who'd stepped into a situation way beyond his depth.

The Americans made contact with the Royal Canadian Navy in Esquimalt. I was issued temporary I.D. and a flight by Naval Air Force to San Francisco, then to Tacoma, Washington and bused to Vancouver. At HMCS Discovery, I was issued a new rail pass to Halifax.

All this came out of my pay, of course. Both of my parents

were furious when I told them of my misadventure.[10]

I arrived at <u>HMCS Stadacona</u> in Halifax looking forward to my first ship and to excursions to exotic lands. But on the 18th of December, 1951, I was sent back to Montreal to work in the Recruiting Office at <u>HMCS Donnacona</u>.

With a living allowance, I took a permanent room in the YMCA nearby. Everything was conveniently located on Drummond Street: <u>HMCS Donnacona</u>, the YMCA, and Sir George Williams University, where I decided to take courses in my spare time. (I had possible company. The Pay Writer at that time studied at Sir George Williams, to qualify for Officer Training.) When I applied for the spring semester, I was informed that, as I was a mere eighteen years old and had not completed grade nine, I would have to finish high school first. Since my work at <u>Donnacona</u> also included some evening "watches", I applied to study by correspondence. Before long, I began a course in basic English.

Mother and Papa were upset with me when I decided to live at the "Y", rather than use my living allowance to board at home. Perhaps it appeared to them as if I were wagging my finger in their faces. But now I enjoyed my new freedom and wanted to distance myself from my parents and the constant struggle to win their approval. I gave up trying to be a success in their eyes.

On July 27th, 1952, I was transferred back to <u>Stadacona</u>, where I was to remain until October 15th. Halifax provided good friends, summer weekend camping, sailing, and hitchhiking trips. I visited Prince Edward Island and Sydney, Nova Scotia.

On October 15th, I was assigned to my first ship, the aircraft carrier <u>Magnificent</u>. The "Maggie" had been given to Canada by the British government and was undergoing refit at <u>HMC Dockyard</u>.

Since I desperately desired to fit in, I joined several of my new messmates for a skirmish ashore. Though I knew I didn't have to get as drunk as they did, one of the fellows I respected the most – a three-badged, able-bodied seaman, twelve years a salt-water sailor, Battle of the Atlantic and all that – fully intended to drink himself silly.

We entered through a restaurant into a noisy, smoky private

club. My "friend" sauntered over to join a group of sailors, none of whom I knew. Exhibiting more "courage" than I really felt, I followed. This elicited swift reactions from the strangers: "Hello sweetie. What brings your little cherub face in here? Looking for your daddy?"

"Buzz off, junior. Sea cadet night's been canceled."

"Run home, sonny. Your mother's looking for you. Time to change your shitty diapers."

"Hey! You heard the man. Fuck off before I come and break your face."

Shaking in my boots, embarrassed and betrayed, I beat a speedy retreat. A short while later, I walked into the Seagull Club on Barrington Street. There I met a couple of my previous mess mates from the <u>Naden Supply School</u>.[11]

Halifax also gave me the opportunity to learn to drive. I passed my driving test on the hilly streets of the old city. While I took the test, a drunk ran out from a tavern and hit the side of the car. He said he wouldn't lay charges if I gave him some money. A policeman arrived on the scene. At first, I thought I'd be in trouble. For sure, I thought I'd failed my driving test. But the drunk overdid his act; he argued so loudly with the policeman that he was escorted to the hoosegow to cool his heels.

My driving examiner who had observed the whole incident and was probably waiting to see how I reacted under stress, drove the car back to the licensing office and asked me to wait on a bench. A few minutes later he came out of the inner office with a big smile on his face – and my brand new driver's licence.

There were so many people coming and going on the <u>Maggie</u> that I had no chance to make permanent friends. The ship swarmed with rats, however, and they were friendly enough. They ran from mick to mick while we tried to sleep at night.

Every now and then, we sailed out past the Harbour so the planes could practice takeoff and landing. Then we returned to the Dockyard so that the refitting work could continue.

In the ship's office, I got into trouble with a midshipman. Better known as "snotties", midshipmen were sent to the Royal Navy for part of their training. Some of these sub-lieutenants then returned to Canada, thinking very highly of themselves – more

British than the British.

Once, when I answered the telephone, a voice asked, "Are you theah?" I couldn't resist. "Just a moment, sir, I'll go and see." I thought this was a great joke until I was brought up on charges for "gross disrespect and insubordination to a senior officer". To make matters worse, when I stood before the captain, I couldn't hold back a fit of giggles. The manner in which the young officer read out my offense in his phony accent was just too funny.

I got seven days of "# 11" – extra work details and curtailment of leave. As I got off lightly, I was relieved. I'm sure the captain recognized the humour.

On November 7th, my second leave began. This time, I had a few dollars put aside which had been a gift from my aunts and uncles in Quebec City. Once more, I would hitch hike.

New Brunswick presented miles and miles of forest, icy rain and few cars. Boston and New York were cold and miserable in November. However, New York was certainly different from any city I had ever seen. I walked gingerly in a bedlam of movement and gabbling voices, afloat on a nighttime sea of writhing sidewalks. Without a tour guide, I stepped past drunks sprawled on steamy grates, clasping brown paper bags from which they swigged rot-gut wine beneath a thousand neon veins. All around me, smells of armpits, after shave, garlic, liver and onions, and various intensities of sickly perfume, blended with carbon monoxide and urine. Transcending the blaring of taxi horns, strands of indecipherable music mixed with laughter, shouts, and curses. From dusty shop windows, feminine undergarments and sex toys assaulted my eyes in myriad shades of pink and black.

Finding my way at last to the Empire State Building, I took the elevator as high as I could without charge. Then I climbed the flights of stairs to the top of the Statue of Liberty. With my fear of heights, I couldn't stand close to the edge of the lookout.

During a rushed trip to the "lights of Broadway", I met an American airman on his way to Washington and looking for someone to help out with the driving. I was delighted to accept his offer.

We pushed on to the sunny skies of Washington, D.C., where I changed to summer uniform. The uniform was still blue but the dickie shirt (like a cotton t-shirt with blue band at the neckline) was white and much cooler than the jersey top. I spent a day visiting "must see" attractions, including the White House, the Lincoln Memorial, and Arlington Cemetery.   Compulsively,   I needed to keep moving. By November 14th, I had arrived at the USO branch of the YMCA in Norfolk, Virginia. For me, counting destinations on my personal score card seemed more important than stopping long enough to absorb the culture and surroundings. Was it lack of money that kept me from stopping for very long in one place? Maybe. But I don't think so.

In many areas of the Southeastern United States, people were surprised to hear Canada had a navy. Canadian snowbirds had not yet journeyed south in great numbers. So many Americans, ignorant of our country, asked me, "Canada. What state's that in?"

Sometimes, I was picked up by state troopers who gave me rides to neighbouring counties. It was against the law in many counties and states to hitchhike. But I was a serviceman from a strange country.

In the South, I did begin to absorb my surroundings. Some of what I saw made a lasting impression. Especially the "whites only" and "colored" signs posted everywhere. In one town, curiosity got the better of me and I took a look inside a "colored" washroom – just a hole in the ground. The stench was overpowering. The only time I saw a coloured person in a white washroom was the lady with a bucket and mop, cleaning up after sloppy white folks.

Near Savannah, Georgia, I stopped to contemplate the Savannah River – so wide, so smooth. Where had she been? Where was she going? What secrets did she hide? Would I were Tom Sawyer, innocent and free to sail my craft, fight off pirates, search for hidden treasure.

I removed my shoes and socks, dangled my feet in the water, and watched bits of wood slowly drift by. The current caressed my calves. Soothed me.

Lazily, I glanced upstream and brutish reality invaded. A small stream plopped its cargo into the muddy river: the corpse of an orange cat, caught in a tree branch and half submerged. Then I saw a giant pipe dribbling yellow effluent onto the muddy shore. The heavy drone wasn't traffic in the distance. It was bluebottle flies gorging on the sewage. I whipped out my feet and struggled quickly to the top of the bank, anxious to put distance between myself and that floating death. The spell was broken.

The further south I travelled, the shorter the rides. At a rickety country store, I stopped to buy a bottle of soda. The scene was bucolic, picturesque. In a large rocking chair on the porch, legs spread out, a good ol' boy sat snoring, mouth open. A fly flew into his mouth. Without awakening, he snorted and spat onto the dust, right beside a thirteen or fourteen year-old girl, who sat on the porch step rocking back and forth.

With a voice as low and dark as weathered oak, soft as a feather pillow, the girl hummed a pretty tune while she repeatedly brushed back a wisp of blond hair that hung across her right eye. Her lips were full, sensuous, and inviting. I muttered a low greeting. "Hi!" Her little brown-button eyes flashed alarm. Then I saw it: beneath her cheap blue dress, a baby grew.

A cat padded across the road. For a moment, it stopped to find out why I was there. Then it jumped onto the steps and sat beside the young, pregnant beauty. At this moment, a rough man in dirty, slung-over jeans exited the store. He glared at me, then at the girl.

He spat out a stream of tobacco juice and pointed a filthy index finger at me. "What y'all gawkin' at?"

I shrugged and moved on. For days afterwards, the girl's face lingered in my mind.

Florida was warm and foggy when I arrived for my free glass of orange juice on November 16th. A big sign at the border read "Help keep Florida green. Bring money". By November 18th, I arrived in Miami. Apart from the beaches, many of which were marked "private property" or "whites only", there was little to see. So I took off up the west coast of Florida. In the Everglades, I saw Seminole Indians, living and cooking on raised platforms above the swamp and selling souvenirs made of alligator hide. They raised baby alligators in big muddy pits and charged visitors admission to see them. The Seminoles owned almost nothing except a few pots and pans – and the alligators.

After many short rides, I arrived in Tallahassee, where I got a lift with a preacher. When we weren't singing gospel songs, he regaled me with a fundamentalist Christian doctrine I had never heard before. Every now and then he refreshed his vocal cords with a swig from a bottle tucked beside his seat.

On our way from Florida to Louisiana, we met the swamp-dwelling descendants of Acadians. They lived not only in Louisiana, they lived in other swampy parts of the deep South too. They couldn't understand my Canadian French any more than I could understand their Cajun French. Fortunately, we all spoke "American".

At last, after navigating through swamps and over many long, single-lane bridges, we arrived in New Orleans. My host invited me to a gospel meeting where he was going to preach. The congregation, entirely "po' white trash", brought the roof down with their singin', 'n' stompin', n' praisin' Jeeeesus! I loved it!

Following the meetin', I booked a room at the local YMCA and went from there, by invitation, to attend a New Orleans funeral. The members of the marching band started off slowly and solemnly, then got livelier and livelier as they marched away from the cemetery.

In the cemetery, all the caskets were placed in above ground vaults, in rows, stacked one upon the other. I was told that when the rent didn't get paid, the bones were placed in a huge common vault. Then on Resurrection Day, people would call out, "Who got my arm?" and "Where's my leg?" and "Can't find my hipbone."

I was impressed with the spirit of joy present when attendees celebrated the life and qualities of the person who died. Death, to them, was a joyous liberation from earthly toil and suffering. To prove this, they threw a big party at the end of the march.

I enjoyed New Orleans – especially the music. I particularly remember one young black trumpet player who seemed no older than twelve. He was absolutely amazing. I sensed a certain togetherness among the people. Yet, paradoxically, I sensed that everyone was being careful. On Sunday, I went to church at the Catholic cathedral. During that service, blacks knelt at the back of the church and did not come to the railing for communion. This shocked me. Maybe someone brought them communion where they were. I'm guessing.

A series of rides took me to Baton Rouge, then through Lafayette, and onwards to Houston, Texas. From Houston, I travelled south to Freeport. At Freeport, I intended to see the Gulf of

Mexico, up front and personal.

Why had I not gone to St. Petersburg on the west coast of Florida? Maybe next time. For now, a dusty, isolated stretch of road alongside the Gulf of Mexico would have to do.

The ocean beckoned with mighty waves. The sheer remoteness of the setting bade me pause.

"Enjoy the view. Watch out for water moccasins!" Spitting tobacco juice from the window, the truck driver stopped his rig and dropped me off. Then, with a friendly wave and loudly protesting gears, he disappeared southwest, along the coast.

At first, I sat on a grassy bank and looked at the beach and the sea. The salty foam carried with it odds and sods of material. As they tumbled back and forth, back and forth, I wondered how long it took to wear them all down into smooth sand. I was one of those bits of flotsam, tumbling back and forth, back and forth in the sea. A great glittering wave, venting her anger, crashed down, frothed on the sand, and retreated, to leave bits of shells, polished glass, driftwood, and bone. Would I survive long enough to get as smooth as all those shiny little objects?

I walked along the grass and pebble beach. The ripples beckoned me: remove your shoes and socks; cool your aching feet. Only ankle deep beyond the pebbles, golden flecks danced on white sand. Silver minnows tickled my toes. The experience was sensual, almost orgasmic.

I wanted to get naked with nature. I had to get naked. I looked about. Not a soul in sight. I stripped. I tossed my Navy jumper, shirt, pants, and shorts onto the shore and plunged into the sea and sun.

This was about as far from anywhere as I had ever been in my life. Here I could stay forever. Nobody could ever find me. One full hour passed in one mere moment.

Way off in the distance, I heard a truck. Hurriedly, I donned my clothes, grabbed my shoes and socks and hat and bag, and stuck my thumb out.

Just in time. The trucker who had dropped me off now was on his return leg to Freeport. In Freeport, he knew a "feller" who had to drive to Houston. He'd arrange a lift for me.

Houston to Dallas. This was oil country. I saw rigs everywhere: on front lawns, beside churches, beside the roads.

Dallas to Fort Worth was thirty-three miles. From Fort Worth I got a service flight to El Paso, and saved 597 miles of desolate roadways. At El Paso, I was asked to drive a drunken sailor who already was AWOL from his base in San Diego. I had intended to travel northwest to see the Grand Canyon, then north through Aztec country. Instead, we took the shortest route to San Diego. Flying was out of the question. The sailor, obviously, would be better off arriving late, with his own car, than getting a military police escort from El Paso.

When we arrived in Benson, Arizona, I had already driven for many hours. My eyes stung and my back ached. My host/ passenger treated me to a steak supper. Then we hit the road again. I drove all through the night. The sailor slept through the blaring radio, without which I also would have slept – while driving.

Somewhere, I can't tell you where, a baritone voice urgently called out to me, "Benjamin Bunny, stop the car!" Believing the sailor was going to throw up, I braked to a stop. But when I turned around, I saw the sailor was still sound asleep in the back seat. "Must've been the radio."

At that moment, a freight train roared out of nowhere and rushed loudly across the section of road on which we would have driven, had I not stopped.

I got out of the car and stood for several minutes, stock still in the freezing desert night, as the locomotive whistled off into the distance. I had seen no road signal to warn of its approach. Nor had I seen a flashing light. It didn't help that I had become mesmerized by the long, straight blacktop, with nothing to distract me. The train had materialized from behind a long bluff or ridge, smack dab in the middle of the wasteland.

The sailor slept through the entire event. When he woke up, I chose not talk to him about what had happened.[12]

On Route 66, snow and sandstorm were yet to come. But I delivered my charge to the naval base in San Diego in one piece. By way of thanks, I was given a bunk for a few hours, followed by a hot shower and a good navy meal.

The next day, I headed north. I visited Los Angeles briefly. Still exhausted, I headed to Sacramento. The routes north of Sacramento were snowed in and too cold and dangerous for hitchhiking. So I got a long flight from McClellan Air Force Base to Amarillo, Texas, and a shorter one to Albuquerque, New Mexico, where I hoped to get a flight northeast. But as everything was snowed in, nothing was moving.

Before I knew it, I found myself on Route 66 again, but this time hitchhiking to Oklahoma City. December 4th found me heading towards Montreal via Saint Louis. I left Route 66 when I got a ride with a trucker to Pittsburgh, Pennsylvania.

On the far side of Pittsburgh, I stood well into the night without a single ride. A cold drizzle whipped at me with each passing motorist. Struggling to keep my eyes open despite the night chill, I slipped into a truckers' greasy spoon for a cup of coffee. At least, I could get warm there. Better yet, maybe I could meet a diner willing to give me a lift.

The door squealed on rusty hinges. The place seemed deserted. I cleared my throat, loudly. A sleepy waitress in stained apron, buttoned cardigan, and hair in curlers oozed up to the counter from behind a shabby green curtain. She glared at me sleepily, mouth open. Enough to catch flies.

"I'll have a cup of coffee, please."

I rubbed my hands to work the chill out of them.

She pulled her cardigan tight around her throat, reached for the near-empty pot on the two-ring burner, and poured me a cup. As she pushed it across the counter, much of the bitter fluid sloshed onto the saucer.

"Do you have any cream?"

She dragged her slippered feet to the far end of the counter, grabbed a small pitcher, and slammed it down.

"Thanks for the warm welcome."

She scowled at me. I swear she would've thrown me out, if she could.

"That'll be ten cents. Jar's fer tips." With that she returned to the back room and left me to drink my coffee in peace.

Nursing the lukewarm cup, I kept an eye out for approaching traffic – any approaching traffic. Nothing. When I felt warm enough, I headed back out to stand my vigil once more. The café – actually it looked like an abandoned school bus – sat at a crossroads.

As soon as I reached the highway, I discovered I had lost my sense of direction. I was at a crossroads. To me both roads looked the same. I had jumped around so much trying to keep warm that I couldn't remember from which direction I'd arrived. My brain was numb with cold.

Back to the café. The waitress reemerged. As soon as she saw me, she narrowed her beady little eyes.

"I'm sorry to bother you. But which direction is northeast?"

She shook her head. She had a real loser here. Wordlessly, she pointed.

"Thank you."

Fingers crossed, I returned to the highway. Minutes felt like hours. A wind rose, cold and menacing, threatening snow. I looked at the stark silver sky and full frigid moon and smelled wood smoke – alder, maple, some fir. Occasionally cars whizzed by. Nobody pulled in at the greasy spoon. Nobody stopped on the road.

When the sun finally rose, bright and cold, it brought with it the sounds of a new day. A train whistle wailed, long and low. In the distance, someone chopped wood. Someone else revved up a chain saw. A dog sent his message down the line: an intruder had entered his domain. Another dog, with a deeper voice, recounted his night adventures. Still others boasted their various pursuits: a rabbit maybe, a cat on a fence.

A train drew near, warning chickens and foxes and sleepy farmers away from the tracks. Half an hour later, an egg salesman gave me a lift to the outskirts of New York City.

I headed into town for a YMCA-USO where I could catch some sleep and prepare myself for the last stretch to Montreal. At breakfast, three fellows who introduced themselves as NHL hockey players offered me a ride all the way to Montreal. I didn't know the first thing about hockey but I enjoyed the ride. At Montreal Station, I boarded the train to Strathmore.

Home at last! But I could stay only for one day. In fact, I barely had time to get back to Halifax; to get there, I had to hitchhike through snowy weather. When Mother told me Naomi had run away from home, I was glad to leave.

I felt blamed and therefore guilty. I also felt a terrible sadness for my sister. As I had done before her, she had fled.

I remembered a conversation Mother had with me during my

last leave home. She told me how unmanageable Naomi had become and wondered, seriously, if she were "possessed by the devil".

The problem was, since a barrier had arisen between us, I couldn't talk to Naomi. I had no idea what her problem could be.

Yet I should have known what it was. After I departed for the Navy, the increased number of household chores, compounded by Mother's outbursts, likely made her life unbearable. Alone, she would have had to do all the baby-sitting, and all the washing and drying of dishes.

Understandably, she would have felt full of rage.

In the face of horrific possibilities, I mustered only shame and self-pity. Since I held myself responsible for "abandoning" my sister, I held myself responsible for her running away too. Naomi's pain became my own.

Yet I attempted to rescue myself alone. Enfeebling and time-consuming, guilt and shame morph into sick substitutes for action.

If only I could have turned back the clock. In our early years, Naomi and I had been so close. Then we pulled apart – separate schools, separate friends. Most damaging of all, we came to vie for Mother's scant love. We felt certain we could win this love, only one at a time.

In the end, neither of us won it. Ever.

Now my sister was gone. Now even more guilt and shame overcame me.

Using her birth name, Naomi had joined the WRENS – the women's branch of the Royal Canadian Navy.

I don't know how she enlisted without our parents' knowledge. Being underage, she would have required a parent's signature to join up.

Maybe our parents did know how she signed up, but decided not to tell me. Maybe someone else signed for her. I don't know.

Because we used different surnames, nobody in the Navy would have connected the two of us. Partly because of this, we were destined not to see each other again for many years.

It never occurred to me to look for the name Nuttall-Smith. My father was dead.

The next morning early, I made my way through Montreal and got a ride all the way to Quebec City. My aunts and uncles greeted me warmly, as always. I told them I had to leave as soon as possible or I'd arrive AWOL and get in deep trouble. They served me a good supper and insisted I stay the night. The next day, Uncle Emilien paid for a ticket and put me on a train for Halifax. I got back just under the gun.

From December 17th, 1952 until January 6th, 1953, I was stationed as a replacement Admin Writer at HMCS Shearwater, Naval Air Station, Dartmouth, Nova Scotia, across the bay from Halifax. While others took Christmas and New Year's leave, I sat in a drafty office at the back of one of the hangars. The base was nearly deserted. I had little to do except read and look forward to my next posting.

Thankfully, on January 7th, I was transferred to the Cruiser HMCS Quebec (another gift from the Royal Navy). The "Old Man" was Mr. Seamanlike Manner himself – Captain Budge. On the Maggie, I had been disappointed not to have visited foreign ports. This posting promised travel at last.

In February, we put to sea on a Caribbean Cruise. First stop: Bermuda. February 14th, several chums and I rented mopeds to tour the most beautiful island I had ever seen. I gazed at waters, crystalline aqua blue – the colour of emeralds over white sands, and lavender where rocks lay below the surface. Houses, every colour imaginable, hung above cliffs and nestled at the foot of hills. Aromatic flowers – rose, oleander, rhododendron, and azalea – grew everywhere, especially over the low walls and hedges that lined the sides of the narrow roads.

It took me only a short time, even with stops for photographs and souvenir shopping, to circle the island. If there were automobiles on the island, they were few and far between. I don't recall having seen any.

Following exercises involving American and other navies, we dropped anchor off Tortola in the Virgin Islands. Those not on duty got permission to go ashore by cutter. There we could swim in warm waters, collect coconuts, and look for girls. We kept our fingers crossed that our duty shifts wouldn't fall on days when the ship visited an exotic port of call.

Watches were divided into eight-hour periods, first port, second port, first and second starboard. With four divisions, we rotated eight hours on and had twenty-four hours off.

Duty watch patrolled the ship and took responsibility for cleanup. Each mess organized one member of the watch to act as duty cook. Depending on the hours of his watch, the mess cook drew supplies from the ship's stores, such as bread, butter, peanut butter, jam, and cocoa. Duty cooks washed everything twice each day, before "lights out" and following breakfast, before inspection. Other members of the duty watch did the cleanup after lunch and supper. The racks on the bulkhead contained all the plates, mugs, cutlery, and other equipment for the mess.

Since inspection could be called at a moment's notice, it was crucial for the mess to be spotless at all times, especially in port, where stoppage of leave could hurt – a lot.

Although most duty officers were reasonable, we occasionally got caught off guard. On one white glove inspection, the officer of the watch noticed a smudge of peanut butter on a mess bench.

"Chief, what is that?"

"Just a minute sir, I'll see. Leading seaman, what's that?"

"Just a minute, sir, I'll see. Able Seaman. What's that?"

The able seaman ran his finger through the peanut butter, put his finger to his lips, and sampled the taste. "Shit, sir."

The next day we had one more ordinary seaman in our ranks.

My messmates on the Quebec were all supply ratings – writers and stores personnel. We slung our micks crisscross over the mess table. Soon we became the best of buddies in the cramped quarters. In the evenings we drank hot cocoa and dined on toast with peanut butter or jam.

Ships at sea carried movies which were exchanged in port. Sometimes we saw the same movie several times. We whooped and whistled during love scenes or when an actor or actress said a phrase that could be given a double meaning. Mostly we read pocket novels – Erskine Caldwell was popular – and played cribbage at every opportunity.

For our meals we took trays up the gangway and along the ship's railing to the galley, then returned to the mess as quickly as possible. In calm weather this was easy. In rough weather, food got soaked with salt spray or even washed from our trays.

We had one messmate on the Quebec who, no matter where we were, managed to get pissy-eyed drunk. We forever held him steady for inspection and covered for him in many other situations, both on board ship and ashore. Though old enough to retire, he still was an ordinary seaman. On a previous cruise to Tortola, he'd buried a sealed coconut filled with molasses. So he was anxious to get ashore. But the Officer of the Watch stopped his leave after he arrived on board in a disorderly manner from an outing in Bermuda. Despite that, he still managed to duck ashore and retrieve his potent "treasure". As a result, we kept him under wraps, pissed – with scarce a leg to put under him, until we docked a few miles from Port of Spain, Trinidad. At that time, his stoppage of leave was over, and he was free to join his messmates ashore for more shenanigans.

Some of the taxi drivers who came to meet our ship had a reputation. They drove unwary passengers by a circuitous route and charged a much higher than normal fare. Our driver turned out to be one such crook. Having previously visited Port of Spain, a member of our group knew what to do. At first, he said nothing. Then, when we drew close to town, he announced, "Stop, quick! I'm going to be sick." As soon as the driver stopped, we all bailed out to "help" the poor fellow.

"One, two, three!" We ran like hell, leaving the taxi driver cursing the fate he so richly deserved.

In Port of Spain, shopkeepers vied for attention. One called out, "Dirty postcards. You want dirty picture, Johnny? You like?" (The monicker "Johnny" came from the wartime comic strip – Johnny Canuck.)

I tried to ignore the little man in the long yellow shirt and orange turban. But he persisted, grabbing at my sleeve with his grubby hands.

"No, Johnny? You no want? I give them to you cheap. Look! Look!" He shoved the cards into my face.

I glanced at the black and white photographs – very explicit.

I shook my head. "No, thank you."

One of my Navy buddies helped me out. "Fuck off. He's not interested."

Another in our group haggled with the man. When he sensed he'd gotten a bargain, he bought the pack. The triumphant vendor melted into the crowd of hawkers. Persistence pays off. In the safety of a quiet corner, we all crowded round to view the purchase. The first five photos were what we'd seen; the other nineteen were just ordinary postcards.

Wherever we walked on the streets, young boys of eight or ten ran up to us, tugged at our Navy whites, peered up at us with big, appealing eyes and earnest faces. "You want girl? You want fuck my sister?"

Our refusals didn't stop them. "Johnny, you want my mother, my brother? You give me money."

Through all of this, I didn't realize a group of my messmates had taken up a collection to help rid me of my virginity. When they treated me to a rum and coke at a rough wooden table outside a motley collection of straw huts, I should have suspected that this was where my "rite of initiation" was to be conducted.

After we laughed and chattered a while, a black girl, maybe sixteen years old, sat down to drink with us. Her thin cotton dress exposed her small, firm breasts; the hemline passed just below her aureolas.

My breath shortened. Extraordinarily, to me at least, she snuggled up, held my hand, and gazed right into my eyes. I felt flattered – and horny.

Meanwhile, one of the guys paid "the man". "Go get her, tiger!"

Mesmerized, I followed the girl's swaying bottom and bare feet. Inside a dirt floor hut, I saw a room with several curtained-off sections. My companion took me behind one of the curtains and whispered into my ear, "Take off your shoes." Shaking like an overeager puppy, I obeyed. She undid my pants buttons, removed my bell bottoms and shorts, and gently washed my privates with a warm solution. My knees nearly buckled.

All the while she gazed into my eyes. Oh, what love!

At last, she removed her dress and stood before me, stark

screaming naked. Never before had I seen a female body in such magnificence. This was beyond my wildest dreams.

She led me to the nearby cot, lay down, and pulled me on top of her. Suddenly, horror of horrors, my equipment shrank to the size of a raisin. No matter what this gorgeous creature did to arouse me, "wee Willie" would not cooperate. She placed my hand on her wet fur and writhed, groaning in my ear. Nothing! I wanted the dirt floor to split open and swallow me up.

In the face of my utter failure, I turned into a whimpering child. "It ... it must be the rum."

Eventually, the girl's pimp got impatient; other customers were waiting. "No more time. No more time. You get dressed Johnny."

When I exited the hut, I sensed the whole world stared at me, this sailor with the pea-sized penis. I raced back to the ship in a taxi on my own.

Though I scrubbed and scrubbed in a long, long shower, I couldn't get clean.

Right away, I wanted to tell my buddies, "Sorry, guys, you wasted your money." But I couldn't. By this time, they had gone to pursue pleasures of their own. Despite this, the word got out that maybe I was queer. More than likely, my buddies had talked to the prostitute and her pimp.

Though I lost friends that day, I gained others. The bargain proved to be a good one; my new shipmate friends turned out to be quieter and more contemplative.

Navy life certainly had its cruel turns. One day, one of the supply ratings was accused of stealing from a messmate's locker. A group of men held him down and stomped the fingers on both his hands to a pulp. He told the ship's doctor that a hatch had crushed his fingers. No longer able to write, he was handed a medical discharge.

Another time, three stokers decided to take a side trip to Venezuela. Several months later, they were brought back to Halifax where they were sentenced to six months in the army detention barracks. There, the Army Provost Corps used every method imaginable to break the spirits of unruly soldiers, sailors, and airmen.

Some inmates even broke their own arms to escape time in

detention. First, new arrivals had their heads shaved. After that, things got worse. Punishments were exquisite. Scrubbing decks with toothbrushes. Spending hot days running up hills carrying packs loaded with rocks. Digging deep holes in icy weather, then filling them in, and digging new holes elsewhere.

Those who did time in detention seldom behaved the same after their release. Depending upon the original charge or charges, dishonourable discharge usually followed. Some poor souls had their sentences lengthened for attempting escape. Detention was reserved mainly for striking an officer, theft, desertion, and sleeping on duty.

On duty watch, talking to the seagulls for hours and hours, I sometimes found myself dozing off. It is a dreadful feeling to fight drowsiness on pain of major punishment. I heard about one seaman who stood watch during the wee hours of the morning. He had just dozed off in a standing position when he looked up to see the officer of the watch standing before him, the padre at his side.

"Sleeping on watch, my good man?"

"Just saying a short prayer, sir."

"God bless you, son."

Following further exercises at sea, we sailed from the Gulf of Mexico into the muddy waters of the Mississippi River and docked at New Orleans, quite a way inland.

I went ashore on my own. While I looked at art hanging in a small gallery, an artist offered to pay me if I would permit him to paint me in uniform. The portrait would hang in the window of his art shop. Thrilled by the thought of being an artist's model, I said, "Sure!"

The man painted a remarkably quick portrait, then suggested we relax for a while. At this point, I realized he had other intentions. I refused his advances and asked for the money he promised to pay me; instead, he threw me out and threatened to call the police. I fled the scene, angry and cheated.

Before returning to the ship, I bought a small set of oil paints, turpentine, a couple of brushes, and three small cardboard canvasses. The next day I remained on board ship and tried my hand at painting.

I spent the afternoon covering a canvas with a fair impression of the New Orleans dock. When several shipmates returned onboard after having spent the day in local bars, one of them remarked favourably on my painting. Another ran his hand across the wet canvas and wiped the paint on my shirt front. Someone yelled, "Hit him, Slim!" Quickly a group of spectators assembled.

Everyone yelled, "Fight! Fight! Fight!"

I stood, shaking. A rating in the shouting circle calmly urged, "Count to ten, Slim, then hit him!" Another sneered, "Ah! He's too yellow."

I could no longer lose face. These were the messmates with whom I lived day after day. Anything to avoid a fight? Laugh off the ruined painting and the paint on my shirt? No, not this time. This was the time to take a stand.

Suddenly I felt the excitement of the moment. I counted. "One. Two. Three ..." Before I reached ten, I drew back and swung with all my strength – and connected.

Displaying a look of utter amazement, the fellow reeled, dropped to his knees, tottered, and fell forward, oh-so-slowly. In the vernacular, he "wound up with a faceful of floor".

Everyone cheered. Though I shook like the last petal on a dead tulip, I felt elated, dangerously dodgy, and heroic. Messmates slapped me on the back and gave me three rousing cheers. A few seconds later, my knuckles and wrist began to hurt like hell.

Slowly, menacingly, the inebriate hoisted himself from the deck and tried to get back at me. Luckily for me, someone held him back.

No way could I have done the deed twice.

Attracted by the commotion, the officer of the watch appeared and demanded an explanation. Fighting on board ship was a serious offense. There would be no excuse for what I had done.

Next day I was brought up on charge. Captain Budge asked the customary "Do you have anything to say for yourself, son?"

"No, sir!"

"Fourteen days number eleven. And ... congratulations!"

Was I now a man? If so, my stepfather's mandate had been met! No matter. I had now gained acceptance by the crew, and several of my messmates approached me to voice their support. Even the fourteen days of punishment involved only light duties.

They were a mere formality. Best of all, the fellow I hit came to shake my hand. We didn't become the best of friends but I had certainly gained his respect. At last, I fitted in.

When I returned to Halifax, I was transferred back to Stadacona. The Quebec prepared to sail to Portsmouth for the "Spithead Review", when ships from all parts of the British Empire sailed by in honour of the newly crowned Queen Elizabeth II. Though King George VI had died early in 1952, the coronation of the new Queen wasn't held until June 2, 1953. I was bitterly disappointed not to be going.

At this point, disheartened with the Navy, disappointed with my parents, and angry with God, I did something I later came to regret. With strong encouragement from a Protestant padré, I officially renounced my Catholicism before the congregation of a Presbyterian Church in Halifax and then was received warmly as a newfound "Christian". That was my last visit to any church for a long time.[13]

I made my statement all right. But I paid a penalty for it: I lost many of my closest friends. As I thrashed about, lonely and confused, I applied for a discharge from the Royal Canadian Navy. I wanted to return to school and make something of myself, far from constant disappointments, far from the bullying, the threats, and the stench of drunken messmates.

When the Quebec returned to Canada in September, I was reposted to her. Almost right away, we sailed through a hurricane to take part in Exercise Main brace, where we played war games with ships and submarines of the American, British, and other Commonwealth navies. I had reached my twentieth birthday that June, and was now eligible for the daily tot. Without that daily rum ration – a drink so strong that the first gulp almost pulverized me – I would not have survived the seasickness that attacked many of us from the moment we left our hammocks at wakey-wakey. The Navy rum mixed with Coke gave us the appetite we needed to eat a hearty lunch. This, in turn, set our stomachs straight for the remainder of the day.

Sometimes, when the weather was especially rough – as it was during that hurricane – many of us not on watch unrolled our hammocks and slung them from iron hooks. Set into the cross members of the deck head, the hooks were spaced enough to permit each man a regulation eighteen inches. Swinging gently as the ship rolled at sea, the hammocks provided a fair amount of comfort.

Each morning we rolled our hammocks ("micks") into tight, cylindrical shapes, secured them with rope lashings, and stowed them for the day. On stormy days, following morning inspections, many of us reslung our hammocks and left them that way for the rest of the day.

Following a rough crossing, we anchored off Greenock, Scotland. Glad to touch solid ground, every one of us who wasn't on duty boarded the train for Glasgow. Though I was free for the weekend, I didn't get permission to travel with a group of my buddies past Glasgow, all the way to London. So I went to a dance in Glasgow instead. The dance was crowded with sailors from several national navies. A fight broke out between Australian and American sailors. I escaped with my dance partner.

I had met the first love of my life. Molly invited me to spend a weekend at Millingavey – "Moguy" – in her parents' home. We walked along the glen, talked, and held hands. When we kissed, her mouth tasted like honey. I was in heaven. Unhappily, when we attended a movie and stage show in Glasgow on Saturday night, I picked up some lice. I made several frantic trips to the theatre washroom, even removed my pants, turned them inside out, and shook them thoroughly. Nothing could rid me of the annoying itch.

Molly's parents cooked a beautiful dinner, then left us to spend a romantic evening alone. Apparently they not only liked me, they trusted me with their daughter. And I respected that trust. I had never before spent such an intimate time with anyone.

When I boarded the train back to Grenoch, clutching the apple Molly gave me with her last kiss, I swore I would love her forever and one day come back to Millingavie and my true love.

Forever ended, all too soon. My true love never answered my love letters. (I'm sure I was the butt of Molly's parents condemnation, when they discovered pesky insects in the bedroom where "that wretched Canadian sailor" had slept.)

Not long after my return to Halifax, I again was transferred to Stadacona. My honourable release had officially been granted, effective November 22nd, 1953. I had thirty-two days to wait.

Those final days in the Navy proved to be the unhappiest and most confused of my life. I could have remained in the RCN and retired after twenty years – after all, I only had a small taste of world travel. Instead, I had ended my career as a failure, without friends and without any reasonable prospects. I bitterly regretted my hasty decision to leave.

* * * * * * * *

[1]   *In those days, it was fairly common for boys my age to leave school. No formal withdrawal was even required.*
Maybe my parents thought it would be a good lesson for me to earn my keep for a while. Maybe they thought it would give me a better appreciation of the perks I had at home. Then I could return to school and complete my education.

[2]   *The war took away Mother's financial independence. No longer did she feel secure or adequately protected. Having money became vitally important to her.*

[3]   **Beaumont**, Francis, and **Fletcher,** John; *Love's Cure (act II, sc. 2), in* Familiar Quotations, Bartlett, John, comp., [Boston: Little, Brown, and company, 1919], p. 199

[4]   *Zoot suiters (post war youth gangs) wore a long, loose coat with wide, padded shoulders, pants with wide legs and tight ankle cuffs, worn very high above the waist, an oversized bow-tie, sometimes a wide-brimmed hat, and a long, hanging watch chain.*
Throughout the Second World War, there had been many battles between zoot suiters and members of the armed forces. The law was almost always on the side of the servicemen even when innocent youths were attacked.
After the outbreak of the Korean War, turmoil surfaced once more as swarms of servicemen invaded dance halls and attracted local girls.

[5]   *"Make and mend" is a traditional Navy half-holiday granted for the care of clothing. This time out may also be used for personal shopping and shore leave.*

[6]   *It did not occur to me that the Navy thugs who beat me up might have viewed me as a pervert who preyed upon little boys. I was too aware of my own pain to have considered this possibility. Perhaps I was naïve.*

[7] **Stevenson**, Robert Louis; *Travels with a Donkey in the Cévennes;* [New York: Charles Scribner's Sons, 1905], p. 63

[8]   *The American sailor played a dirty trick on me. And he knew it. A gay steam bath is not an overnight residence! My anger grew toward men who continued to threaten and take advantage of me. On the other hand, I clearly had not learned to recognize or even to say "no" to predators and their advances. It was this fact, more than any other, that made me feel dirty, stupid, and cheap.*

[9]   *Mexican customs and immigration welcomed uniformed servicemen to their border towns, passports unneeded. Servicemen were an excellent source of hard currency. Deeper into Mexico, passports or visas, were always required.*

[10]   *My allotment was sent home until I turned twenty. All that remained after taxes was nine dollars monthly. Since it had to cover all personal expenses, it left almost nothing for entertainment.*
    Even ten years earlier, nine dollars a month might have been sufficient for a single fellow who had food and lodging provided. Our parents remembered the depression when nine dollars would have been a fortune to any man.
    Pay back would have to come from my allotment home.

[11]   *The Seagull Club was a drinking and dancing club for Canadian sailors .*

[12]   *The only person ever to have called me "Benjamin Bunny" was my own father – when I was very young. I'm sure the name came from the Beatrix Potter books he read to me in my early years.*
    see **Potter**, Beatrix; "The Tale of Benjamin Bunny", in *Peter Rabbit, the Flopsy Bunnies* (New York: Random House, 1988)

[13]   *When I gave up my faith, some said I was disillusioned. In a literal sense, this meant I had emerged from illusion. This was inaccurate.*

Chapter Ten
Sparks and Sputters (1953/55)

"If it's worth doing, it's worth doing well."
– My stepfather.

A few days after my arrival at <u>Stadacona</u>, I was paid out, with advance funds included for annual leave. I sent my kit bag by train to Montreal and headed for the highway, in civilian clothes to hitchhike west.

My intention was to leave my navy gear at my parents' home and travel to Victoria, where I would find a job and attend night school classes. Foreseeing no difficulties, I brimmed with idealistic plans. I had worked with Cubs and taught swimming at the "Y", and enjoyed both. I set my sights on becoming a teacher. My future lay ahead. I was free to make my own choices and ready to set the world on fire!

With more money on my person than I ever had in my life, I divided the larger bills and placed them flat in both shoes for safekeeping. Though this felt uncomfortable, I welcomed the sense of security it gave me.[1] Then with my light carrying case and Navy burberry (light raincoat), I headed for the highway. It was late afternoon before I got my first ride. My hands and feet were frozen. But the cab of the transport truck soon warmed me. And the driver was equally warm.

As I didn't want to spend money on motels, I decided to keep on traveling. The trucker dropped me off near the far side of Moncton, New Brunswick. Following a lengthy walk to a suitable lift site, I got a short ride with a group of partying college students. They left me on a lonely stretch of highway, before taking off up a gravel side road.

Occasionally a car splashed by. The night grew dark and windy; gradually I turned into an icicle. I was alone in Siberia. Confidence seeped from me as minutes turned into hours. The wind caterwauled with whistles and shrieks. The banshee!

Then, silence, until the moon peeped out from behind a heavy snow cloud and bathed the trees in ghostly light. A crow flew down from a pine top, cawing and flapping over the glistening roadway. Birds and other creatures of the night joined in the chorus.

The moon hid her face once more. With the renewed blackness, silence returned, punctuated only by the periodic hooting of an unseen owl. A nearby river reinforced my fear. As though pursued by wolves, it gushed out of the forest and tumbled helter-skelter over rocks and tree limbs.

I stood, stamped my feet, ran on the spot, sang into the dark – anything but walk away. I couldn't walk away; I'd be swallowed by encircling forest. Toes, fingers, ears throbbed with cold. Then, from a bush beside the road, I heard the distinct song of a robin.

In this frozen wasteland, he too was alone. Ah, poor bird. This place is too cold for thee and me.

> *The frosty ways like iron,*
> *The branches plumed with snow, –*
> *Alas! in Winter, dead and dark,*
> *Where can poor Robin go?* [2]

In the small hours of the morning, a logger and his girlfriend picked me up and took me as far as the Greyhound bus station in Fredericton.

After a hot cup of coffee, I inquired about bus fares, then went into the washroom and took out enough money for a ticket to Quebec City via Rivière du Loup.

Three pleasant days in Quebec with Pat and Madeleine, Louis and Emilien provided the breathing space I needed before facing my parents. As the weather in Quebec was exceedingly cold, I paid for a train ride to Montreal, trusting my funds would hold out until I got to Victoria. I picked up my kit bag at the Montreal Windsor Station and purchased another ticket for the short train ride to Dorval. During the previous October, the family had moved to a new home on Claude Avenue. Since I had no idea where that was, I splurged on a taxi. This was something I'd never done before and would not repeat for many years.

When I informed my parents of my intention to travel west and eventually return to school, both were skeptical. They were especially unhelpful when I said I wanted to study to become a teacher: "It requires character to be a teacher! Why don't you apprentice for a trade? You'd be a good carpenter".

After my brief visit, I left navy gear and other belongings in my mother's care, picked up an extra jersey, a heavier coat, and an old pair of brown shoes – all of which were too tight and would soon have to be discarded. Then I gave Mother most of my money for safekeeping and set out to hitchhike to the Pacific Coast. I wanted to leave the cold climate – of parents and the Canadian winter both.[3]

Instead of travelling north of the Great Lakes, I decided to head for Windsor and take the southern route through the United States. But I was no longer in uniform; hitchhiking was very difficult.

On the outskirts of Oshawa, a traveling salesman invited me to share a motel room. He registered as a single, and I stayed without charge. There was only one bed. The salesman took a bottle out of his travel bag and poured each of us a drink, neat. Soon we crawled into bed in our shorts. Hesitatingly at first, then with increased aggression, he tried putting his hand inside my underwear pants.

I got up quickly, put my feet on the cold floor, and lit one of his cigarettes. Trembling from the cold and from the feelings of revulsion and anger that churned in the pit of my stomach, I hurriedly dressed without saying a word, grabbed my belongings, left the cigarette to smolder on the salesman's jacket (which he had tossed across the chair), and departed. During all that time, the salesman glared at me. He did not move, even to extinguish the smoldering cigarette. I left the door open, hurriedly backtracked through the cold drizzle, and waited for a fresh lift.[4]

Kitchener, Ontario was as far as I got. That friendly town became my home until the following spring. Hitchhiking in winter was too much.

November 23rd, 1953, I began work as a medical attendant on ambulance service with the Kitchener-Waterloo Hospital at thirty-five dollars per week. Mine was the morning shift (7:00 AM to 3:00 PM). I was to pack a bag lunch to eat en route. I found room and board with a German-speaking family on Louisa Street.

My first ambulance trip, I helped bag the remains of a person cut to pieces by a train. A police officers on the scene became violently ill. While he vomited, I picked up body pieces and carried them to a plastic sheet. Latex gloves had not yet been invented. At least, they weren't available on the ambulance. This experience didn't bother me until weeks later, when nightmares returned.

On another trip, I sat beside a Mennonite and read <u>The Bible</u> to him. He died before reaching the hospital.

On still another trip – some déjà vu here – I helped deliver a baby en route to hospital.

Between calls, I emptied bed pans, changed catheters, and administered enemas. This was a messy job. Once in a while, I got splattered or had a major cleanup. I needed tact and a sense of humour without which I risked overlooking human dignity.

Over the weeks and months, I befriended musicians, conductors, teachers, farmers, doctors, and paupers. It never failed that the dying were anxious to tell their life stories. Every day, I found inspiration in a milieu where all walks of life are levelled.[5]

I was told I had a gentle touch. I shaved patients for operations or for the pleasure of helping an elderly soul. I read to people, held their hands, prayed with the dying, and took the deceased to the hospital morgue. With the elderly, I was frequently the only "relative" present. One patient urinated on my hand as I took his rectal temperature. Then he died.

My favourite part of the hospital was the children's ward. I read stories and sang comical songs from my own childhood. But when a child died, I was devastated for days.

When I left the Navy, I had developed an annoying stutter. Since I wanted to get rid of this, I decided to emulate Demosthenes. I placed marbles in my mouth and practiced speaking clearly. (The Greek had used pebbles. Close enough.) One day I swallowed a marble. However, the marbles worked.

Public speaking of a kind soon followed self-improvement. A friend introduced me to James Mitchell, manager of the Kitchener-Waterloo Broadcasting Company. Mr. Mitchell offered to try me out as part-time announcer and disk jockey. Soon I was working the afternoon shift at CKCR, doing newscasts and being "Mr. Musical Sunshine" from four until "God Save the Queen" at midnight.

My salary at the radio station was thirty-five dollars per week, no matter how many extra hours I worked, no matter that I worked on weekends and holidays or not, and no matter that I filled in for other announcers. I was happy. On air I was someone special. And Kitchener was my home.

The weather for the day had to be located on a huge record disc with many grooves. Among those grooves, winter snow was situated close to summer heat waves. Most commercial jingles were prerecorded on audio tape. Everything had to be cued to the exact spot and turned on at the right moment. All of this got aired in the intervals between popular songs. "Oh Mein Papa", "How Much is that Doggie in the Window?", and other popular requests of the day were all preselected by each announcer, for his own airtime.

We also delivered live commercials and chatted happily with an unseen audience. Some people loved me and phoned in to tell me so. Others couldn't stand my English accent. When I got a terrible cold, several listeners suggested I keep my new voice – "a cod id by dose". It was the deep huskiness they liked.

Excellent rapport existed amongst the staff. Occasionally, when a special guest came to town, we threw a late night party at the Press Club. On Sunday mornings, I often got called in to broadcast live church programs, including "Maxwell House Coffee Presents Everybody's Favourite Gospel Singer".

One night, just before closing, I was alone in the station when an ex-employee turned up high as a kite. He begged me to let him do the traditional station closing. "This is CKCR, AM and FM, broadcasting from the Waterloo Trust Arcade Building in downtown Kitchener. We are on the air from ... etc. Ladies and Gentlemen, the Queen." I was crazy to let him at the controls. Instead of playing the preset recording, he stayed on the microphone and, in a high pitched voice, intoned: "Hello, Canada. So glad to be heah!" I prayed no one heard. Sure enough, the company received several indignant phone calls. Following my contrite explanation, I was warned to keep the door locked when working alone.

Actually, nearly every announcer made bloopers:

"Everybody's Favourite Gospel Slinger, Sinner, er... Singer"

"Where's that damned tape? Oops!"

Though I was happy with both my jobs, I exhausted myself with long hours and lack of sleep. It all caught up with me. I fainted pushing a corpse down a hospital corridor on a gurney. Corpse and gurney went crashing against swinging doors. One of the hospital administrators told me I could not keep up two jobs. I would have to make a choice. I chose to stick to radio.

On February 21st, 1954, I bid farewell to all the nurses, doctors, fellow orderlies, and hospital staff, and went to prepare for my afternoon programming at CKCR.

Not long after that, on my way to work, I passed a group of people standing near an apartment building. Smoke poured from an open window. Someone had heard a baby crying. Slim and light, I volunteered to be hoisted through an open window several feet above ground.

Once inside, I saw smoke pouring from a pot on the stove. I put the pot in the sink and turned on the tap. Then I turned off the element and unlocked the apartment door. (There was no baby.)

Firemen and policemen entered with an inebriated owner, who promptly ordered me arrested for breaking and entering. I was not charged. However, a story in the local newspaper the following day reported "Local announcer held in break and entry". My fellow workers found the event amusing – a certain amount of rivalry always existed amongst members of the media – and I laughed with them. Trouble was, my only suit stank of smoke.

After filling in for fellow workers on several occasions, I had a few days off owed to me. I also had loaned another announcer one hundred dollars. On the Friday, I was due to take my few days off, I was let go without notice. Though I never got my money back, I was given a letter of recommendation, signed by Mr. Mitchell, recommending me as "an able operator".

In those days, employees had no recourse. Jobs were scarce; competition was keen. Bosses and owners were all-powerful. A more experienced disk jockey, who left the station at the same time as I, went to a radio station in Toronto.

Despite the fact I had done fairly well as an announcer, I had to work hard to find a job. I went to Montreal and applied at CFCF. Then I took a CBC bilingual audition and was told to call back in a few days for the results. Finally, I went to CJAD in Montreal, where I was given a job as technical operator on a trial basis. I moved back into the YMCA. My life seemed to be back together.

One day a message came for me at the front desk of the "Y". I was to contact the CBC. Vancouver had an opening for a bilingual announcer at the new television station. The people at CJAD congratulated me and I left immediately for Vancouver.

It was now spring. As always, I was short of money. My parents "could not afford" to lend me the fare, let alone give me the money they were holding "in safe keeping" for me. So I hitchhiked west, and arrived in Vancouver about a week late. The job at the CBC was already filled; besides, my level of education was "far below par". "Come back when you have a university degree".

I traveled all over the west coast and applied at every radio station. No luck.

Back in Vancouver, with just twenty-five dollars in my wallet, a policeman handed me a twenty-five dollar ticket for jaywalking, payable on the spot.[6]

Now I had no money. And no job. And no place to stay. That first night, I slept in Stanley Park. Starting at dawn the next morning, I combed the streets looking for work.

That evening, desperately hungry, I entered a restaurant and ordered pasta with meat sauce. I worried so much about not being able to pay the bill, I developed a stomach ache before I finished. I checked out the bathroom and the surrounding area and found no back door, except through the kitchen. Instead, vowing to return and pay my bill as soon as I could, I walked straight out the front door without glancing back.

I felt like a criminal. Not a vagrant, though; I was too well dressed for that.

In desperation, I entered a phone booth and tried a reverse-charge call to Dorval, to beg for temporary funds. Mother hung up. Following a second night in Stanley Park, I saw a help wanted sign at a car wash. I was ready to do anything.

I vacuumed and cleaned inside cars. A few times I found loose change on the floor or in the ashtray. I considered the money a tip. Before long, someone complained, and I was let go without getting paid. "Go! Or I'll call the police". I left.

With no more than small change, I returned to the restaurant where I had stolen the free meal. Introducing myself to the manager, I explained my situation and offered to pay the skipped bill. Fortunately for me, the manager was impressed. He gave me a job as a dishwasher and all the food I could eat. Soon I had enough money to find a decent place to sleep.

I hated the work; the waitresses and busboys held me in low

130

esteem. But I decided to stick it out until I had enough saved for the ferry to Victoria.

Vancouver was unfriendly compared to the Victoria I had known. I got into an argument with one of the busboys over a tip that supposedly had been left under one of the plates I was washing. He accused me of taking money I hadn't even seen. The threat of physical violence made me decide it was time to move on. When I received my next pay, I thanked the restaurant manager and resigned. I said nothing about my altercation with the bus boy. Navy training taught me to keep my mouth shut.

Also, I had never learned to stand up for my rights.

In Victoria, I took a room at the YMCA and found a job selling yard goods at Eaton's.

In June, the "Y" was preparing for summer camp at Camp Thunderbird, in the Sooke hills. As I had been a volunteer swim instructor, I was offered the summer position of camp waterfront director. A week later, I quit my job at Eaton's and was driven to camp to prepare for the season. My job was to repair the docks and get the canoes, swim float, and all other waterfront equipment into running shape. A couple of canoes required patching. And the swim area had to be raked and cleared of winter debris.

Camp Thunderbird had been established on property that once had belonged to a Japanese fruit farmer. At the start of the war, a vigilante group stormed over from Vancouver and hanged the old man from one of his apple trees. Or so the story went. It was a good one for late at night around a camp fire. Of course, the man's ghost could often be seen at night – sitting near the dock or strolling down the road with a swinging lamp! Every summer camp must have its ghost. It's obligatory.

The hill on the camp property boasted a long stairway, at the top of which was a chapel for Sunday services. Usually the camp director, Clayton Cameron, conducted the service. But occasionally the duty fell to me. I enjoyed the honour of being chaplain for the day. As I led the campers up the steps, we sang "We Are Climbing Jacob's Ladder." I pointed out the wonders of God's creation to all the restless campers and dreamt of becoming a missionary.

When camp was over in August, 1954, I got my job back selling yard goods at Eaton's and took a room with the Cameron family. I taught swimming and diving at the "Y" and became "Akela" – Cub leader, for the 1st Fairfield Cub Pack. The following Christmas, I didn't think of going home. For the time being, my ambition to return to school was set aside.

Shortly after the winter snows and cold weather, the Cameron family moved to Calgary. So I moved back to the YMCA, where I was told of an opening on James Island packing explosives. The pay was better than what I was making at Eaton's, so I took the job. I commuted back and forth with a fellow worker in his yellow Cadillac convertible.

Working with dynamite produced terrible headaches and nausea; I was told this would pass as I accustomed myself to the fumes. My coworkers chewed Copenhagen snuff to help them deal with this. They tucked chaws behind their lower lips and spat out the juice. I tried doing this but swallowed some of the juice and became even sicker. Headaches and nausea persisted.

On March 19th, 1955, I got a break. After returning with my pay from James Island, I saw an ad posted on a bulletin board in Victoria harbour. The William J. Stewart, a hydrographical survey ship, required a steward. I walked on board and signed up. As the boat was scheduled to sail within a couple of hours, I had to run. I picked up my few belongings at the "Y" and signed out. Then I left a hasty message for the Fairfield Scout Group Committee, regarding my resignation from the Cub pack. I made it back to the ship just before the gangplank was hoisted up.

The first few weeks were great. My duties were light. I cleaned the captain's cabin, made up his bunk, and served meals in the officer's mess. As I could type, I helped out with correspondence and other paper work. In my considerable spare time, I read, fished, and admired the spectacular scenery. With a large hook and a strip of bacon rind, I caught a huge halibut. Several hands helped haul the fish on board, and the cook immediately went to work cutting it up. We caught many red snappers too. But as bottom fish, they were considered garbage – much too bony. So they were thrown back, to float away on the surface. The surveyors often returned with clams and oysters and the occasional abalone, a shellfish that was beaten with a meat mallet and fried. We ate very well indeed.

We stopped at Namu, Bella Coola, and Bella Bella, and

charted the inlets of the Queen Charlottes. The other steward – with whom I shared a cabin – told me he planned to disembark at Prince Rupert and make his way north to where "the big money" could be made.

He nearly convinced me to join him – before he showed his sadistic side. In excruciating detail, he described how he tortured his wife by beating her, urinating on her in the bathtub, and pouring cold water on her while she was sleeping. When he asked if I "did special favours for the captain", (implying I was gay), I feared he might want to beat me up.

This short, wiry man could have been handsome, that is, if he had taken care of his body and mind. As it was, with his acne scarred cheeks, cigarette stained teeth, long, dandruff-flaked black hair, and malevolent eyes, he repulsed and terrified me. He hated himself nearly as much as he grew to hate me. This meant that, since we had set out to sea, I had to stay out of his way as best I could.

Why did the man come to hate me so? Did my looks rub him the wrong way? Or my manner of speech? Maybe he noted my distaste for loud, smelly men with greasy faces, huddled in the boiler room, brandishing wrenches. Maybe he took this as an affront.

Then again, maybe he had no particular reason at all to dislike me. Hatred sustains itself exceedingly well without benefit of cause.

It wasn't long before I realized that he wanted to kill me.[7]

He was jealous. His job was heavier than mine. He had to wait on the surveyors, their helpers, and other ship's crew. He really wanted my job.

One day, he turned on me and put the boots to me. While I delivered a tray from the galley to the officer's mess, he knocked the tray from my hands and tossed it and its contents overboard. Then he knocked me to the deck and kicked me savagely. I woke up in sick bay with the captain applying ice to my bruised and bleeding face.

I didn't say a word. Instead, when we returned to Victoria on June 5th, I signed off.[8]

I had worked at Eaton's for only two short periods. Since I hadn't built up a suitably lengthy employment record, the store wasn't interested in rehiring me. I looked in vain for another job. At Camp Thunderbird, another waterfront director had been hired, and all other staffing positions were filled. Someone advised me I would have better luck in Calgary; jobs were opening up throughout Alberta. I traveled with another fellow in the same position as I and shared driving and gas costs.

Thanks to a recommendation from Clay Cameron, my former landlord and camp director from Camp Thunderbird, the Calgary "Y" hired me as a group counselor at Camp Chief Hector Crawler, located on Bow Lake in the Foothills.

Unfortunately, I had to wait for two or three weeks before starting. A crew had already been signed to do all the required preparation work, such as setting up teepees, preparing the waterfront and main lodges, and cleaning the grounds.

* * * * * * * *

[1]   *With my discharge, the allotment to my parents was also terminated. However, I knew nothing of banking, never having had money to bank, so my entire "fortune" was carried in cash.*

[2]   **Allingham,** William; "Robin Redbreast", in Flower *Pieces and Other Poems* (London: Reeves and Turner, 1888), pp. 82-83

[3]   *Mother convinced me that carrying the amount of money I had on my person was unsafe and I easily could be robbed. So I gave her a goodly portion, withholding enough to get me to the West Coast where a man with my talents would easily find a job.*

[4]   *I had a right to be angry. Once more I was taken advantage of by an older man who had, in effect, lied to me. He offered friendship under false pretenses. And of course, I judged him in the light of past injustices. But I could have expressed my anger in a less violent manner than by burning his jacket.*

[5]   *I understand the dilemma of those in the caring professions. When they become too attached - too involved - they easily can succumb to depression and burnout. Doctors and nurses have to find a happy balance – meaning support within their professional groups and teams.*

[6]   *At that time the Vancouver police had a reputation for extortion and kickbacks.*
see **Macdonald,** Ian and O'Keefe, Betty; *The Mulligan Affair,* (Surrey, B.C., Heritage House,1997) pp. 17-20

[7]   *In Herman Melville's novelette, "Billy Budd", Claggart demonstrates an insane hatred of the young sailor Billy Budd. Melville's examination of the spiritual roots of Claggart's hatred is incisive, as is his observation that the innocent and inexperienced offer tempting prey for those who cynically have surrendered to their own darkness within.*

[8]   *So often, I allowed bullies to get the better of me. I ran, rather than staying to fight. Feelings of shame convinced me I deserved the beatings and emotional abuse. My victim mentality invited torture. And I would be tortured for years.*

Chapter Eleven
Bed Sheets and Matches (1955)

> *In Thy light, we shall see light.*
> *- Columbia University motto.*

June, 1955, while waiting for camp, I volunteered to help out in the YMCA youth office. I typed, filed, and provided general assistance in exchange for room and board.

One of the staff introduced me to a well-spoken black fellow, a Quaker – member of the "Society of Friends". I shall call him *Winston.

Winston was in need of a volunteer to assist with correspondence and to accompany him on a brief visit to the Tenth Anniversary Commemoration Celebration of the United Nations, to be held in San Francisco, from the 20th to the 26th June, 1955. His involvement came through the National Association for the Advancement of Colored People. Winston explained there would be no payment involved. But I would be welcome to live comfortably in his home, where I would be well cared for. And the experience would provide me with an opportunity to help my fellow man. Winston handled the arrangements with the "Y" for me. I would work at Camp Chief Hector Crawler for the six weeks of camp, during July and part of August. But first, I would attend the San Francisco Conference. Without second thought, I jumped at the opportunity.

Winston's house in Calgary was in a well kept neighbourhood. I thought I'd be very comfortable. There was just one problem. Winston invited me to sleep with him. In response, I asked to sleep on a chesterfield or in one of his spare rooms. Immediately, I was shown to a private bedroom. But that didn't stop me from planning my quiet departure. I had made a terrible mistake.

I waited, fully dressed, until I thought my host would be asleep. Carefully, I opened the bedroom door and headed for the front entrance. I had to pass through the living room. To my dismay, Winston sat at his desk, going over papers.

He spoke in a soft, steady voice, without looking up. "There's no need to sneak off like a thief in the night! Come and sit down."

I shook uncontrollably, almost in tears.

"What is it about me that frightens you?"

I couldn't answer. I just stood there, confused and dazed, and looked at my hands, my bag on the floor in front of me. I thought I'd throw up.

Winston swiveled around to face me. He spoke in an even tone. "I promise you that who I am and how I live has no bearing on what I do or the cause I work for. You told me you want to fight prejudice. Do you really know what prejudice is?"

He paused for an answer. I couldn't speak.

"You judge me by people you've known before. Maybe they've hurt you. Well, I'm not them. I'm me. So accept me as I am, or ... do something else with your life. Since I respect you for who you are, I'd expect no less from you."

Knees buckling, I felt like an absolute fool. I fought back tears. I felt as though I'd been caught stealing from Christ Himself.

Winston continued. "If you still wish, you may leave, but allow me to drive you to the Y. You'd probably get lost from here."

Stammering, "I'm really sorry," I took a deep breath and shook my head. I tried to still the quaking in my knees. "I made a hasty judgment. I'll stay. If I may. I really am sorry."

Finally, I sat down, feeling sick and dizzy.[1]

I felt humiliated and vulnerable and terribly, terribly wrong. Winston offered his hand. I took it. "I'll get you a cup of coffee. I think we need to have a good talk."

At about three in the morning, Winston and I made our way to our separate bedrooms. For the first time in years, I felt a sense of purpose. What an introduction! I had so much to learn. I even felt a sense of excitement: "Yes, Mother. I'll be a hero yet."

The next morning the sun beamed through the curtains. I heard a knock at my door. "Are you going to sleep all day? Come have some breakfast; we've got work to do."

Before long I was busy taking dictation and typing letters.

Visitors – and there were many – always knew, without a word being said, that I was "straight". Winston had many friends, both men and women. Most were dark skinned. Since everyone was kind and considerate, I felt increasingly comfortable working and learning. But there were times when I wondered if people at the

Calgary YMCA "knew" – and misunderstood – about Winston and me. I had a terrible fear of being labelled "homosexual".

I enjoyed Sunday afternoon barbeques and relaxed with Winston's guests in the warm sun. One very dark woman told me why people of African descent cover up with big hats, long sleeves, even gloves. "We burn in the sun just as white folk do. Our dark skin attracts the burning rays. Light colours reflect the sunlight and keep us cool." Embarrassed at a slipped remark, the same lady said "Man, is my face red." I also enjoyed the humour.

I learned many lessons in the short period of time I was involved with the "Friends" and the civil rights movement. The Quakers had founded the American Friends Service Committee in 1917 to assist black servicemen during World War I; in 1947, the committee won the Nobel Peace Prize. I learned also that the Friends served in many countries worldwide as doctors, nurses, and teachers, during the Second World War and during later civil wars, long before Medecins Sans Frontiers (Doctors Without borders), the American Peace Corps, and United Nations Services were formed.

"Justice is truth in action."
– Benjamin Disraeli (1804 - 1881), [2]

I had already seen some of the conditions that "people of colour" had to suffer, not only in the South, but even in parts of Canada – such as near Halifax where I had black friends during my days at <u>Stadacona</u> and <u>Shearwater</u>. Although, during my travels through the United States, I never stopped long enough to really observe what was going on, I heard stories of how non-whites were insulted openly as "black cows" and "black apes". I was told how they were forced to pay their bus fares, then get off the bus to enter by the back door, and that sometimes drivers were encouraged to drive off without them, with their fare in the box.

In some states, there were separate theatres for "negroes". Their films were always a couple of years or more behind what the whites had already seen. I had seen the separate toilets and drinking fountains and knew that only whites were permitted to eat in good restaurants or stay in decent hotels or even swim at public beaches. I felt very uncomfortable when blacks stepped off the sidewalk, to allow a white person to pass by.

Somewhere around 15th June, 1955, Winston and I left for San Francisco. First, we drove west to Vancouver. I didn't realize at the time the difficulties posed for mixed races travelling together that we might have encountered had we taken a more direct route through the Northwestern States.

While at the Commemoration which opened June 20th at the San Francisco Opera House, I had the privilege of being introduced to Paul Robeson. The famous bass singer was active in Civil Rights for much of his life. He was also a good friend of my mother and father in Finchingfield, when I was small. Mother's oil portrait of him hung in our home for many years.

Robeson remembered my parents and repeated what Mother had once told me, that when I was born, a witch doctor foretold I would one day work for his people. Again I entertained visions of traveling to Africa. This man's influence was primary in convincing me to commit to the struggle for justice in the United States.

After San Francisco, I attended the Calgary YMCA Camp as a section counsellor.[3] Not having gone through orientation with the younger counselors and having replaced a more popular fellow who had been "let go", I found myself unwelcome.

The counsellors at Camp Hector Crawler were rougher than their counterparts in Victoria. Campers who wet the bed were dumped into the lake. I protested, and the practice was not repeated in my section. Although the Camp Director was likely unaware of the way some counsellors treated their young charges, I was told by my fellow staff members not to try to change traditions that were "none of my business".

I tried to introduce the ceremonial campfire lighting we had used at Camp Thunderbird. On a tin plate, we placed a piece of magnesium and covered it with fine kindling. Then we ran a rubber hose up an incline to a spot behind a tree. When water was poured into a funnel, the magnesium ignited. Campers knew only that the fire was started by the sacred words of the Camp Chief.

By age old tradition, the campfire at Camp Hector Crawler featured a flaming arrow shot by a senior counsellor from outside the ring. My suggestion fell on deaf ears.

The YMCA had a contract with some local First Nations to provide ponies at the camp. Most of the horses were mild and even-tempered. Only a few were frisky and shied at the slightest provocation. Campers and counsellors went riding bareback along narrow trails in the steep foothills. My first time out, someone flicked my mount with a branch he was using as a whip. My horse took off at breakneck speed. I held on to its neck as long as I could, but got thrown onto a rocky path. I returned to camp on foot. My pony grazed unconcerned in the paddock.

The next time we went riding, the pony crew assigned me an ancient nag, separated from her skeleton by just a few pounds. When I urged her to get moving, she broke wind and wafted me with the aroma of her impending death. I ended up so far behind even the most timid camper that I turned old Bessie 'round, returned to camp, and passed up the entire excursion. Though I felt not a little guilty – the group for which I was responsible was off in the mountains somewhere without its "fearless leader" – I enjoyed a day without responsibilities.

A few nights later, a group of hooded counsellors yanked me out of bed and tossed me into the freezing waters of Bow Lake. This was an embarrassing situation. I was supposed to be in a position of authority, but had lost all respect. What was I doing at that camp? At Camp Thunderbird – the Victoria Y camp – I had been effective as a youth leader. Here, in this violently macho atmosphere, I was lost.

I was happy when the season ended. I didn't hang around for cleanup.

Winston suggested I try my hand at teaching native children unable to attend regular or band schools. Once more, I jumped at the opportunity.[55]

Special schools had been established for Status Indians; those without "Status" could not attend. My teaching experience was something like this: I usually sat with two or three of the youngest children and helped them stumble their way through a primary reader. "Lessons" never lasted longer than fifteen or twenty minutes before my charges ran off with a whoop. Sometimes several such groups would be brought to me in succession by insistent mothers.

Many of these people lived in squalor. On weekends, beer, whiskey, cheap wine, and lemon and vanilla extract turned up and fights broke out. Invariably, I got beaten up by someone or other.

Every time I got beaten up or treated unjustly in some other way, I asked myself, "Why? Where is God when I need Him? " I was a mouse in the jaws of a vicious, playful cat, who permitted me to revive only so the game might go on.[4]

> *As flies to wanton boys, so are we to the gods*
> *who kill us for their sport.*[1]
> – William Shakespeare, *King Lear; Act IV, Scene 1*

Some, perhaps many, of those Native Canadians, who had served in the Canadian Army in Europe, had learned to drink with their comrades. There they had become accustomed to being treated like everyone else. Back home in Canada, however, they "broke the law". The RCMP routinely raided and seized whatever they could find.

One Friday afternoon, I was asked to drive a fellow who had lost his licence to Calgary. En route, a truckload of screaming youths harassed us and tried to drive us off the road. The only thing we could do was keep going at a steady rate, being careful not to break speed limits.

I was invited to attend a "sweat lodge". I thought this would be a great honour. Naked, I entered with several other Native men. The lodge was steamy and hot. Women and children were already inside. All eyes were on me. How long would I last? It would be unwise to leave ahead of the women and children; I would be lesser in their eyes. As they splashed water onto hot stones, the steam made the air difficult to breathe. It became apparent that everyone was putting me to the full test. As they chatted and laughed in their native tongue, my skin felt on fire. I thought of the Jesuit martyrs, tortured at the hands of the Iroquois.

I survived and enjoyed the icy dip that followed. Later, I attended a feast of meat roasted over an open fire. That was one of the best meals of my life. The chief presented me with doeskin pants, top, and moccasins, hand-stitched by his wife. I had passed the test.

During my stay, I became one of the few white men permitted to see a sun dance lodge. The Sun Dance ceremony, however, had already taken place during the summer.[5]

I had mixed feelings when Winston and another Friend drove up and the band came out to bid me farewell. My work with Winston and the Alberta Friends was complete. It was time to move on to another assignment.[6]

I had been preparing for this a long time. My "missionary" zeal was soon to be tested to the extreme. I was to be driven by various people to New York City, where I would work with one of the Friends in Harlem.

When we arrived, we climbed several flights of stairs in a noisy tenement. A knock at the door provoked loud barking and "Down, boy!" We identified ourselves and a gray-haired matriarch in a wheelchair opened the door. She had no dog! She did her own barking!

For the next several weeks, I typed letters, delivered messages, and ran for groceries. I soon learned why I lived with such a vicious guard dog! In that neighbourhood, muggings and break-ins were an everyday occurrence. At night, I laid awake, listening to the sounds of poverty. Babies cried endlessly, sirens wailed, unhappy voices screamed at one another. But not all was sadness.

On Sundays, we went to the Baptist Church where the singing and preaching and "amens" and "Praise Jesuses" were sweeter than I had ever heard in my life. In Harlem, I felt a love and acceptance from everyone I met, at the church meetings as well as at various private gatherings in people's homes. I never did get to attend a Quaker "meeting" either in Calgary or Harlem.

Apart from what I wore, I had scant belongings. I had an electric razor – which I still used only twice a week at most – and a toothbrush and comb. Everything fitted into my well-worn Navy carry bag. In my wallet I kept my old Navy I.D. and British Columbia driver's licence. There were no credit cards and S.I.N. numbers in those days. At the most, I had a few U.S. dollars I had been given "for emergencies", and some small change. When I was finally called for by a well-spoken white fellow, about my age, I was ready to go.

We drove through Philadelphia and Baltimore. In Washington, we switched to a car with southern licence plates, joining two other volunteers, one white, one black, about our age. My companions were college students who had taken a year off to work in the "Movement". Not all volunteers were members of the Quaker Church. Many had no religious affiliation whatsoever. All were idealists.

Now and then we stopped at safe houses to freshen up and get fed. The term "safe houses" made me think of the safe houses in Harriet Beecher Stowe's story of the underground railroad in <u>Uncle Tom's Cabin</u>.

Every now and then, a fifty miles per hour speed limit would suddenly turn to fifteen miles per hour and a police car would be waiting behind a billboard. Fines were paid on the spot or "with expenses" before a local judge the following day.

While we drove, I learned a lot more about the Movement. My companions talked of Gandhi and nonviolent resistance:

"Evil can only be overcome by love."

"It is better to be the recipient of violence than one who inflicts violence."

"Communism resulted as a protest against hardships and injustices suffered by the underprivileged in many countries."

No, my driving companions were not Communists!

We drove through Lynchburg, Virginia. What a name!

Instead of taking a southwesterly route through mountainous territory, we headed directly south. We took turns driving, sleeping, and looking out for speed traps. We crept through Charlotte, North Carolina, and turned southwest toward Atlanta, Georgia, "Gateway to the South".

Late in the day, a heavy rainstorm forced us to pull over and stop in a rambling community of tumbledown shacks.

Everywhere, rain dripped like tears from leaning gutters. In front of one shack, a mother sat on a porch step under a yellow tarp and dandled her baby. Two toddlers, wearing only ragged t-shirts, floated sticks in a puddle at her feet. When we stopped, she got up and called her children inside. The screen door slammed behind her.

We sat in our car and waited out the storm.

Occasionally, we passed chain gangs cutting ditch grass with scythes. For what I was about to do, I wondered if I might end up on a chain gang.

We stopped to eat at a restaurant in Birmingham. It seemed all eyes were fixed upon us. Not one of us said a word. Our volunteer guide, who had come from the south, ordered for us all.

Later, as we drove southwest towards Tuscaloosa, I learned about Montgomery even further south. It was in Montgomery, the Alabama state capitol and "Cradle of the Confederacy" that Jefferson Davis, the first and only president of the Confederate States of America, raised the rebel flag that now flew in such abundance in every town and hamlet.

I didn't know at the time that Martin Luther King Jr. had, that August, become the pastor of the Dexter Avenue Baptist Church, located just across the street from the state capitol – cradle of American apartheid.

Early in the morning, we left the main road and drove over dusty back roads to a small community that, at first sight, looked abandoned.

Here, well off the beaten track, I saw maybe one hundred and fifty metres of battered shacks. None showed as much as a single curtain in their windows.

Five cement steps led up to the front door of a sad, red-brick bank with a clock in the wall above a big, dusty window. Next to the bank sat a general store with a sloping front porch; in front, a Pepsi sign hung teetering on one rusty chain. At the end of the road, I spotted an unpainted wooden church with a single wooden spire topped with a plain wooden cross. Behind it, a grove of dwarf spruce spread their branches through a white picket fence. Amazingly, the fence appeared freshly painted. Not far from the church I saw a handful of grave markers. They all looked so dreary – yet, in a strange sort of way – picturesque. Many lay flat, smothered now by thistles and nettles. Behind the graveyard, a turd-brown river slithered along under a rickety wooden bridge.

The entire village seemed deserted.

Caught up by the depressing nature of this place, we hurriedly whispered our goodbyes. One of the fellows grabbed his scant belongings and sped out on foot to follow a path from the

144

church graveyard, across the rickety bridge, and into the woods. He knew where he was going.

I was glad this wasn't going be my assignment.

My own rickety bridges and torpid rivers were to come later.

From Tuscaloosa, we travelled northwest and crossed the state line into Mississippi. Before long, we drove off the main road and into a small community of clapboard houses. Everything was neat and clean. The porches were unlittered and the gardens well cared for. Many of the homes looked freshly painted.

We got out of the car before a plain looking wooden church. The heat baked the tops of our heads. A black man walked by and lifted his wool cap. "Sho is hot enough. Aint it?" A white cat padded down the street carrying a mewing kitten in her mouth. She placed it on the dusty ground by the church steps and proceeded to wash it.

The minister came out of the house next to the church, introduced himself, and invited us inside to meet the handful of people who had turned up to welcome us. The place looked pleasantly comfortable.

We sat on straight-back chairs and sipped ice cold lemonade. The minister was thin, tall, and shiny bald, with a forehead furrowed like the grooves on a pine fence. While he spoke, a big red Labrador walked in and planted himself at his master's feet.

The Reverend chatted away but, tired from the long drive and distracted by the dog, I missed what was said. The dog bit at his fleas, scratched an ear with his hind leg, got up and shook himself, and circled back down into a doze. A large orange cat then walked in, rubbed herself against the Reverend's leg, and curled up beside the dog.

The barefoot minister extended his toe to scratch the scrawny feline under the chin. Just as he made contact, the beast got up, stretched, jumped onto the back of a large easy chair, and tore at her fur with a sandpaper tongue. Suddenly a flea crawled across the dog's nose. The dog flicked his head and pounced on it.

After introductions were made all 'round, we all got up to depart. I left with the woman at whose home I had been invited to stay. My travel companions drove on to their assignments in Louisiana. I never saw any of them again.[7]

Apart from whisking me to and from church on Sundays, my hostess expressly warned me to remain indoors throughout my entire stay.

Mostly I taught reading and writing on a one-on-one basis, with people who had worked in the cotton fields since childhood.

Mine was a tough job. But, I had patience and a will to succeed. Still, in a milieu of fear, I could smell my own fear, and it made me ashamed. I struggled to be heroic.[8]

The neighbourhood had remained peaceful – on the white man's terms, that is – for years. These people certainly didn't want to be labelled "troublemakers". Even if they passed the "literacy test", many of them knew they wouldn't be allowed to vote.

Despite the danger, some were eager to learn. Others, who couldn't overcome their fears, told me, "Why can't you white folks just leave us be? Things was peaceful before you come along." Some evenings, four or five showed up for lessons. Other evenings, only one or two.

One day I asked my host why he and his wife didn't teach friends and neighbours themselves. He told me he and others like him were teaching many in the community, but that it took a great deal of persuasion for others to accept help. Without "qualified teachers" – students from northern universities, for example – no one could persuade them to attempt to change the status quo.

"Qualified teachers". Why had I allowed everyone to think I was educated? No one had ever asked me for a resumé. So I just stepped in, deeper and deeper. And here I was.

My speech, despite my lack of formal schooling, was refined. This, combined with my confident attitude, more than made up for what I lacked in the certification department. Inside, though, I felt much different. What if my students or the Society of Friends discovered that I had not even completed high school? What if they found out that there was no comparison between me and those young heroes with whom I had driven to Mississippi?

I was a phony. Worse, I jeopardized the lives of my students. When I fretted about this – which I did often – a sense of doom overcame me.

I had lived in the Old South only a few weeks when, late one night, a rock was tossed through the front window. With much whooping and laughter, a truck screeched off into the dark. Trembling, I helped my hostess pick up the shattered glass. Fortunately, the draperies were closed, so most of the glass lay close to the window although the projectile had travelled, through the split in the curtains, to the centre of the room.

"Don't you worry none," she told me, although I could tell she was shaken. "This just goes to prove you're doing a good job, and some people are taking notice."

I wasn't so sure I wanted them to be taking notice of me. That night, I lay awake listening to the moaning and wailing of the wind. Whipping the tree branches against the cracked window pane, it played a wild fugue, sometimes dropping to pianissimo, sometimes rising to frenetic crescendo. Occasionally the porch door slammed, screeched, then slammed again.

The next evening, no one showed up for instruction.

Since I was probably the reason for this fear tactic, I knew I had to move! Nobody wanted to put me up. The black people were afraid that their church would be burned down if I stayed where I was. But how could I get away without someone to pick me up and drive me to another location? Despite the fact that I had remained in hiding, the white hierarchy had found me out! Now I was terrified. And so, I believe, were my hosts.

A few nights later, while I was sleeping, some men broke into the house and smashed their way through each room. I hid under my bed. They found me, pulled me out, and wrapped me up in a rough blanket. Sticks, boots and fists flew at me from all directions. I smelled smoke.

My attackers threw me into the back of a pickup truck. With a screech of tires, we sped off.

Laughter and more blows from boots and sticks followed. The shouting and violence went on and on. I lost track of it only when I lost consciousness.

The rest is a strange nightmare.

Somewhere in the black of night I heard laughter, bright as polished brass. Then I saw them. Little black boys and girls emerged naked from the woods and danced in a circle around me. They held out their hands to me and called in high, tinkling voices. Then another materialized out of the forest. This boy wore a long, loose-fitting

147

white shirt. He took my hand and led me into the dance, his face oddly familiar.

"Dance, dance," he called, in singsong fashion.

"I can't," I replied. My legs were moored in oozing mud.

"You used to dance with us ... used to dance ... used to dance ... used to dance." As the children retreated into the trees, his voice trailed off. The trees glowed as if on fire.

"Please, don't go." The more I struggled the more my legs sank deeper into the mud. I thought I would be swallowed up.

Shrill laughter echoed from the flaming forest. The children reemerged, now albino white, shrouded in white robes. They attacked me with clacking, sharp teeth and pulled at me with hands that morphed into animal claws. I screamed, loud and long.

Suddenly, the little people vanished. The forest melted. I sat up alone, naked and cold, shivering violently. I tried to open my eyes. But they were glued shut.

I must have passed out again.

When I came to – minutes later? hours later? – I vomited, alone, in the blackness. After a while, through eyes puffed almost shut, I saw stars in the sky. I groped around and found my pajama bottoms. When I stood up to put them on, I felt dizzy and blacked out again. Much later, I awoke to a gray dawn, shivering cold and racked with pain. I expected to see signs of the burnt crosses I had heard so much about. Instead, I saw a garbage dump.

With difficulty, I walked to a dirt road. When I passed a shack, I thought I heard voices. So I knocked on the door. Nobody answered. I walked on, shivering and crying in pain and fear.

Eventually, a police car drove up and stopped.[9]

Much of this is recalled only in nightmares. The rest remains blank. I can only imagine the kind of treatment I must have received at the hands of local law enforcement and judges. How I escaped being sentenced to a prison farm with long days on a chain gang, I'll never know. I vaguely recall somebody driving me to Windsor, Ontario, then to Toronto. From Toronto, somebody else drove me to Dorval. I don't remember if I was driven by Canadian policemen or by people from "The Society of Friends". But I do remember being reminded constantly that I should thank God for being alive.

I arrived at my parents' home somewhere around the ninth or tenth of December, without money, without having brushed my teeth for days. I wore ragged clothes and desperately needed a bath. My head and face were badly bruised. I needed shoes, socks, underwear, pants, shirts, and, above all, a coat.

I was greeted with disgust and few words. I made my way to the basement where I'd left my belongings stored in boxes. Most of my clothing was gone. When I ran back upstairs and asked Mother where my things were, she told me she'd thrown out my Navy gear a long time ago. And since my doeskin outfit stank of wood smoke and stale sweat, she got rid of that too.

All I could do was return to the basement and scrounge around. I found a pair of grubby Navy boots and brushed them off. I tipped out the rag box and found a couple of Papa's old shirts. I also found a pair of better fitting pants of my own as well as some underwear. Then I spied, hanging on a nail inside a spider web, my Navy flight jacket from <u>Shearwater</u>. Since I found no socks, I screwed up my courage and asked Mother for them. She dug out a pair from the laundry hamper, walked to the top of the cellar stairs, and threw them at me. (Not to me – at me.)

No money, though. "Sorry! As a matter of fact, Benoit, you can consider yourself disowned."

I felt too ill to argue. I managed only to whisper, "When have I ever <u>not</u> been disowned?"

Until now, my stepfather had stayed out of the whole thing. He walked to the top of the cellar stairs and looked down to where I stood, two steps down.

At this point, I hoped Mother would just shove me down the stairs. Then I could hold her responsible for all my troubles. But this didn't happen. I actually stayed just out of her reach. Otherwise, I believe she would have shoved me.[10]

Papa François stood to one side and pointed toward the front door. He looked furious. Never a loud man, he uttered just two words: "Leave, now!"

I stared at him, open mouthed, not daring even to walk past him.

Then he shouted: "Out!"

Mother had opened the front door. I darted to it and slammed it shut – from the inside. Now I too was angry. I'd face the dragon lady even if it killed me.

At the top of my lungs, I shouted, "Fuck you!" Then I burst into tears. Luckily, since they were in school, my little sisters were spared the rancor. Mother wasn't done with me yet. While I stood at the door trembling, feeling sorry for myself, she gave me the biggest dressing down I ever got from her. As she did so, my stepfather returned to his newspaper; as far as he was concerned, this was strictly between Mother and me.

This time, she didn't shout. I felt all the frustration and venom of her attempt to kick me out of the house. Now she stood between me and the front door. I had no choice but to stand there and take it.

"What the hell did you think you were doing, interfering like that in a situation you know absolutely nothing about? You go into somebody else's country with some asinine idea in your head that you can convert the world to your way of thinking. You know absolutely nothing about the people. You have no understanding of the situation. You interfere and create havoc and do nothing but upset everyone. All this so you can be some kind of hero. Well, you might think you can set the world on fire, but don't you dare – don't you dare – come running to us for more matches. You've gotten yourself into this situation. Now you're bloody well going to have to get yourself out of it. Furthermore, when you break the law, you bring shame not only on yourself but on your family, too. We're not going to let you shame us any further. Now, take your belongings and go cry somewhere else."

She stepped aside. I couldn't even look at her. In my anger and humiliation, I shook all over. If I were by a highway or a railway line, I gladly would have thrown myself before an oncoming locomotive. I felt like a stick of dynamite with a lit fuse. I dashed out of the house without knowing which direction to take.[11]

My tears blinded me. Safely out of hearing distance, I threw my bag of clothes to the ground and screamed, at the top of my voice, "Bitch! Bitch! Bitch! Fucking, fucking bitch!"

Yet – as always – not one decibel of sound passed my silent lips. Even at a safe distance, I had no safe distance. My silent scream begged for an audience. My chest ached; I could barely breathe. The world spun about as in a kaleidoscope. I took deep breaths; gradually, I regained my composure sufficiently to pick up my things and head for the highway.

Now I felt resolve. Clearly, suicide wasn't the answer I'd show them. I'd bloody well show them. I'd gone this far. I can go all the way.

I walked the frozen miles to Montreal; it must have taken me several hours. My toes were numb with cold. I don't remember even arriving. I don't remember where I got to. I don't remember where I stayed.

Someone must have taken me in. Perhaps the Salvation Army sheltered me. I only know I ended up, after several days and nights, at H.H.C.S. Donnacona on Drummond Street looking for work. I'd come to the right place.

On December 13th, 1955, wearing an ill-fitting uniform, I again found myself as a Reserve at HMCS Donnacona, filling in as a Leading Seaman Admin Writer in the recruiting office, while one of the regular staff went on thirty days leave. Luckily for me, because there was a shortage of staff over the holiday season, the recruiting officer was able to push through my papers without delay. And the pay officer gave me a small advance on my future earnings, so I could get a room at the YMCA on Drummond Street.

Until Christmas noon, the holiday season had been the loneliest and most unhappy of my life. Christmas dinner turned out to be a hamburger at a fast food joint.

That's when everything began to change within me. I felt a desperate need to survive.

While I sat in a plastic booth at Harvey's Hamburger Grill, the Christmas spirit yanked me forcibly from the doldrums. I felt suddenly delirious. I took a sprig of plastic holly from the decoration on the counter and crowned my hamburger "turkey". Then I placed a salt and pepper shaker as candles at each side of my regal platter. I even splurged on a glass of Pepsi-Cola. Better wine I never tasted.

Tucking a paper serviette under my chin, I took a knife and fork and skillfully carved. After watching me for a while, the waitress sat across the counter from me. Maybe she doubted my sanity. She no more than I. Or maybe she thought I was drunk. Well, maybe I was.

"Happy, happy Christmas," I said and toasted her with my first sip of magic wine. She smiled, got up, and walked into the kitchen. I savoured my first bite of festive bird and mashed potato bun. Delicious!

The waitress returned with a slice of lemon meringue pie and placed it before me, with a ceremonious curtsy. "Christmas pudding. Compliments of the house." She smiled and raised her eyebrows, as if to say, "I understand."

Yes, it was Christmas. I had much to be thankful for, although I hadn't figured out just what or where my good fortune lay. I felt deliriously happy. Before returning to my room at the "Y", I strolled St. Catherine Street and took in the joyful sounds of the season – Christmas concert, courtesy the merchants of Montreal.

I slept well that night.

On January 14th, when the regular Admin Writer returned, I was dispatched to Stadacona in Halifax for a fortnight. Since I saw nobody familiar, I felt uncomfortable. The regular ratings seemed to be laughing at me, the reserve replacement, so out of place. A nonresident in a scratchy, ill-fitting uniform, I forever was "moving on" or "hanging about", in corridors, empty offices, even the lavatory.

I felt like a homeless tramp in a large railway station. I had one consolation only: I had managed to pocket a few dollars to help me get started when I returned to Montreal.

I applied to reenter the regular force at Stadacona. But, since I had left before completing my original five year stint, I was turned down. Also, since the Korean conflict had ended, there no longer was the same need for personnel as in 1950.

In mid February, I returned to Montreal, went onto the Emergency Call-up List, found a job at Eaton's selling men's shirts, and took a room in Snowdon, the Jewish section of Montreal.

* * * * * * * *

[1] *Never before had I been given a such a lecture. Right and wrong had always seemed so obvious to me. I was about to be violated; therefore, I had to run and hide. That was the only way I could say "no". Now my imagined assailant was the good guy. I was the jerk.*

² **Disraeli,** Benjamin; *Speech to House of Commons* [London: Hansard of the House of Commons; February 11, 1851]

³ *Events of that summer are jumbled. I think I even missed part of the camp session. I am unable to recall the trip back from San Francisco to Calgary. Did something happen following the Assembly that I would rather not remember? Winston was black; I white.*

⁴ *God is indifferent to justice as we understand it. When He gave us the gift of life He also gave us free will. Therefore, it is up to us to deal with our own dilemmas.*

⁵ *The sun dance, a sacred Native ceremony, had been outlawed by the Canadian government. (Religious freedom was not accorded to First Nations.) The strips of coloured cloth tied to the many teepee poles represented the lives of every member who had taken part; a person could be killed for removing a "flag".*
Indeed, a couple of hunters had already lost their lives for such an act. The Natives responsible were, of course, hanged for murder.

⁶ *I have searched for the place where I spent time with my Native Canadian friends. Either the construction of the Trans-Canada Highway had displaced the people or my memory played tricks on me.*

⁷ *Larger towns and cities had segregated high schools, many run by church organizations. In Louisiana, some Roman Catholic orders of priests, brothers, and nuns set up high schools for Afro-American students.*
I can't recall if such schools, run by white religious, were in existence in 1956. Nor can I recall where I was at that time. I have examined maps to force the memory back, but to no avail. I only know I was somewhere in Mississippi. Beyond that, if I were to recall more, a thousand devils would return to drag me to unbelievable tortures.

⁸ *In November, 1960, the U.S. federal court ordered the New Orleans school system to desegregate. A little six-year-old girl, Ruby Nell Bridges, walked alone through a heckling crowd to attend an all-white elementary school. Angry whites lined both sides of the way, shaking fists and threatening terrible things if she kept coming to their school. But every morning, that little girl walked, head up, eyes ahead, straight through the mob.*
Now, that's courage.

⁹ *In this memoir, it sometimes seems true and genuine for me to elaborate upon what I only barely remember. At other times, such elaboration doesn't work. In my sleep, old nightmares flash in and out. Buildings appear as looming monsters and I walk in mazes of endless, lost passages that disappear like ghosts in the mist.*

10   *I think I was finally looking for a showdown. Hell! Might as well go all the way. Finish off what the Ku Klux Klan failed to accomplish.*

11   *Why, when I have felt angry and hurt have I had the impulse to self-destruct? Is this the same impulse as the baby who holds his breath until he turns blue in the face? Is this like the child who destroys her doll's house because she's angry at her mother or her father? Or is this simply a cry for recognition, for love? Perhaps I simply wanted to have my feelings recognized as real – and okay – by key people in my life, such as my mother. And since the key people in my life didn't acknowledge my hurt and angry feelings or even that I had any right to possess them, it is possible that this was what caused me to turn inward, against myself, whenever I felt angry, like the suicide who doesn't really want to die but only to be recognized in his unhappiness.*

The tendency to turn anger towards myself – anger that I didn't dare express towards others – manifests itself again and again throughout my childhood and young manhood. But, instead of bringing me recognition and love, it only brought added pain.

Chapter Twelve
Searching For the Fountain. (1956/58)

"Go to friends for advice;
To women for pity;
To strangers for charity;
To relatives for nothing.
– Spanish Proverb.

In February or March of l956, I began night classes at Darcy McGee High School in Montreal. The classes were taught by the De La Salle Brothers of the Christian Schools. I had not seen the inside of a Catholic church since I had turned away in protest three years earlier. But the Brothers were kind men and I enjoyed learning under them.

I sped ahead and completed my secondary English and French the following June. I was informed at exam time, however, that since I had not done the full year of studies, I would not be permitted to write the final examinations.

Defeated again, I stormed into a nearby church. Then I knelt, sobbing before a statue of Mary. I must have been there a long time. An old priest put his hand on my shoulder. I sat down with him and, like a river breaking through its dam, I sobbed out my failures, my shame, my anger, and my inability to please. I don't recall the old priest's words, only his sense of peace and love. As I sat with him, I felt quietness and peace enveloping me. I wanted to touch God. Through this gentle priest, God reached out and touching me.

I knew my life was going to change. I could succeed! I could prove myself. But I needed help to do it. I don't recall when the old priest left. A caretaker came to where I was sitting. "Monsieur, c'est tard. Il faut barrer les portes pour la nuit." (Sir, it's late. I must lock up for the night.) The church was empty. Before I went to the "Y" and my little room, I walked about for a long time. I wore myself out enough to sleep well.

One of the Brothers had loaned me a copy of Thomas Merton's "Seven-Storey Mountain".[1] As I began to read Merton's story of conversion to Catholicism and of his journey to the monastery, (*Merton became a Trappist Monk.*) I saw parallels in my own running from and search for God. That book, more than any other, had a profound effect on me.

Recalling the words of the African witch doctor, Paul Robeson had confided to me in San Francisco, "One day you will return to help my people.", I sought information about the White Fathers of Africa, where I could study to become a missionary priest. My birth certificate bore the name Bendt Nuttall-Smith; I was Benoit Boucher. Inquiries had to be made. At almost twenty-two years of age, I still needed a letter of explanation from my parents regarding my change of name. Furthermore, I needed to complete high school before entering the seminary.

I knew I'd have to consult Mother about my latest ambition, and the prospect terrified me. At one time, Mother had mentioned the witch doctor's prophecy. This was at about the time I was considering the navy. Subconsciously, I still was trying to gain her approval. Maybe I could make the prophecy come true, and she would love me as she did when I was a little boy. Maybe even Papa would be happy that I had, at last, found my vocation.[2]

A short visit home brought me more pain than I had experienced in the American South. "You, a priest? Benoit, you do not have the character to be a priest. We've given you every opportunity, and you have squandered your life. What have you ever done to show any appreciation for all that we have given you? Be thankful we brought you to Canada. You and Naomi were brought here out of love and kindness, yet you have never tried to belong! You ran off to the Navy, but couldn't even make a go of that. Because of you, Naomi ran away, and we have no idea where she is. We've given you everything and you have only given heartache in return."

Blinded by tears, I fled the house and walked for many hours. Finally, I went back to the White Fathers and was told, very kindly, that under Canon Law, illegitimacy was a permanent impediment to ordination to the priesthood. The order would not be able to accept me.

I had been "born in sin".[3]

I prayed. I offered my life to God. But God did not answer my prayers.

I was Catholic enough to accept the miracles God sent my way, but not enough to accept divine plans that contradicted my own.

A Brother who taught night school was the only person I could confide in. I told him how I wanted to be a missionary and how I struggled to prove myself over the years. I even told him of my visit to my mother and stepfather. He asked, "Do you really want to dedicate your life to God?"

My answer was quick in coming. "Yes, I'll do anything."

The Brother took out a sheet of paper and began taking notes while asking me specific questions such as place and date of birth, Baptism, First Communion, Confirmation. I did not know the dates for the last three. But how could I face my parents again? Surely, I could just sign up and not have to face my mother again until I'd proven myself. No! I had no choice but face more skepticism and further rejection.

I was due for a shock.

For the first time in many years, this new direction – to be a Christian Brother – passed muster. It even got a warm reception!

In the coming weeks, I realized I had won favour with Mother. Just before I joined the Christian Brothers in Scarboro, she confided in me.

She told me I was not the first to be born illegitimate and that it was nothing to be ashamed of. Perhaps I'm confused as to whether or not she too was illegitimate, but she did tell me her grandmother, my great grandmother, and others before her, came from fascinating liaisons.

Mother also told me how her mother refused to acknowledge her as a daughter, passing her off instead as a niece. Mother told me she compensated by getting into all sorts of mischief.

To keep her out of trouble, her older sister, Ruth, looked after her until she could be sent off to boarding school and out of her mother's hair. In Mother's words, "Ruth was more a mother to me than my own mother. She looked after me and introduced me to art. Still, I got into all sorts of shenanigans. While boarding at a convent, I took a dare from some classmates and crawled under the bench in chapel to see what the nuns wore under their habits."

Mother told me her father, Oluf Weber, died when she was just nine. He was not only a sea captain, he was Mayor of Svendborg, a very popular and jovial man and a doting father. My mother was devastated when he died and especially when, not long after his death, her mother remarried.

Illegitimacy runs in families. According to Mother, my grandmother was born out of wedlock. Mother told me great-grandmother was involved romantically with none other than Edward VII, during that time period when he sowed his wild oats all over Europe.[4]

Was Mother putting me on? Perhaps.

Grandmother was known as Lady Ruth de Bath. Was this a title bestowed by British Royalty for favours received, or was it handed down to the daughter of a royal rake?

Even further back, mother spoke of a Polish Jewish connection – Polish royalty no less. I have searched the Weber family tree as far as I have been able but have not been able to solve the mystery of my ancestry. I've only found snippets from letters and notes. For example, the Weber family had for many years attended numerous functions with the Danish royal family. Mother's favourite Uncle Theobald Weber sometimes sent her generous gifts.[5]

According to Mother, she was scolded several times as a young girl for refused to curtsy to the Danish queen.

While she told me all of this, Mother wept. More than anything else, this compelled me to believe that she told me the truth and not mere figments of her ever active imagination.

My life had taken a major turn. How far I had come from that unhappy day, eons ago, when I formally renounced my Catholic faith in Halifax. After making a full General Confession – privately, with a Catholic priest – I now was back in "a state of grace".

On June 2nd, 1956, just prior to my twenty-third birthday, I was accepted as a postulant in the Brothers of the Christian Schools and driven to the Novitiate in Scarborough, east of Toronto. I now was entering a holy order, devoted to the education of poor boys. This was what I longed for. At last, I could become a teacher.

The Christian Brothers' Mother House was a huge brick building with a bell tower at its center. It was built on land donated by Senator O'Connor, the founder of Laura Secord Candies. Since the Senator's hobby had been breeding race horses in the farmland suburb of Scarborough, the property was sizeable.

Boys, who indicated a desire to become Brothers, were provided high school education as well as room and board. Enrollment in the Junior Novitiate peaked in 1956-57, with over one hundred boys, some as young as thirteen and fourteen. At age seventeen, these boys entered the Postulancy, where they prepared for acceptance into the Novitiate. The Postulancy lasted for three months, at the end of which candidates "received the Habit", i.e., became Novices.

Novitiate lasted one full year. After taking First Vows of Poverty, Chastity, and Obedience – Novices then became Scholastics. In the Scholasticate, the new Brothers studied Dogma, Moral, Worship, Church and Bible History, and the History of the Institute. Also, they were permitted to continue their higher education, either at Teacher's College or University.

Besides myself, just two other Postulants had not come directly from the Junior Novitiate. One had worked in comedy with the CBC in Toronto; he left a few weeks into the Postulancy. The other was a fellow from P.E.I. whom the novices nicknamed "Spud". He and I became very good friends during my time at Scarborough. All the other Postulants were in their teens.

The day began at 5 A.M. with the sudden scare of a loud clanging bell and "Live Jesus in Our Hearts" to which we were to respond "Forever!". Another bell rang about fifteen minutes later to call us to chapel for morning prayer and meditation. After a short break, Mass was held, followed by breakfast.

During the meals, every novice and postulant was invited in turn to stand at a podium and read. When I read, my pronunciation was often corrected. I was sure my version was correct, still I had to repeat the correction as an exercise in obedience and humility.

Reprimands were frequent in those early days. "You were heard singing in the shower!" "There will be no singing!" "The brother's eyes are to be cast downward at all times." "There is to be no laughter." "Only the devil grins. A serious look must replace that hideous smile."

I was reminded by the Director that I had come to the Brothers with several strikes against me. I had been a Navy seaman and a radio announcer. These occupations were not in my favour. And the accident of my birth was another point he would "not be sufficiently uncharitable to mention in public".

The day was filled with conferences (sermons), rosary, prayer, benediction, and manual labour. I scrubbed washrooms and ran a heavy polisher over miles of ceramic hallways. On sunny afternoons in late summer, we all trekked to the fields to bring in truckloads of baled hay.

After lunch we had a short siesta, then recreation. Sometimes we teamed up for baseball. One sunny afternoon I connected bat to ball. This was such a surprise to everyone in the game that I managed a home run. All were shouting directions at me: "You missed a base!" "Go back!" On another occasion, while we played football, I caught a pass and ran for a touchdown – to the wrong end! The Postulants, having developed their sports skills in the Junior Novitiate, used a special interpretation of the rules which outsiders could not discover.

Sometimes I felt as adequate as an umbrella in a swimming pool. But I was not alone. Before the year ended, one of the novices thought he was John the Baptist and was taken to the mental hospital at Penetanguishine.

I also had fun moments on the sports field. Once, when I was up at bat, the pitcher teased me – as pitchers are wont to do. "You hit it and I'll catch it."

"If you do, don't swallow it." My reply scored a point and everyone laughed, even the pitcher.

Though we learned a lot about religion, only a few developed any degree of piety. I'm being judgmental here, I know. But the development of this judgementalism in me accompanied my twelve years of training with the Christian Brothers.

Every Sunday, we were permitted to write one letter to our parents or, with approval, to a close relative. The only close relatives I had, apart from parents, were my aunts in Quebec City. I liked writing to them and wanted to impress them. Every week I wrote a letter home, too.

In my letters home, I spouted prayers for my lost sister and praise for my God-fearing parents. My correspondence was terribly sanctimonious, especially after my "salty" navy letters. I became convinced that finally I had gained my parents' approval. Despite the fact that they never found time to answer my letters, both Mother and Papa came to Scarborough for the Novitiate admission ceremony – "taking of the habit".

Every prospective Novice had to select a saint's name from a list. I selected St. Francis and was given the name of his first follower, Bonaventure. Just in case I would be too comfortable with that name, I also was given a second name, "Tatwin". Later, some called me Tatwin instead of Bonaventure or Bonnie.[6]

Here is a stroke of irony. Was it this little known Saint Tatwin who influenced my disposition to write poetry?

On the day we postulants received the habit and became novices, the novices who had just completed their year of novitiate made their first vows and became scholastics. We were not to have any communication with the scholastics until the end of our own year of Novitiate. Our year of preparation would be one of total isolation from outside influences. The scholastics, in turn, would look down on us "mere mortals".

While my parents were leaving following the reception, Papa remarked that the Christian Brothers' House of Formation was on the Maryvale Stud Farm. He called out a cheery "Keep your pecker up, son!" (The term "pecker" in Canada has a different connotation from the English "Keep your chin up".) An innocent enough remark, but, the Director was not amused. He made sure to mention the irreverent remark during his next Conference.

Before leaving, Mother gave me a copy of Thomas A Kempis, *The Imitation of Christ*,[7] "as a source of inspiration for meditation and personal prayer". Translated from its original Latin and carrying the Church's full approval in form of Nihil obstat and Imprimatur, I thought I would be permitted to keep the one gift and token of approval I had received from my parents in many years. However, *The Imitation of Christ* remained at the Mother House when I moved on.

We were each given one good habit for chapel and meals, and another for manual labour. Because our robes were seldom laundered, they soon began to smell like dead skunks. For manual labour and sports, we hitched the bottom around our waist, no matter how hot the sun. We also wore a little skull cap called a calotte.

On Fridays, we stood for breakfast and, later in the day, we each knelt before our confrères, arms extended, and begged them in charity to point out our faults. I didn't consider it charity when a fellow novice blurted: "It seems to me, my very dear brother, that you sometimes look over the divider when another brother is in the washroom!"

I squirmed in silence. Brother Director intoned: "You will thank your brother for his kindness!!"

Still I remained silent. I felt angry and embarrassed. Of course, the accusation was untrue.

"You will thank your brother for his kindness!!"

"I thank you, my very good brother, for having had the ... kindness ...."

Increasingly, I found myself alone in the chapel, in frustration and tears. I felt alone. Some mornings I was so exhausted that I slipped a note under my door: "I'm sick". As the year wore on, I sent out more and more of these notes. I was not alone. The urge to get a little extra sleep was strong.

In chapel, I wrote poetry. It just came to me, as though dictated. Some poems were amazing. When the Brother Director discovered what I was doing, he ordered me to burn what I had written and resist "temptations to pride".

> Poor pagan world!
> How little do you realize
> The emptiness in all your day to day
> Attempts to please naught but, in reality,
> Your own mind's eye.
> Can you not see, above yourselves, a greater aim
> Than all earth's mortal fame?
> .....
> Poor pagan world!
> Look yonder where the convent walls
> Hide earthly beauty for a greater prize.
> Open your eyes!
> 'Tis this that keeps the earth's rotation swift
> That keeps the stars on high, else they would fail
> And bring us all to no avail.
> Look about! On you 'twould dawn
> The whole world runs on love:
> All else is but sham.
> .....

THE SEARCH

I sought the Fount of Youth,
Spring of Everlasting Life.
I searched, Oh, how I searched:
.....
A burning thirst for love unquenched.
In each young face, searched greedily
to find a spark of truth.
Truth was not there ... And then ... I turned to prayer.

Poor, weary soul, come rest a while,
Here, from whence in youth you fled, here is your goal.
Yes, I, this spotless Host, I am the Fount of Youth,
The Spring of Life Eternal.
In your self-seeking, you saw Me not,
And still I waited patiently.
Now, in fervent, penitent love, come back to Me.

Despite their content, these poems (abbreviated here) were worldly distractions. We were to resist "the World, the Flesh and the Devil". Though I nodded "yes", I continued writing in secret. I hid what I wrote, and my collection grew.

Poetry was my only disobedience apart from the occasional cigarette. Cigarettes were not hard to come by. Many of the retired Brothers smoked. One old Brother smoked cigars. When he died, novices had to clean out his room. The smell of cigar smoke was sickening. Our director of Novices smoked a pipe; eventually he died of cancer of the mouth. One day, "Spud" and I were tattled on for smoking whilst out for a meditative stroll. Brother Maurice, breath reeking of pipe tobacco, told us it was a downright sin to smoke when we should be praying. I asked if it would be all right to pray while smoking. Humour not appreciated. I don't recall the resultant penance, but Spud and I chuckled over that one for days.

Apart from tobacco, the only other worldly pleasure that was apparent was alcohol. We had wine on feast days. On weekends, the Director of Novices and other Brothers smelled of more than wine. One novice wore after shave and covered his facial blemishes with a medication that his aunt brought to the Mother House on her monthly visits (the limit allowed).

Several novices left during the year. We were told how shameful it was to throw a vocation back in the face of God. I could never leave at such peril to my immortal soul. Somewhere, St. Paul had said that we were to "knock the dust from our sandals" and forget those who had walked away. (*He didn't really say that. See Matthew 10:7-15*)[8]

Sometime later, I met Harold White, music specialist for the Montreal English Catholic School Commission. We became good friends. But White was unwelcome at the Brothers' residence. He once had been sub-director of novices, but had left and married – a woman!

"The word 'woman' comes from Woe to man."

"Eve brought God's curse upon human flesh."

"The worst sins are of the flesh."

"Never look a woman in the eye."

When we showered, we were to wash down as far as ... And up as far as... And to leave "as far as" alone and to permit only cold water to fall on those unmentionables.

Every morning, before Mass, a line of sleep-eyed novices queued up to unburden themselves of their steaming sins.

"Bless me Father for I have sinned. I accuse myself of lack of prayer, feeling angry towards my brothers ... and ... I've sinned against purity."

"Alone or was there someone ... ?"

"Just me, Father."

Personal friends were forbidden. Relationships could lead to temptations.

I wanted to say, "I only touched it, and it exploded." No matter how I struggled against my youthful sexuality, it got the better of me. Needless to say, I soon got seriously terrified of "failing the test".

For me, nothing less than perfection would suffice.

"My son, the devil is a sly one who comes when we let our guard down. You must pray, pray, pray to remain steadfast in the struggle against evil. Now, for your penance, say five Our Fathers and five Hail Marys. And make a good Act of Contrition."

"Oh, my God, I am heartily sorry ..."

In the daily director's Conferences, we were told the lives of those saints who gladly inflicted their bodies with scourging and hair shirts. These were men and women who died in the "Odour of Sanctity". My robe had the odour of sanctity.

In the Royal Canadian Navy, recruits were told, in a paraphrasing of Alfred Tennyson's *The Charge of the Light Brigade*:

> *Yours is not to reason why.*
> *Yours is but to do and die.*

In the Novitiate the wording was different but the message was the same: "Dei sacrificium intellectus" [sacrifice intellect to God]. But was the Director of Novices God? He told us, "I am the voice of God." So we obeyed. In contrast, before joining the Christian Brothers, my motto would have been: "Omnibus disputandum" (question everything).

With no one in whom to confide, I had to face my doubts and confusion in frightening solitude.

Our district sent brothers to mission schools in Nigeria. Brother Maurice thought this a waste of time. According to him, "Satan mated with a gorilla and produced the black savage." Near the end of the novitiate year, we received a very black postulant from Nigeria. He was a short fellow who often came to chapel barefoot. Brother Anselm Uba earned a university degree and was posted to St. Michael's College of Education in Malta. Brother Maurice treated the young postulant kindly. Had he been putting us on?

Finally, we went into an eight-day closed retreat. The silence and intense prayer – broken only by the peal of bells – were intended to prepare us for our first vows.

These days I can live with silence. But back then, I was different. I vainly attempted to stem the deafening void, the ever-present roaring in my mind. I clapped my hands over my ears. I even whispered to myself. I had to have sound to drown out the ghosts that whispered to me from the dark recesses of my mind.

Anything to drown out the sounds of silence.

Following graduation from the novitiate we truly would be brothers and scholastics. Some scholastics would go to Teachers' College or to University. Some would obtain their master's degrees and even doctorates before becoming teachers. Others would remain at the Mother House and complete senior matriculation. Some would remain to work on the farm and look after the retired brothers.

First, we all travelled to Brothers' Island on Lake Simcoe, near Orillia, where a week of well-earned holiday had been planned by our director of Novices. During the week, I discovered snapping and painted turtles, frogs the size of my hand, and slithering garter snakes. Dragonflies skimmed the water amongst black flies and bothersome mosquitoes. Swallows swooped and darted. With beakfuls of insects, they returned to their nests in the eaves of the main cabin.

One day, we novices sat on the dock and hoped for a turn on our one pair of water skis. Brother *Harold finally returned to the dock, out of gas.

"Maybe tomorrow. Rosary's in twenty minutes."

"Shit! It's not bloody fair."

Novices don't swear. So no one heard that.

Brother Director offered solace. "The Basilians have their island close by. They have more water skis. And a boat with gas in the tank. Tomorrow we'll pay them a visit."

As promised, we visited the Basilian Fathers. But we didn't water ski.

One day, we left the island to attend a funeral at Saint John's Training School in Uxbridge. One of the young brothers had drowned in a small lake nearby. Following the funeral, we were treated to wine, sandwiches, cake and other goodies. Then we were given a tour of the school.

I remember the "blue room" where boys were sent to cool down after running away or for certain other infractions. Though the paddle and strap were used, the dedication and love the brothers showed for the unfortunate boys was obvious.

Today, any form of corporal punishment is out of place. Thank God, we are living in a totally different age. However, St. John's was without fences, and I do not recall locks on the doors. Many of the boys were from abusive homes or had been deemed incorrigible by teachers and parents. Given the opportunity, they would run off in a staff car or terrorize residents in neighbouring communities while they were on the run. They required a mixture of discipline and love, which the Brothers appeared ready and able to supply.[9]

During the Scholasticate year that followed, I completed my final year of high school as well as religious studies. Our time was well scheduled, and we had very little to distract us.

Sometimes during the Scholastic year, we went to see school plays or such suitable movies as The Robe or Bernadette of Lourdes or Court Jester with Danny Kaye. On such outings, we wore black suits with Roman collars. The older Brothers wore Roman collars on what were known as "dickies". (A clerical dickie is a front piece that ties around the waist and, under a jacket, looks like a full black shirt and Roman collar.) On a busy Sunday in Toronto, a very holy old Brother saw that he'd closed a car door on his dickie. He yelled at the driver, "Stop the car. My dickie's caught! My dickie's caught!"

When the Bishop of Toronto got hit by a beer truck, I remarked "the drinks were on him!" No one laughed. My jokes were never considered funny. That jest cost me a full day in chapel, kneeling in front on the cold tile floor.

One Saturday afternoon during the May / June period of final exams, we went to a matinee dress rehearsal of Gilbert and Sullivan's "Trial by Jury" at De La Salle "Oaklands" High School. During the performance, I fell ill with an allergy or food poisoning. My hands, feet, face, and throat swelled up, and I had difficulty breathing. In panic, I asked to see a doctor. The Brother director gave me two aspirin and sent me to bed. I recovered in time to write my Algebra exam the following Tuesday morning. Nothing lost but study time.

When the exam results came out, Brother Romuald, head of the Order in Canada, gave me permission to attend St. Joseph's Teachers' College in Montreal. First, though, he sent me to spend the summer as entertainment director at De La Salle Camp on Jackson's Point, Lake Simcoe.

De La Salle Camp served the sons of those who could afford the fees. Thus it provided a source of funds for the upkeep of the Mother House, among other projects. This annoyed me. I thought I had joined the Christian Brothers to teach poor boys, not rich brats.

My judgmental attitude notwithstanding, I enjoyed a busy and productive summer. At last, I felt useful. I helped the campers produce skits for entertainment nights. I organized campfires and led singsongs. During the day, I supervised activities such as moccasin and wallet making, the painting of plaques (which I made and sold to campers), finger painting, and nature study (about which I knew little).

* * * * * * * *

[1] **Merton**, Thomas; *The seven storey mountain.* (New York: Harcourt, Brace, 1948)

[2] *Sometimes Mother could be deeply religious. At other times she rejected Catholicism and turned to beliefs she encountered through reading. And Mother was an avid reader. She was fascinated by treatises on Tibetan Buddhism, written by the Dalai Lama. She lent me books by Edgar Cayce, the "sleeping prophet".*
On a trip to Virginia Beach, I made a point of visiting the Edgar Cayce Institute, in order to see what it was that so inspired my mother's enthusiasm. The vast library of books and huge array of newspaper clippings turned out to be too much for me to deal with in just one day. However, I was impressed by what I saw and read and went on to read some of Cayce's books.
In my turn, I became infatuated with Rosicrucianism, the "mysteries of the Rose Cross". In newspaper and magazine advertisements, the "Invisible Order", "AMORC", the "Ancient and Mystical Order Rosae Crucis", this religion which was "not a religion", promised to improve my memory, develop my will power, and unlock for me the secret wisdom of the ages. The "Rosicrucian Digest" offered me lessons on "mental vibrations", "mystical comprehension", "the life force", and on many and various other occult subjects. I happily passed the literature on to Mother.

[3] *A new Code of Canon Law, effective in 1983, declared that being born out of wedlock would no longer bar an applicant from any position or office in the Church.*

[4] *Known as "Roué Rex", Edward VII developed a risqué reputation for indulging himself in sport, food, drink, gambling, travel, and women. He married Princess Alexandra of Denmark in 1863, who bore him three sons and three daughters. Alexandra, turned a blind eye to her husband's extramarital activities, which not only continued well into his sixties, but found him implicated in several notorious divorce cases.*

[5]   *Theobald Weber carried on his brother Olaf's* (my grandfather's) *engineering and boat building business and remained lifetime friends with Prince Knud and Princess Caroline-Mathilde of Denmark.*

A nephew has been tracing the family tree. Apparently a book written in Danish documents the Jewish connection but has yet to be translated into English. To date, I have found no trace of a royal connection.

[6]   *St. Tatwin (TATUINI) was Archbishop of Canterbury. He died on July 30th, 734. The Venerable Bede describes him as "a man illustrious for religion and prudence and excellently instructed in the sacred letters" (Hist. Eccl., V, xxiii). After his death, miracles were wrought through his intercession. He is also said to have written some poems in Anglo-Saxon which have perished.*

[7]   **Kempis**, Thomas à; *The Imitation of Christ* (Milwaukee: The Bruce Publishing Company, 1940)

[8]   *See Matthew 10:7-15, in* **The Holy Bible** *[King James Version]*

[9]   *Years later, I read with shock and dismay of physical and sexual abuse. I knew some of those charged. Many former brothers and many who remained in the order suffered the torture of guilt by association.*

There were days when I had a terrible fear that I, too, would be charged. Although innocent of abuse, I remembered the countless boys and girls to whom I had shown natural affection. Never had I done anything that I would have judged inappropriate. In my nightmares, I waited for that phone call or for the RCMP visit.

How many others suffered those same nightmares? When people would relate the details of abuse of children by clerics, I wanted to shout out: "No! It's not true!!" But, yes it was true.

I am an affectionate and loving man. I know that this side of my nature is innocent and blameless. Like other men who have this side to themselves, I'm sure this has been misinterpreted at times. Especially in the present-day, supercharged atmosphere of suspicion, men such as myself must be very careful.

Chapter Thirteen
Hamsters, Guppies, and Knights of the Road

> *For I was hungry and you gave me food, ...*
> *I was naked and you clothed me*
> *– Matthew 25:35*

In the last week of August, 1958, five shiny new Brothers drove from Scarboro to Montreal. We brought with us our meager possessions and, on my part, an overflow of enthusiasm. I was introduced to *Brother Osmund, the director and principal of St. Dominic's Elementary School on Delormier Street. The Brothers' residence was attached to the school. This was convenient. Lessons could be prepared in the classrooms. I was to prepare immediately to teach grade five and would not attend St. Joseph's. Brother Osmund assured me that the grace of God would be sufficient. He reminded me that obedience not only was the greatest of all virtues, it was my vow.

I loved my class and learned with my students as I taught. Never did I divulge my lack of training. When we fell behind in the curriculum, I made up for lost time by introducing extra-help sessions. Usually, all my boys attended.

My weakest subject was still Mathematics. Now I discovered shortcuts to replace learning by rote: Nine is ten minus one. Eleven is ten plus one. Eight is ten minus two. Five is half of ten. Multiplication and division made sense at last. It made sense to the boys.

Teaching of religion called for memorized Catechism with very little explanation and less understanding. We used the standard Baltimore Catechism. All prayers were to be memorized in English and Latin. Those who attended mass before school received a gold star to paste to a chart at the front of the class. Money was collected for missions and children could buy black and oriental babies to paste on their mission chart. The sticky cutouts represented the souls of the "heathen" the school children were saving with nickels and dimes.

Teaching History, Geography, English Language and English Literature was an adventure. Grammar was learn-as-you-go.

Recalling my enjoyment of the weekly story at St. Pat's, I made sure to include a weekly reading of <u>Tom Sawyer</u>, <u>Treasure Island</u>, and poems such as <u>Evangeline</u> and my favourites from Robert Service.

I got to know the families of all my boys and visited their homes. I was sometimes invited to stay for dinner. Parents and teachers worked together to help the boys succeed. I seldom met parents who were not totally supportive.

All the teaching Brothers had been issued black leather straps, usually carried in one of our two deep robe pockets. After trying the strap out on myself, I decided it would best be left at the back of my bottom desk drawer. I carried candy as rewards for work well done.

Some of the brothers used a paddle rather than the strap. To me, this was far less primitive.

When I judged it necessary to go further than a scolding, I, too, paddled behinds, acting *in locus parentis*. Parents in those days approved, even expected their sons to be punished at school. No boy I spanked was unable to sit following a spanking.

The boy caught cheating on a test was paddled on the seat of his pants and given the test to write again after school. He was not punished in front of his peers nor verbally shamed; he was not sent to the principal's office. Parents weren't notified: "Your son cheats. He will probably end up in jail." Punishment was swift and forgiving; the matter soon forgotten. A child kept his healthy mind and hopefully learned that dishonesty is not acceptable.

But strapping and caning, in my mind, were always cruel, and my knees still turned to jelly at the thought. Still, in my English public school days, I'd have been considered a wimp by the other kids if I ever complained about a caning. "Whacks" were as much part of the curriculum as cricket and Latin. In my English boarding schools, some headmasters proved more adept at caning than others. I remember the "bacon-slicer", a vertical downward slash that inflicted far more pain than the downward swat. It seemed some headmasters enjoyed visiting pain on rude boys. They either performed the rite with absolute indifference, even boredom, or they pretended sorrow: "I hate to do this, old chum. You know it will hurt me far more than it will hurt you." Boys hurried to the dorm to display their welts with talismanic pride, like Prussian duelists boasting scars: "Wow, nice grouping!" But don't ask me if I'd ever like to go through that again.[1]

St. Dominic's was a blue collar, immigrant school. I taught a Pasquale Pietrantonio and a Roberto Ricci and a Luis Delaporta. Some of my Sicilian students later filled the ranks of the Montreal Mafiosi. But they were good boys when I knew them. At lunch time, they ate enormous sandwiches with sausage and cheese and drank green wine from Coca-Cola bottles. Very few brought milk to school.

In those days, Roman Catholics in North America were supposed to abstain from meat on Fridays. (No longer the norm.) Most of my students were freshly arrived from Italy, Sicily, and Hungary. People from Italy, Ireland, and a number of other countries ate fish regularly and were not subject, in their home countries, to meatless Fridays, except for Good Friday in memory of Christ's passion and death. Still, during lunch periods, big, redheaded *Brother Roger examined all the sandwiches and made the boys throw their meat into garbage cans. Anybody who resisted earned a smack upside his head then and there. I hated to see good food go to waste, so I permitted my boys to eat in the classroom, while giving extra help where required. I did not examine sandwiches on Fridays. Nor did I confiscate the wine, which I recognized as part of the cultural upbringing in Montreal's "Little Italy". My students noticed that I did not go to the "residence" for lunch. So they quite often brought an extra sandwich and a bottle of vino for "the Bro".

Once I did appreciate Brother Roger's gruffness. This happened when he summarily dealt with a cigarette company representative. After parking his company car by the gate, the man – no more than nineteen himself – walked onto the elementary school playground. Pockets jingling with coin, he struck up conversations with the schoolboys who swarmed about him, and handed out free cigarettes. Any boy who chanced to own a packet of the favoured brand "hit the jackpot": He received a free cartons of cigarettes.

I'll never forget the scene. An angry Brother Roger, somehow bigger than I ever saw him before, stormed over to the fellow, seized him by the back of his neck, and literally booted him off the school property.

Secretly, I cheered.

Horace White, whom the Brothers called "Duck" White, came to see if all classes were being taught to sing. The prescribed curriculum included "God Save the Queen", "Holy God We Praise Thy Name" and selections from well-worn song books. Other inspectors from the Montreal Catholic School Commission appeared without warning to ensure that our registers were up-to-date and that all boys had clean hands and nails. From time to time, a nurse also came by to check for head lice. The parish priest dropped by to question the boys on Catechism.

At times like these, I often felt more nervous than the boys. The parish priest might ask "What is Matrimony". He received a memorized answer from the Baltimore Catechism. Sometimes the answer to "What is Matrimony?" could turn out to be the answer to "What is Purgatory?" "Matrimony is ... Matrimony is a state of temporary punishment ..."

Except for some experience as a choir boy in grade school, I had absolutely no knowledge of music. It was logical, therefore, that the leadership of the parish boys' choir fell to me. If it weren't for Horace White, I couldn't have done the job. He helped me with basic conducting and taught me the rudiments of music theory.

To this day, I don't know how I did it. With a signal and slight wave of my hand, I launched the boat – and treble voices, now in motion, rose upon a crest, moving forward on waves of sound.

The boys sang like angels. I was in heaven! I organized the Christmas concert and teamed up with a sister from the girls' school to put on HMS Pinafore in the spring. When Sir Joseph Porter came on stage, a proud papa cried out "Thats'a my Tony. Bravo, Antonio!"

Science went well, too. I repaired an aquarium and, with the help of several parents, acquired the needed plants, guppies, and other paraphernalia. Soon after, we got a cage of hamsters and a terrarium filled with baby turtles. When a local fish shop donated a huge aquarium to my class, we started breeding guppies and black mollies by the hundreds. I sold baby hamsters to buy pet food. "Making classroom money on sex. "

The classroom became my life. My boys did well in all tests administered by Brother Osmund and the school board. When refugees arrived from Hungary following the 1956 revolt, many of them came to my class. I gave them the extra attention they needed. As a result, I had little time to spend with the other Brothers.

At the end of the school year, I applied to take music courses at St. Michael's Choir School in Toronto. Permission was denied. My services would be more valuable as entertainment director at De La Salle Camp. The director at St. Dominic's made it clear that music courses were not "masculine endeavors".

In my second year of teaching, I was moved to a grade seven class. I had to leave all the equipment I had procured during the previous year, and start from scratch. I left a bright, well-decorated room, for a classroom with a cracked blackboard and few library books.

Brother Roger took over the choir which then fell apart due, in the brother's words, "to the boys' previous poor training". But he did say I might be called on to help with the spring production. That year, no spring production was held. And a lie was relayed to the parents: Brother Bonaventure does not wish to continue with the choir." Under vow of obedience, I was forbidden to tell say anything. I was to mature in the religious life!

I also was forbidden, as before, to waste my time writing poetry. When my poem "Poor Pagan World" was published in Saint Joseph's Oratory Magazine, I had to return the cheque, together with my apologies.

Despite such irritations, I enjoyed teaching the more challenging grade seven students. Everyone passed the provincial examinations. Top provincial marks in religious knowledge went to a student of mine, a Jewish boy!

I made sure the boys understood what I taught. I insisted they pronounce every word clearly. As children frequently misinterpret and misspeak words, I simply accepted full responsibility. I had heard kids reciting the "Act of Contrition" – "O my God, I'm hardly (heartily) sorry for having offended you, ..."

When I was three or four years old, I asked for a blazer for my birthday. Clothing was the last item on my mind for a birthday present. Little boys like teddy bears, trains, and tricycles. When my birthday present turned out to be a blue jacket, I was terribly disappointed. I wanted a blazer to shave like my daddy. He lathered up and shaved with his blazer.

> Attention, all you Catechists
> And lectors also, heed.
> The ears of little children
> Hear precisely what you read.
> So frequently the humble
> Misinterpret what you mumble-
> From the AXE of the Apostles,
> From Gladly the cross-eyed Bear,
> From poor bandaged children of Eve.
> To the simple prayers they hear.

Once more I set up an aquarium for fish and scrounged another aquarium for the care and breeding of hamsters. This time a public health nurse from the school board visited the class and told the Director that hamsters posed a health hazard. Normally, I wouldn't have thought much about this. But Brother Osmund explained that children could be bitten while handling them. When my blackboard notes got erased after I had prepared special lessons over a weekend, I began to believe somebody didn't appreciate the extra work I put into my teaching. Was I paranoid?[2]

Greater challenges lay ahead. A new boy, a refugee from Hungary, came to school during cold weather, with ragged shoes and no coat. I asked the Director if anything could be done for him. He responded "Our job is to teach and pray." This wasn't good enough for me. I spoke to the pastor at our church. He told me to get in touch with the Saint Vincent de Paul Society. They in turn said the boy could turn to refugee agencies for help. "We already have provided these new families with lodging and food. Nothing more can be done at this time."

I became aware of many poor people in Montreal. Their situation was desperate. I knew, at least, I had to try to help this boy. After school a few days later, I walked him down to one of the clothing shops on the Rue St. Joseph and asked the store owner to fit my charge with boots, pants, sweater, coat, gloves, and toque. When the owner wrote out the bill, I said I didn't have any money but that, without proper clothing, I knew the lad would fall ill.

I didn't know any other way. My only hope was that, as it

was getting close to Christmas and Hanukkah, someone might help with a little charity. I guess I believed in miracles. I said I was from St. Dominic's School, signed the bill, thanked the merchant, and left.

The next day, Brother Osmund ordered me to take the boy back to the store and return the clothing. I told him I couldn't. Although I had now sinned against my vows of obedience and poverty, I was obstinate.

In the end, the store owner allowed the boy to keep the clothing. He couldn't now sell it to anyone else anyway. When I next passed the store, he looked at me with a smile and shook his head.

We "poor" Brothers each were given a carton of cigarettes every week. The Molson's truck delivered beer to the residence on Fridays. The hypocrisy made me rebellious. Like all my fellow brothers, I had sworn a vow of poverty. Yet I had to ask, "What poverty?" I was reminded, "Jesus said, 'The poor we have always amongst us' (Matthew 26: 11)." I countered: "I was hungry and you did not give me to eat; naked and you did not clothe me. (Matthew 26: 11)." But I couldn't win the argument.

Saying, "Satan himself uses Holy Scripture to lure men into the sin of Pride," the director ordered me to chapel to pray, adding "You are in very grave danger, Brother. Pride is the sin of Lucifer himself."

I was kneeling in the company of Saint Francis. I was happy.

My rebellion came to a head on Christmas morning. While the aroma of turkey wafted from the kitchen below, the Brothers kneeled in the chapel and attempted to concentrate on prayers. Someone insistently rang the front doorbell. Usually Brother Roger or the sub-director answered the door. But this time nobody moved. I went to the door.

A "knight of the road" stood outside, shivering. The old man wore rubber boots, baggy pants, and a ragged coat fastened by two large safety pins. His white hair stuck out in strands from under a filthy Toronto Maple Leafs toque. His stubbly, frost flecked whiskers and rugged eyebrows framed the flinty eyes of an explorer, a survivor of life's Arctic blizzard. Brother Roger usually sent such beggars across the street to the rectory. In turn, the good pastor sent them back to the good Brothers.

A standing joke.

The poor fellow greeted me with a cheery "Joyeux Noèl" and asked "s'il vous plait, le charité, pour l'amour du bon Dieu." (Please, for the love of God, have charity.) Indicating the direction, I quietly asked him to go to the lower side door. Then I went to the kitchen entrance and invited him in. The turkey was ready. I prepared a plate with a bit of everything. Brother Osmund came down, asked me what I thought I was doing. He told the beggar to leave. I wrapped the meal in wax paper and newsprint and gave it to the man who thanked me and left.

Brother Osmund sent me to chapel for the rest of the day. I had given my Christmas dinner to the derelict. Stubborn as I was, I didn't mind the sound of tinkling glasses and laughter from the refectory. I did mind that I was not permitted to visit my parents. I wasn't even allowed to phone to wish them a happy Christmas. Even on Boxing Day I wasn't to visit. I was to say I had decided not to go. To make sure, the brother director monitored my telephone call.

A few days later, I arrived at chapel late for morning prayer. The brother director announced that the brother who had "condescended" to join his dear brethren in morning prayer kindly would repeat the morning offering for all to hear. I began, "Behold, O kind and most sweet, sweet, sweet Jesus, I cast myself upon my ass – knees – in thy sight, and thank you that I live with such holy and loving men..."

So, in this order of God-fearing brothers, I was judged to be suffering from psychotic delusion! Lickety-split, right after the holidays, I was sent off to visit a psychiatrist in Montreal. Special permission was obtained from the provincial, Brother Romuald.

The psychiatrist was a kindly Jewish doctor. I told him of my struggle with disillusionment. I said I got angry when the Molson's truck pulled up in front of the residence to deliver beer on Friday afternoons. I only wanted to work with children and help the poor. He asked me if I ever thought of leaving the order. I answered that such a thought was out of the question. I might have been confused. But I loved teaching.

When I had visited the psychiatrist several times, Brother Osmund announced I no longer was allowed to see him. When the date for my next visit came up, I boarded the streetcar on Rue St. Joseph, even though I had no money. The driver let me on without paying. I arrived at the office a few minutes late. The doctor was on the telephone. He hung up, surprised to see me. Brother Osmund had just told him I refused to continue seeing him. The doctor wanted to know why.

I discovered other lies. I had "refused" to attend teachers' college. I "disliked" teaching grade five. I "didn't wish" to teach music. My application for summer courses "was never sent". I had been a "constant troublemaker". I was "not well-suited" to the religious life.

The doctor recommended to the Provincial that I change my community. But I wanted to complete the year with my grade seven class. I promised to do my best to keep out of Brother Roger's and Brother Osmund's way.

I spent another summer at De La Salle Camp.

In September, after three years of elementary school teaching, I was transferred to Bishop Whelan High School in Lachine. I would teach French, English, Vocal Music, and Art from grades eight to twelve. Brother Roger also was transferred to Lachine, but now seemed a lot more friendly. Still, I'd try to avoid him.

I began teaching teens, having barely completed high school myself. I certainly had no teaching diploma. I faked it successfully, mainly because I loved my job and loved the kids. Nobody guessed I had not been an honor student at some teachers' college or university.

My arrival at Bishop Whelan and the Lachine community brought promises of a new life. Bishop Whelan was an all-boys school employing a dozen brothers, complemented by lay teachers. (Similarly, Resurrection Girls' School, near the parish church, had sisters and lay teachers.)

At first, I taught French and directed the Glee Club. I also registered for my first evening course at Sir George Williams University. Several of us carpooled once a week to our various courses.

Apart from assorted hockey sticks and pairs of skates, the Lachine community owned several pairs of skis, boots, mitts, and goggles. One day I joined a carload of brothers for a skiing trip to

Mount Orford in the Eastern Townships, approximately one hour's drive southeast of Montreal. Having mastered the slopes of the Grove Hill Golf Course as a teenager, I was enthusiastic.

Orford's vertical drop of 1,770 feet was accessible from top to bottom by a double chair lift. Though it included several expert runs, I elected to ski the long, winding roadway that descended gradually from the summit to the base of the mountain. As I gained confidence, I sped faster and faster down the windy trail, yodeling like a Swiss mountaineer. Through soft, fluffy powder, I flew over moguls. As I tore by, I waved at less daring novice skiers.

All too soon, the sky turned purple-pink. I saw fewer people on the slopes. The wise skiers packed it in for the day and headed to rendezvous points for the drive home. "Just one last run. Then I'll be on my way to the car lot to meet my confrères."

As I rode to the summit, the chair lift was almost deserted. A cold wind bit through my parka. At the drop off, I paused to warm my fingers and to drink in the view. Below, lights twinkled in cottages. "The brothers will be waiting. Better speed it up."

I traveled faster than I had dared on any previous descent. On a sharp turn, I miscalculated and barreled into a shrubby bank.

"Crack!" I lay still. Something felt wrong. My ankle was on fire.

Spraying a cloud of snow, someone came to a halt beside me. "Ca va? Es-tu blessé?"

Yes, I was hurt. I nodded weakly. "Attends. Je vais chercher de l'aide." The man pushed off down the hill to get help.

Meanwhile, another skier stopped to keep me company. Then Brother Ralph found me. When I failed to turn up at the car at the designated time, he had returned to search for me. I told both men someone had gone for help.

When three ski patrol fellows pulled up beside me with a sled, the hill had turned quite dark. They asked where I hurt. Pain tore all the way from my foot to my stomach. The young men packed my leg tightly between slats of wood, then lifted me onto the sled. I lost consciousness. I remember nothing of the ride down the mountain and only briefly recall being loaded into an ambulance.

The hospital at Magog, five minutes from the ski hill, was run, with much bustling, by nuns. Morning and night prayers rattled over loudspeakers in French. I lay for a long time on a trolley in a hallway. Draped in a sheet and alternating between gas pains and explosive relief, I developed an uncontrollable fit of giggles. Close by, a sign pointed to "Maternité". I raised the sheet over my stomach. Thank God my good friend, Brother Ralph, stayed with me and shared my strange sense of humour. Anybody else would have wondered what was so funny. At last, a nurse gave me a needle and put me to sleep.

The next morning, I was wheeled in to surgery. The doctor inserted a pin into my ankle to secure a broken bone. That pin was destined to become my personal weather vane.

Following my operation, I spent six lonely days in that hospital. I was overjoyed to be transferred to Lachine General, where friends and students visited me, loaded down with books and magazines.

I wore a cast for a long time. For the rest of my days in the Christian Brothers, I never skied again. The equipment I used on that fateful trip had disappeared.

The following July, I attended St. Michael's Choir School to learn Choral Techniques, Music Theory, Music History, and Vocal Training. In August, 1962, I joined a group of the remaining brothers who had been my confrères in the Novitiate. Together we made another thirty-day retreat before taking our final, solemn vows, promising to dedicate the remainder of our lives as Christian Brothers, serving the poor. I returned to Lachine with added enthusiasm and love for my vocation.

During the summer of 1963, my music training continued with Music for Children at the University of Toronto. There, I studied Orff, Kodaly, Jacques Dalcrose, and more theory. I was happy to be back on track with part-time studies. I would not only complete a Music Specialist Diploma at the McGill Summer School of Music, I would also advance towards a B.A. at the University of Windsor.

Horace White helped me to compose and arrange music. In turn, I directed "HMS Pinafore" with the St. Mary's School of Nursing and assisted with a baby-sitting course in Montreal. I also became a District Cub Leader for campfire singsongs and skits. My friend, Peter Dawson, played the banjo.

Peter had taken part as a senior student in my first production at Bishop Whelan. He eventually became a teacher and was my best friend for many years. Another student, Chuck Baranowski, played Sir Joseph Porter in my second production, <u>H.M.S. Pinafore</u>.[3] Chuck also became a teacher and lasting friend. Following <u>Pinafore</u>, and most likely at Peter Dawson's instigation, the cast gave me a guitar.

* * * * * * * *

[1]   *Today, the issue of corporal punishment is so culturally loaded that I tremble to admit that I too paddled boys' behinds. Did that make me a child abuser? The answer is "Yes". And I shudder at the thought.*
        Nothing can justify the use of physical punishment. I just don't believe the paddle really accomplished anything other than fear. But I can't deny the past. And I can't use the sad fact that I was physically abused as an excuse for my own behaviour. I wish I had stuck to handing out candies.

[2]   *I have learned from other educators who have used creative and novel approaches in their classrooms that artistic teachers, especially men, often are discouraged from "artsy" teaching methods. Perhaps the novel approach threatens left-brained administrators, accustomed to orderly and better disciplined classrooms.*

[3]   *Gilbert and Sullivan operettas were always popular in schools because their production required no payment of royalties. There were seldom funds for school plays and musicals.*

Chapter Fourteen
Flying With Angels

> *God gives all of us a voice to use as an instrument for good. To children, especially to boys between the ages of ten and fourteen, He gives a clear bell with which to ring His praises.*

In November of 1962, I chose twelve boys from my eighty-five-member school Glee Club, to sing in a local production of "The Man Who Came to Dinner". These youngsters proved especially dedicated and continued to practice with me daily before school. By the end of that year, we had polished a small repertoire of French and English songs. With the active encouragement of Mayor Louis Joseph Gaston of Lachine, the group became known as "Les Petits Chanteurs de Lachine".

The following spring, a member of the E.Z. Players of Dorval introduced me to Joe Hart of Hart Motors who agreed to be our sponsor and to supply the boys with their first set of uniforms – grey slacks, sky blue jackets with crests, white shirts, and blue and gold striped ties. We adopted the additional name "Hart Singers of Lachine" and soon were performing in four-part harmony for charity performances, on radio, on television, and live. In the fall of 1963, the number of boys had grown to twenty-six.

In 1963, Resurrection School became a coed elementary school and Bishop Whelan a coed High School. I was assigned to teach Music and French in both schools.

The children I taught were my great joy. Natural, happy, and sincere, they responded to me with trust unshattered by trauma. With them, I rediscovered my own innocence. It was a simple matter to build a bond with them, devoid of threat. I did not lose patience. When a child failed to understand, I just found another way to explain, to illustrate.

Most of all, I loved teaching Music. We sang. We played instruments. We danced.

We not only sang songs created by adults for children, but also improvised songs to go with play. We made up silly songs too; after all, music is fun.

In my French lessons, I adopted the same technique. We sang our French conversations, creating simple melodies as we went. Soon we were writing words and music on the blackboard – but not until they were established in memory.

I wanted to use Karl Orff's Method of Music for Children, but I had no funds to buy instruments. So I began experimenting. My students and I improvised our own instruments.

By June 1964, the Hart Singers sang a twenty-minute program, entirely in French, for the St. Jean Baptiste celebrations at Fletcher's Field in Montreal. Several thousand people heard "Les Petits Chanteurs"!

Accompanied by Peter Dawson, Chuck Baranowski, and a Brother Cyprian, I began an annual one-week music camp at the French Brothers' "Camp de la Salle" at St. Alphonse de Joliette, on Lac Rouge in the Laurentians. By hiring the brothers' camp crew, we acquired professional chefs and a qualified infirmarian. And we ran a Red Cross inspected waterfront.

The boys slept in heated cabins and participated in a wide range of activities: boating, water skiing, canoeing, bicycling, music instruction, and local performances. The Hart Singers attended this camp for thirty dollars, transportation included. Other boys were welcomed for ten dollars more. Youngsters whose parents couldn't afford the fee were given a free week, with tuck money thrown in.

Every school year, I taught guitar classes on Saturdays for one dollar per student per class and showed Walt Disney movies on Friday evenings. Although some of these proceeds went towards school sports, the bulk of the money paid for camp costs, group travel, and additional uniforms. In short, I was able to subsidize my school music program.

Happily, I missed the rowdy sessions with the other brothers as they watched hockey games. On one occasion, I returned early enough to find one bottle of beer left on the table. As I put the bottle to my mouth, Brother Roger claimed the beer as his and, when I resisted, punched me. I fled with a bleeding lip.

Fortunately, I had the Hart Singers and my work to keep me involved and away from the "community".

A parent served as business manager for the Hart Singers. All its banking and financial dealings were also scrutinized by the

Brother Director. My life was full. At last, I had found success and acceptance. When some older girls asked to join the Hart Singers, we formed a second group known as "The Young Set". By that time, quite a few of our singers also played guitar.

When the Vienna Choir Boys came to perform at Place des Arts in Montreal, we were invited to join them during part of the program. The epitome of our group's success was reached when we performed several times during Expo '67. We sang in various languages and even belted out our own Expo song, which I composed in both English and French. That fall, we sang at the Parliament Buildings in Ottawa. During the winter, we spent a weekend in Quebec City. We also produced a long play recording.

Because I often sang the Gregorian Masses at the French church in Lachine, I was invited to join the brothers from L'Académé Piché for breakfasts. The brothers served huge breakfasts of sausage and steak and eggs and hash brown potatoes. I made many good friends at Piché.

I usually went straight from Piché to my morning classes at Resurrection School. By that time, the Hart Singer practices had been changed to after school, three days a week, at Bishop Whelan.

I was very happy teaching Music and French. I enjoyed the Lachine community and had many good friends. However, dark clouds began to appear on the horizon. My happy world once more was threatened.

At Bishop Whelan, *Brother Mathias taught mathematics. He was an alcoholic. But he loved the opera on Sunday afternoons.

Once he remarked to some Native Canadian students – from the Kahnawake Reserve – that they had the brains of savages. Retaliation was not long coming. When he made an appearance in the school yard, several Native girls pelted him with snowballs.

I always got along with the Native kids and sometimes visited families on the reserve. I was present when the snowballing incident occurred, and I knew why it occurred. When the Brother Director called me to his office and demanded a list of names, I said I didn't know. Brother Mathias knew differently.

The following September, a change of Directors brought changes in teaching assignments. I was no longer assigned to teach music. Worse, my music room at Bishop Whelan became part of the school cafeteria. This meant that the Hart Singers' uniforms had to be hung elsewhere. We had to use a regular classroom for our practices. I was also told to become involved in other extracurricular activities besides music and drama. Something "more manly".

One of my assignments was to lead a group of art students in building a snow and ice sculpture. Not only was this an entertaining project, our sculpture won a prize in the community! Though I taught more English, I still managed to retain some French. But at the expense of Music.

A favourite colleague of mine was Gordon Blickstead, a lay teacher at Resurrection School. Gordon sang, helped with the Hart Singers, and provided an annual trophy for top performer in the group (the Mister "B" Trophy).

During Christmas holidays, 1967, Ron Garinther (at that time Brother Ralph) and his cousin, Gordon, invited me to join them on a trip to Florida. Ron asked for leave to visit his parents for the holidays. I asked to spend Christmas with my aunts in Quebec City. Both requests were granted. We drove to Florida and had a great time swimming and enjoying the night life. When we returned, people asked me where I got the sun tan. When I said Florida, they knew I was lying. I had used a sun lamp.

Gord took the rejected football tryouts from Resurrection School and turned them into a winning team. He even purchased uniforms. However, his success inspired jealousy. When the school coach and physical education teacher wished to recruit Gord's winning players, the principal announced that Gord's team uniforms were school property and that Mr. "B"'s team should be disbanded.

Gord spent a lot of time with extra coaching and with what he called the "STA Club". STA referred to the new mathematics program "Seeing Through Arithmetic". Gord's club was "Ships, Tanks, and Airplanes".

The privilege of belonging to the STA club had its price. Every member had to promise not to smoke or do drugs. When a couple of boys were caught smoking, they were suspended from the club and from the football team.

The disgruntled boys spoke to their friends. Somebody said, "Oh, Mr. B.'s a fag!" That got into the football team argument. When the principals of both schools questioned students about the comment, they made it clear that there was only one truth and anyone who lied would be severely punished.

It took months for the real truth to come out. Meanwhile, some insisted, "Where there's smoke, there's fire." I wished to speak on Mr. "B"'s behalf. But the Brother Director would not permit me to get involved. He reminded me that since Gord and I had been close friends, I could be tarred with the same brush. With a feeling of terror, I withdrew my offer. In doing so, I knew I was being disloyal to an innocent colleague.

The entire community split over the issue. But, as such events go, the accusation alone turned out to be enough to damn my friend. He lost his job. His wife left him. And his house was vandalized. Even when every boy testified that the story had arisen from one careless remark, even when the school board ordered that the teacher be reinstated, the school principal was adamant. She would not believe the boys and refused to comply with the order. Gord Blickstead left teaching.

While all this foofara was going on, I retreated into countless hours with the Hart Singers. Better that than deal with my own shame concerning Gord.

During those years of happiness mixed with frustration, I came to know many of the students' families as I had since my first teaching assignment in Montreal. I developed strong relationships with some whom I visited more often than others, enjoying family meals and some of the comforts of home life. Those close moments with loving parents and happy kids helped me to persevere in my otherwise lonely vocation. Sometimes, however, I dreamt of having a family of my own with a loving wife and happy children.

One of the Hart Singers became despondent following the death of his father which followed a lengthy fight with cancer. The lad's mother invited me to supper to discuss her son and see if we could help him pull out of his lethargy. The evening progressed, and the boy went to bed. The mother and I sat up talking. She poured me another glass of wine.

Suddenly, she broke into sobs. I held her hands in an effort to comfort her. I told her I understood her loneliness. Then, I put my arms around her. Unexpectedly, she kissed me. Not on the cheek but fully on my mouth as I had only fantasized for so many years.

We held each other tight, her body burning against mine. She took my hand and placed it on her breast, the nipple of which stood out hard through her soft sweater. I shook with anticipation.

"Wait right here", she whispered in my ear. I stood shaking as she left the room.

Then I panicked. *How did I get into this mess?*

Shame and humiliation overcame me. I grabbed my coat and quietly opened the front door, slipping out into the cold night.

Oh, what a fool to have let myself into this situation. Oh what a fool not to stay and enjoy what I had only imagined so many times. *"On my God, I'm heartily sorry ...."* Oh, how my body ached! I hurried down the leaf-scattered street, praying that no one had seen me. As I escaped, imaginings of dire things to come spurred my feet forward toward the monastic discomfort of my icy bed.

The Lachine community remained divided over the Gordon Blickstead affair. Unhappily for the Hart Singers, administrative support for my music program quickly evaporated, and I was informed that the group would have to be disbanded. Lachine had gone sour. I requested a year of full-time study at the University of Windsor, and my application was approved.

Pete Dawson and I organized one last singing tour. We took the twelve most supportive singers to the Maritimes. I didn't ask permission to do this. It was enough that the parents got behind us. Several mothers sewed white sailor suits as a second uniform for every singer. We left as soon as school was out. Our plan was to camp out and to stay in motels only as need arose.

Somewhere in New Brunswick, the motel we planned to stay at turned out to be full. As we had faced rain for several days, the motel owner told us we could stay in his mother's house, a huge old structure up on a hill. We all had sleeping bags. Pete went upstairs with the younger boys. I slept on a couch in the living room.

Pete told the kids ghost stories to help pass the time before they fell asleep. When he said the motel owner's mother had been murdered in "this very room", a ruckus ensued. It got so loud I had to go upstairs to tell everyone to pipe down. After all, we had a busy day ahead of us. One thing was wrong with this picture: I had wrapped a sheet around myself! A perfect ghost!

We sang at HMCS Cornwallis, drove through the Annapolis

Valley, visited Green Gables and the beautiful sandy beaches of P.E.I., and entertained the officers in their mess at <u>Stadacona</u>. At the end of the trip, only uniforms and fond memories remained. Peter and I gave the uniforms to the boys, including extra pants and jackets.

The music fund had been well spent.

From July 4th to August 4th, 1968, I was given permission to complete courses at MacDonald College while living at the Lachine community. But Brother Mathias had been appointed Lachine community's summer director. He ordered me to stay where I was, to cook and look after the house. Though I didn't say "no" outright, I intended to disobey anyway. While I packed my bags, in preparation for taking the bus to Senneville, <u>Sunday Afternoon at the Opera</u> bellowed from the stereo in his room.

Finally, bags in hand, I stole quietly to the front door. Then, with a horrible sinking feeling, I remembered that I'd stuck my wallet beneath my mattress, for safekeeping. I had to return to my room. While I crept up the stairs, an uncooperative floorboard – you guessed it – creaked.

"Have you got a minute?" Brother Mathias, from his room. I took a deep breath and opened the door.

What I saw made me sick to my stomach. The man looked like a cadaver's cadaver. As he crooned along with the tenor on the radio, his hands flailed about like windmills, first to the crown of his balding head, then to his chest.

He was a singer gone mad. Driven by an excess of bottled energy, he roared, then crooned like an Irish tenor, then lapsed into near-poetic tenderness. At this point, he was almost human.

Finally he turned to me. Thrusting a stubby tumbler toward me, he growled, "Join me." My palms sweated. The glass nearly slipped from my grasp.

"I don't drink rum," I lied. My whining voice echoed back at me. He glowered at the vicinity of my crotch; I felt positive he saw my quaking knees.

"I really don't drink rum. Thanks, anyway." I turned to leave.

He growled like an English bulldog. "Shut up! Take the damn drink. And listen."

My stomach gurgled with misgivings. I was about to be pilloried, exposed to public scorn. Brother Mathias drained his glass and waited for me to do the same.

I had no choice but to obey. "Holy shit!" The straight, over proof rum burned its way down to the pit of my stomach. I was on fire. At least, he drank his mixed with milk.

"Now, do you mind telling me where the hell you think you're sneaking off to?"

I lied – again. "I'll be back shortly."

I just had to get out of there. I flew into my room, grabbed my wallet, and descended the stairs three at a time. Then I was gone.

From my parents' home in Senneville, I wrote to the Brother Visitor (Provincial) and told him that (a) I was terrified of Brother Mathias, and (b) I already had his permission to complete my Music Certificate Program.

The Brother Provincial responded by sending me funds for my courses and for room and board.

Murray Shaeffer, a well-known Canadian composer, wrote music for high schools. I appreciated his creativity, especially when our summer session music class paraded around the MacDonald College campus, playing mezzo forte on invisible instruments in an imaginary marching band. We had so much fun we didn't concern ourselves that the other students on campus, including teachers on summer courses, questioned our sanity.

On one glorious excursion to the woods, we played bells and listened to nature's response. Hundreds of song birds joined in with their own music![1]

One of the most joyful experiences of my life has been flying just above the angelic voices of an all-boys choir while conducting sacred music. To control the ebb and flow of those clear tones is sublime. I have sailed with arms gently waving to the august strains of the Avé Verum and the Panis Angelicus and have been left breathless at the gift of angelic music. I have known the twofold gift of praying with music while conducting the Missa des Angelis and have felt the elation of participating in Palestrina's polyphonic Missa Papae Marcelli while studying Choral Conducting at St. Michael's

Choir School in Toronto.

In response to those who told me that singing is unmanly, I say, "I agree!" Singing is not for men – or women, for that matter. It belongs to the angels. We humble humans are offered a mere part in this. Those who grasp this opportunity are blessed forever.

God gives all of us a voice to use as an instrument for good. To children, especially to boys between the ages of ten and fourteen, He gives a clear bell with which to ring His praises.

Call me unmanly. I have flown with the angels.

* * * * * * * *

[1] *Murray Shaeffer's spontaneity freed me and many other music educators from our inhibitions. He nudged our own creativity. He also taught us to listen carefully and to appreciate the way all nature joins in with pleasant sounds.*

Chapter Fifteen
Tears in the Chapel

> *"If a man does not keep pace with his companions,*
> *perhaps it is because he hears a different drummer.*
> *Let him step to the music which he hears,*
> *however measured or far away.*
> – Henry David Thoreau, *Walden*

While I was in Lachine, my sister, Naomi, returned to Canada with her husband Don and small son Fred. They had been in Lagos, Nigeria where Don worked for Canadian External Affairs. Naomi had developed inoperable melanoma and been flown to hospital in London, England, but too late. Doctors could do nothing for her. She and Don returned to Ottawa where Naomi got a job as a bank teller. When her cancer worsened, she quit work and went to live with Mother and Papa François in Senneville, near Montreal.

Don went to visit Naomi on weekends. One day, he invited me into the village of Ste. Anne de Bellevue for a couple of beers. I was happy for the chance to get to learn more about my sister's life since I had known her as a teen. But the beer turned my brother-in-law into a bully. He harangued me for being Catholic, insisting he knew more about popes and priests than I did. Finally, calling me "queer", he pushed me into a ditch on the way home. Sick with embarrassment, I didn't fight back.

Instead of showing sympathy upon my return home, Mother, Don, and Papa François reminded me that I had spent a lot of time with Sigvard. Apparently, he had died in Denmark, in their words, "surrounded by his little boys". I stood accused. Denying that my Uncle Sigvard had ever touched me, I tearfully fled the house to the accompaniment of their laughter and my own sickening shame.

I did not return to Senneville for a very long time.

Naomi was admitted to Lachine General Hospital to spend her final days. One afternoon I went to visit her, but Mother had left orders that I could not see her unless she or other members of the family were there. Maybe she was afraid I might get preachy. Or so I thought at the time. Later, I surmised that Naomi had some things she wanted to tell me. Perhaps she had discovered what happened to our own Dad.

My mother also ordered that no clergy should be admitted to "bother" my sister. We had a little priest from Ireland, Father Bell, who assisted at Resurrection Church. I spoke to him about Naomi and, before long, he was visiting her regularly. Later, Mother called and told me I could visit my sister too. When I arrived, the entire family was present.

Still, I got a chance to say goodbye to Naomi, but with everyone there. She was in a cold sweat and having difficulty breathing. As Mother had ordered that her lungs should no longer be pumped out, I knew she wouldn't last long.

The next day, the Hart Singers performed at a mental hospital in Montreal. As we boarded the bus, I told Peter I wanted to visit my sister as soon as the concert was over and asked him to drive me. Naomi died at the exact time I spoke to Peter on the bus. As for her son, Fred, he was away visiting a paternal uncle in Ontario. He remained with his uncle until after the funeral. Either my mother or Don thought it better that Fred not attend.

Naomi was just thirty-five years old.

When we were little, Naomi was my best friend in all the world. We were constantly together sharing giggles and tickles and butterflies. Everything felt beautiful in the Garden of Eden.

Granted, like any small child, I knew love in simple terms only. Yet I know I loved Naomi. I would have done anything for her, including defend her.

Though Naomi and I grew apart, she never stopped representing for me a link to my lost joy. Frequently, I yearned for her company. Yet I couldn't tell her anything. Whenever we talked, we were defensive and guarded. She didn't tell me her secrets; I didn't tell her mine.

In boarding school, the teachers refused to allow me to talk to my sister. We lived in different worlds. Whenever these collided, we landed in trouble. Naomi got caned because of me over the "Catholic Truth Society" booklets. Naturally, I had shared the books with my sister and so, she also was caught with "stolen material" and punished.

Then, after Mother married our stepfather, we moved away from London and the worst of the bombing. In Sussex, we walked many miles to and from school. Every day proved to be an adventure. Once again, the two of us looked forward to a wonderfully mysterious future. I felt a lot of my old love – the companionship, closeness, and familiarity part of it – for my sister.

Then came Canada. And things got worse again, a lot worse. I vied with my sister for scarce moments of Mother's attention. At

192

least, I vied for snippets of approval. This resulted in Naomi and I finding ways to get each other into trouble. Mother only had time for one of us at a time, never two. All her real motherly love went to the three Boucher girls. Naomi became Cinderella. I became Cinderfella.

Despite this, we soon shared long bicycle rides. By this time, at the ages of fourteen, fifteen, and sixteen, our personal agendas broadened to include sexual urges and adolescent exploration. The trouble was, whenever my imagination ran wild I felt terribly sinful. On this, I can't speak for Naomi. All I know is that, since she had her boyfriends and her own secrets, I feared she, too, would end up in hell. Instead of "going all the way" with any girl, I masturbated and lived in constant dread of dying in a state of mortal sin.

Later still, when Mother told me Naomi had run away from home, she implied that she did so because I had provided a bad example, by leaving home myself when "things got tough".

During the period of my involvement with the Christian Brothers, Naomi eventually returned – but at a great distance from me. Naomi was dying from cancer. I wanted to see her. I wanted to save her soul. But I had it all wrong. My sister's soul didn't need saving. She just needed me to love her. I didn't really know how to love, though I thought I could. The love I learned in the Brothers was superficial at best.

When Naomi died at the age of thirty-five, I regretted our lost moments. If only she and I had gotten closer during our lost years! If only I had behaved like other big brothers! Then, I thought, I could have rescued her from her miserable life.

When Naomi joined the Navy a year after I did, she had the guts to reclaim our original surname. She must have missed her father as much as I did. Yet she never shared that burden of hers with me; we had grown too far apart.

Louise's younger twin, Nicole "Nickie", joined the White Sisters of Africa to become a missionary nurse. I saw her when she was working with sick children in a West End Montreal hospital. She radiated joy. Still, she left the order before taking final vows. Had she become disillusioned with the religious life?

Before long, while working with a parish youth group in the same area of Montreal, she met and married another volunteer, Roger. Roger started seeing another woman, and the marriage ended on the rocks.

Mother developed a friendship with *Jean Citron, an automobile dealer from France who sold Peugeot sports cars in Pointe Claire. Nickie and Jean developed a relationship. However, he was supporting a wife in Bermuda and took unfair advantage of my little sister.

Ten years later, Nickie developed cancer but, remembering

the grief Naomi's sickness and death had caused Mother, did not tell the family until it was too late. Nicole died alone in the parking lot of the Lachine General Hospital. The year was 1979. Like Naomi, she was thirty-five years of age. The sad epilogue to her life is that Jean ran off with all of her assets, leaving many bills unpaid.

Was Nickie attracted to the White Sisters of Africa in the same way I wished to join the White Fathers of Africa? Did she have the same desire I had to do something special with her life? Was Nickie struggling as I had struggled to please her mother? Why did I feel so guilty when my little sister died so tragically?

The Stockholm Syndrome.[1]

Over the years, in my childhood and adulthood both, I was routinely mistreated by people in authority over me. It wasn't long after I was beaten to within an inch of my life in the American South, and subsequently made to feel by my parents that I brought this horror on myself, that I went "all the way" in the Roman Catholic Church. Since no one thought to offer me professional counseling – indeed, counseling had not reached the degree of acceptability it has today – my unresolved feelings had to go somewhere. So I signed on for more mistreatment, in education and training both, in order to become a Christian Brother.

Did I even think at the time that I would be subject to further abuse? Or did I see the Church as an avenue of escape from my years of loneliness, pain, and frustration? What was it that brought me so deeply into the Church? Was it a subconscious wish for martyrdom? Was I willing to suffer anything to gain approval?

Why did I persevere when I perceived so much hypocrisy and cruelty in the Church? Why did I continue when so many were falling away from religious orders and the Church, like wasps from a burning nest? The answer was obvious to me at the time: It was I who had run away from God. Now God had welcomed me back. Since my faith was a simple one, I lacked the sophistication to question it.

My two years at the Christian Brothers' Mother House provided me with opportunities for spiritual reading and meditation. I often went to chapel, suffering from terrible headaches. My vision blurred, I gazed at the ten foot crucifix hanging before me. There He was, with nails in His hands and feet, a gaping wound in His side, and thorns piercing His head. How could I complain of a mere headache? Here were love, forgiveness – and healing – personified. In the chapel, the symbols of love were everywhere. The statue of Mary. The Stations of the Cross. Often I meditated on Christ's suffering and death by following the stations around the chapel's interior perimeter. During my first thirty-day retreat at the Mother House, I penned a sixteen stanza "Via Crucis" and "The Pieta". Here is a brief segment:

I   With Christ I trod the same weary way
        That He trudged from His trial.
        In silent grief I heard Him pray
        That long and bloody mile.
            .....

        I followed Him along the way
        All nature was forlorn.
        To die upon that fateful day,
        The Lamb of God was born.

PIETA

On feeling the bitter twinge of sorrow
And pangs of self-commiseration gnawing at my soul,
I find myself, in spirit, standing
before the Thirteenth Station.

How could my greatest grief in least compare to hers?
As even a dewdrop to the ocean's depth,
Or as a firefly to the brilliant, blazing sun.
Yet she now has taken my affliction to be her own,
Pleading my cause with her beloved Son.

It was during thirty days of silent prayer on one of those summer retreats, that I was finally able to balance the beauty of religious life with its absurdities, cruelties, and contradictions. At least, for the time being.

Faith and love brought me into the Church. Granted, I still had a subconscious wish for martyrdom. I was still willing to suffer anything to gain approval. And I was still attempting to atone for the toxic shame I'd felt since early childhood.

* * * * * * * *

The Stockholm syndrome refers to people who are both abused and rewarded over a period of time until they come to love and obey their abusers, without ever fully understanding the aberrant, exploitative nature of the relationship in which they're stuck.

On August 23rd, 1973, three women and a man were taken hostage in a large bank in Stockholm. They were held for six days by two ex-convicts who both threatened their lives and showed them kindness.

All the hostages resisted efforts to rescue them; in fact they were eager to defend their captors. Several months after they were saved by police, they still had unresolved feelings about their experiences.

Chapter Sixteen
The Times They Are A-Changing (1968/69)

> *When you get into a tight place and everything goes*
> *against you, till it seems as though you could not hold*
> *on a minute longer, never give up then, for that is just*
> *the place and time that the tide will turn.*
> *– Harriet Beecher Stowe*

I brimmed with new and exciting ideas for teaching music. The music program in Lachine was scrapped. I was definitely at a crossroads. My time with the Brothers had been a mixture of joy, sadness and betrayal. Still I held on, looking for the perfect existence. With much to sort out, I cast about for a fresh start.

I had been teaching for more than a decade without qualifications. I had neither teaching diploma nor university degree, despite summer courses and evening classes at Sir George Williams University. Time for a sabbatical.

The Brother Provincial granted permission to complete my B.A. at the University of Windsor (*previously known as Assumption College and still under the auspices of the Basilian Fathers*). I packed my few belongings and said my goodbyes to the friends I had made during seven years in Lachine. The parents of the Hart Singers presented me with a mandolin. I was ordered to leave the gift with the brothers in the Lachine community. I did, however, take my guitar and two harmonicas with me. I knew these would serve me well in the year to come.

Musical instruments had come as gifts from parent groups during memorable years with the Hart Singers. Usually I was permitted to keep them; sometimes not. Though the vow of poverty was hard to swallow at times, I usually obeyed.

I joined sixteen other brothers, many of them fresh out of Scarborough Scholasticate. Most were sent to live at La Salle Hall, on campus. A handful of us went to live several miles from the university, at St. Joseph's, with Brother *Symphorian as director. My good friend, Brother Charles Dennis Berry, who had taught with me at St. Dominic's, lived at the same residence. He now served as an elementary school principal.

Brother Symphorian did not approve of my course

selections, including a Major in Drama and a Minor in Fine Arts. Instead, I was supposed to study "more useful" subjects such as History and Mathematics. "Furthermore," he said, "I will approve no transportation to attend extracurricular activities, such as play rehearsals. Even if you are allowed to take Acting."

At this point, I decided I had been bullied long enough. I registered for Painting, Print Making, and three classes in Theatre. However, I had no money to pay for art supplies. Then, by chance, I was invited to take part in some entertainment at a Friday and Saturday evening coffee house. Thus I made money to pay for canvases, paints, and engraving tools I already had purchased on "credit".

It was the age of Folk Music. We sang songs by Woody Guthrie – he died that year – and Pete Seeger, Oscar Brand, Burl Ives, the Clancy Brothers, and many great entertainers. Other regulars at the coffee house did some fancy guitar "picking".

I got the folks singing. We all had a good time. I made friends and went to parties. I sometimes played harmonica and sang with Pete Cowan's Dance Orchestra, a group that imitated the Harmonicats. I played harmonica for other folk singers, too.

Apart from the vow of chastity, I broke free of the intense control I'd been under for the past twelve years. I certainly broke the vows of poverty and obedience.

Having no paid transportation for my late returns, I hitchhiked, often arriving at St. Joseph's after curfew. I rapped on Brother Charles' window to let me in. Sometimes, we shared a bottle of Crème de Cacao and sat up talking half the night.

Every weekend, one or two of the brothers drove to Detroit to pick up duty-free liquor and cigarettes. As there was no question of staying the required forty-eight hours in the United States, they just slipped back into Canada without declaring what they'd bought. So far no one had been caught.

When it was my turn, I got cold feet. I drove across to Detroit. But I couldn't enter the duty free shop. On the drive back, with a clean car, I was asked to pull into an inspection spot, and the car was searched with all the thoroughness of Canada Customs. When I returned empty handed, the brothers were most unsympathetic. Henceforth, I was cut off from cigarettes, beer, or any form of leisure supplies.

Since I seldom was present for the Friday night parties and since I used my cigarettes as a form of barter – having given up smoking during Theatre courses – I didn't feel the loss much. With the one exception of Brother Charles, I didn't care about my colleagues. Having decided my Canada Customs account was a lie, they returned the sentiment

I was given the grandfather role in the university production of "Angels in Love" and started to grow my own beard and let my hair grow longer. The Brother Director asked me one Sunday morning what I had on my face.

"Where? Where?"

"Go and shave that abomination from your face and get Brother *Cosmas to give you a haircut".

"I'm growing this for a play".

"You are not to be in a play; it's unheard of!".

Tediously, he lectured me on the evils of the stage: "Don't you realize that Satan leads astray the hearts of men in notorious, lewd songs and willful whistling – on the stage? The theatre is the home of intemperance, pomposity, and impurity, where flagrant characters, festooned in fine fripperies, are forever in pursuit of sexual conquests and other and sundry lusts. You imperil your soul with senseless, rude chatter."

"You do not have my permission to take part in such debauchery. I forbid it!"

Enough was enough. I dashed to my room in frustration and drafted a letter to the Brother Provincial requesting a dispensation. I could no longer continue the battle to study and be involved in the arts without the support of my community. I could no longer observe the life-binding vows I had made of poverty, chastity, and obedience. My religious vocation had come to an impasse. Rome could release me from vows.

In my letter, I explained to my Provincial that I might have remained forever had I been permitted to continue teaching music.

I no longer could tolerate the idea that it was unmanly or ungodly to paint or sing or act. When I told Brother Symphorian my decision, he reminded me, "You're throwing your vocation in the face of God".

That was the last time Brother Symphorian spoke to me.

I had to remain in the order until my dispensation came through at the end of the school semester, in April. But that was just as well. I still needed a roof over my head. I rode to the university with the brothers in the morning. But I was no longer given a bag lunch. Now my meals, indeed, my very survival depended on my own resources.

After the final night of "Angels in Love", the cast were all invited to a party in Detroit. On our way over the border, I was called into the U.S. Immigration office. Likely, this was because of my long hair and beard and traces of make-up. The officer asked me to provide identification. I produced my Quebec driver's licence. He took the card into another office then returned and asked for my birth certificate. I had been asked for a birth certificate previously, so I carried a folded photocopy. My birth certificate bore the name Bendt Nuttall-Smith, born in Tanganyika Territory. I showed a Canadian Citizenship card, also under the name Benoit Boucher.

The officers told my fellow cast members to carry on without me. I was ushered into a small office and questioned by two officers in plain clothes. They asked about my affiliation with the Communist Party. I told them I was not and had never been a Communist. I was a member of the Christian Brothers studying at the University of Windsor.

One of the men asked, "Who are you trying to kid?" He looked at my birth certificate. "Maybe we should just deport you back to Tanganyka. Save us all a lot of trouble."

After a long time, I was given back my wallet and escorted back to Canada Customs at the Windsor end of the tunnel. American Customs kept my birth certificate copy and citizenship card.

I had to walk the entire way back to St. Joseph's. As always, Brother Charles let me in, freezing cold and this time in tears.

"What the hell happened to you?"

I told Brother Charles the entire story. While the two of us polished off what remained of one of our famous bottles of Creme de Cacao, I began to see the humour of the situation. The following morning I shaved. Later in the day, I asked Brother Cosmos to give me a haircut. For this service, he customarily demanded a package of cigarettes. As I didn't have one, he gave me a brush cut. My emotionally overloaded reaction to this was "What the hell? Who cares?"

A couple of days later, on the advice of one of my professors, I made an appointment to see a lawyer. After some investigating, the lawyer discovered that, despite having been granted Canadian Citizenship in January 1961, I had never been legally adopted and would have to go to court to change my name from Bendt Nuttall-Smith to Benoit Boucher. *The fact that I had served in the RCN as Benoit Boucher had no bearing.* I would have to apply once again for a new document and required a "Declaration of Heredity" from Papa François to qualify my Canadian Citizenship. As I stood, if ever I entered the United States again, they could deport me to Tanganyka on the strength of my birth certificate.

I was relieved when Papa François provided the necessary document in January 1969. After the customary advertisements appeared in newspapers in Montreal and Windsor, I appeared before a judge to legally become Benoit Boucher in March of that year. My new Canadian Citizenship document was granted in May 1969. Still, the lawyer advised me not to try reentering the U.S. in the foreseeable future. I was on their list of "undesirables".

While still at the University of Windsor, better things happened to me. During Holy Week, several of us drama students played out the passion story in Assumption Church. Some in the congregation were moved to tears by our performance. Part of the production included music. I would have made Stanislavsky proud when I sang out Christ's impassioned "Sitio!" - "I thirst".

I later sang at funerals and weddings, expressing the same emotion and reality I learned so well at University. I played Belomy, the girl's father in "The Fantastics". And got hooked on musical theatre.

Part of my painting course involved painting nudes. Maybe because the class included several sisters, the models were usually homely. Still, to be on the safe side, I kept all of my work at school until my courses were over. One of my charcoal sketches, a linear one representing the strength of womanhood, won an honourable mention in an exhibition. Even better, some of my poetry was published in the yearbook.

A little more than a week prior to the end of classes, my dispensation came through. I was no longer bound by vows of poverty, chastity, and obedience. It was difficult for me to find a defining moment in this. I know of no one else who left a religious order without having been given some provision for transition to secular life. Yet I was provided with none.

Throughout most of the year, I found it necessary to support myself. Fortunately, I managed to save enough to make a down payment on a Volkswagen station wagon. I was not in a position to make the purchase myself, as I was still living at the Brothers' residence. I sent Mother the money, and she made the purchase for me and drove the car to Windsor.[1]

With the help of my good friend Horace White, I was offered a teaching job in Dorval at L'Ecole Sécondaire Jean XXIII to teach English as a Second Language, covering for a teacher absent on medical leave. (She'd suffered a nervous breakdown.)

The only brother to bid me farewell and good luck was my good friend "Chuck" Berry.

During my final year with the De La Salle Brothers, I reached the peak of rebellion. True, I found many grounds for disillusionment. On the other hand, I had lived and worked with countless dedicated and holy men.

I sought perfection in my confreres while I, all too often, broke my own vows of poverty and of obedience (if not in fact, at least in spirit). I judged my colleagues' actions to be inferior to mine; I received so much gratification from the development and sharing of my own gifts. Though I was just as fallible as everyone around me, I didn't trust enough in them to learn this essential truth that the gifts of others are as valuable in their own right as my offerings. I didn't recognize the great Science teachers, the dedicated football and hockey coaches.

Religious orders, like all organizations, are inhabited by saints and sinners both. Sometimes the good wins out. Sometimes the bad. As we see this so much in others, we tend to be harsh in our judgments. Most of all, we see this in ourselves. So we're hardest on ourselves.

Since leaving religious life, especially, I have met many great and generous men and women who carry their goodness and leadership abilities into service of others. Thousands upon thousands of them serve in poverty, chastity and obedience. The reasons why one enters and departs from a religious community, even the priesthood, are as complex as life itself. God is the sole judge of our lives. So God alone knows the answer to this.

What prompted me to join a religious order? Was it an unselfish desire to serve God and fellow man by dedicating my life to teaching the children of the poor? If I could provide an unqualified "yes" to that, I'd be well on the path to sainthood. But I know I also had darker, subconscious motives.

Here, out of the dregs of my childhood shame and need comes the answer. Like so many of my life's decisions, I surrendered to a pattern of attempts to please my mother and win her approval. Later, I transferred this pattern to other meaningful people in my life. This pattern I call "Singing for Mother".

All this did not remove the meaning from what I did. The hardships I faced helped me to develop a spirit of generosity. Sometimes I even reached a point where I could love without expecting return. Agapé.

Most of the time, unfortunately, I could not fully love others because I could not first love myself. In the process of my growth in love, I still had much to learn. But I kept working at it. In fact, this has characterized my entire life.

I joined the Christian Brothers in an attempt to redeem myself from the guilt and shame I felt, day in and day out, since boyhood. This proved insufficient, of course, to sustain, for long, a truly religious and spiritual life. That's why I eventually left.

Two types of men stick it out in religious orders. First, there are those who truly are motivated towards sainthood, for all the right reasons. Second, there are those who look upon the orders as a simpler, less threatening, and more ordered way to live out their lives; of the members of this group, most feel emotionally threatened and insecure by the more chaotic demands of secular life.

I fit into neither group. I desired redemption. I couldn't find it, mainly because I looked in the wrong places. For certain, I couldn't find redemption from the guilt and shame I felt about sex. For me, sex had become dangerous and dirty; it inspired in me much anxiety and fear.

* * * * * * * *

[1]   For the first time that I could remember, Mother provided emotional and physical support when I needed it. She even helped me design and make furniture for my apartment, when I began teaching in Dorval.

She realized I could make a go of life on my own. And for this, she gave me unqualified acceptance, at last.

I want to grow up in a world where little birds nest in the trees.
I want to feel the breeze and taste the cool clean air.
I want to walk down by the river, see the moon among the ripples,
Count the stars and smell wild flowers and know I'm free.

All my neighbours will be friendly; they'll be white and brown and black,
And I'll know each name and show them that I care.
I want my children to be happy and my children's children, too;
I need to know they'll laugh and sing and cry like me.

In that world, we'll fight all wars around a table in a hall
With wooden soldiers and lead sailors in a line.
And then the losers and the winners will invite us all to dinners
Where we'll cheer the referee, a child of nine.

What a world this world will be where I'll need you and you'll need me
And every one we meet will smile and call us "friend".
If we hurry, we'll just make it, change the world before they break it,
Call for love and bring the madness to an end.

April 1969. John XXIII High School, Dorval, Quebec, was shared by two separate administrative bodies – French and English Catholic. A brand new building, the school boasted a huge indoor swimming pool, fully equipped theatre-auditorium, humungous cafeteria, and classrooms with intercom. Everything was up-to-date and subsidized well beyond any school I'd ever seen.

All was not peaceful, however. The separatist movement was well under way, promoted all the more by disgruntled expatriates from Algeria.

I ate with the French teachers and spoke only in French. However, in class, I spoke only English, acting towards my students as though I did not understand or speak French. After all, my assignment was to teach English.

The Language program was taught with tape recorders and earphones. The teacher could switch from pupil to pupil for individual attention or address the entire class.

One senior class consisted entirely of girls.

"Monsieur, est ce'que vous parlez français?"

"I'm sorry; you'll have to repeat your question in English."

The girls flicked spit balls and passed countless notes. While I chose to ignore what was not immediately concerned with the task at hand, I began to understand why the former English teacher went on leave.

"Monsieur, aimes-tu les petites filles?" (Do you like little girls?)

"Monsieur, veut tu coucher avec moi, chez-toi?" (Do you want to sleep with me at your place?)

"Would you care to repeat your questions in English?"

"Monsieur, as tu un gros pitou?" (Do you have a big penis?)

Over the days, the questions, remarks, and roars of laughter grew.

"Monsieur, est ce que tu manges les petites minoux?" (Do you eat little pussies?)

"C'EST ASSEZ!" (That's enough!) I shouted.

Shock!

Then I said in French, "Vous allez tous m'écouter! C'est le seule fois que je vais vous parler en francais." (You will listen to me. This is the only time I shall speak to you in French.)

Disbelief!

"Si vous voulez apprendre l'anglais, les leçons seront en anglais seulement. Cette affaire imbécile est fini!" (If you wish to learn English, the lessons will be in English only. This ridiculous affair is over!) "Now, let us continue in a more serious manner."

Several girls broke out in tears. A couple left the classroom. I continued.

About five minutes later, the two girls returned with the principal. He addressed the class. "Mademoiselles, si vous avez de la difficultée avec certaines mots en anglais, Monsieur Boucher peut certainement vous aider en français. N'est ce pas, Monsieur Boucher?" (Ladies, if you have difficulty with certain words in English, Mr. Boucher could certainly help you in French. Is that not so Mr. Boucher?)

Every girl was grinning. They had won, or so they thought.

However, I continued to teach in English only, but only until the end of the term. The class behaved well and nothing further was said. Fortunately, I had been given a job for the following year teaching on the English side of the school where I reasoned I'd have better support from the administration.

That summer I spent much of my time at Cub Camp with my good friend Peter Dawson and various packs from throughout the Montreal area. In this totally volunteer work, I enjoyed myself immensely.

The following year, I taught Vocal Music, Drama, and Art from grades eight to twelve, formed a mixed-voiced choir for St. Veronica's Church, joined the Lyric Theatre Society and the Lakeshore Players, performing in "The Pajama Game", "Fiorello", and several one-act plays, and ran a special exercise class for expectant mothers on the Lakeshore. One evening a week, I drove to Sir George Williams University for a Theatre History to complete my B.A. Everything was falling into place.

1970, I directed the school production of <u>West Side Story</u>, and in 1971, <u>Oliver</u>. While directing <u>Oliver</u>, I also undertook the role of Henry Higgins in <u>My Fair Lady</u>, with the Arcadians, a semiprofessional group in Montreal. The Director, Alexander MacDougall, did choreography for "Les Grands Ballets Canadiens" as well as for several groups of modern dancers in Montreal and the West Indies. An agile seventy year-old, he was a master of crowd scenes.

At every performance, I fell in love with Elva Hanson who played Eliza. Elva's husband played trumpet in the orchestra. Jack McCutcheon played a magnificent Doolittle. After the show's run, he moved to Australia for a job with the Australian Broadcasting Corporation. Robert Thorpe, the group's president, played the Major. We were a marvellous cast, a team!

Not only did Alex MacDougall teach me to dance, but in doing so, he taught me to fly through the air as though hoisted by invisible wires. He exerted more influence on my acting and directing than any other person in theatre.

Mother attended the opening night of My Fair Lady. She didn't care for the callous Higgins called for by George Bernard

Shaw. I took my mother's criticism to heart; the next night, I softened up and played Higgins with a twinkle. Alex MacDougall approved.

I visited Mother often. She helped me decorate my apartment in Dorval. In turn, I installed a pond and waterfall in her back garden, even supplying the water pump and plants. Mother opened up in a way she hadn't done for many years. She shared secrets about her life during the war. She told me why she was absent for such great lengths of time and why Naomi and I had to stay with Uncle Sigvard.

Mother told me that because she had done so well in the Censorship Bureau, because she had lived much of her childhood in Denmark, because she had attended schools in France and Germany, and because of her fluency in French, German, Danish, and other languages, she was assigned to British Intelligence.

In one of her stories, Mother was in Denmark. She convinced her younger sister, Birgitte, not to take the tram to school. Even though it was raining, she told her to ride her bicycle with her friends. But she couldn't tell her why. Though her stubborn sister didn't like being told what to do, she eventually did what she was told.

Birgitte soon found out why she had to ride her bicycle: the tram was blown up by the Danish underground, probably to eliminate quislings (enemy agents). I'm sure innocent Danes must have died along with those who had to be eliminated.

Married women never got sent on dangerous missions. But Mother wasn't married. Since she had never married my father, my sister and I were illegitimate – and didn't count.

Much later, after she died of Alzheimer's, I wondered if my mother had suffered, over so many years, from feelings of guilt. What a burden to have carried on her conscience for the rest of her life! She had taken the Secrecy Oath; as a result, she couldn't talk about any of this, even if she wanted to.

Neither Mother nor Papa ever talked with us about the war. All Mother ever did was drive her Peugeot at excessive speeds and joke about wearing army boots and driving a motorcycle.

While Naomi and I attended boarding schools, was Mother being parachuted into occupied countries? For certain, she fluently spoke six or more languages and possessed the chutzpah that such activities required. And for certain, she worked as a censor of important wartime documents. Records of some wartime activities just were not kept or are not available. Quite conceivably, she might have been given other jobs to do, too. But now that she's gone, I'll never know.

Anything's possible here. When Mother met my stepfather,

did she need a change of identity and a new life? Her pregnancy certainly would provide the secure status of Canadian bride and housewife.

Despite all this "love", I was still insecure. So, when Mother confided that she was getting increasingly depressed and that, if she didn't get a car to drive, she'd probably kill herself, I caved in and gave her money to buy a Peugeot from her good friend Jean Citron. When she took me for a 100 m.p.h. spin in her new sports car, I became motivated enough to trade in my Volkswagen station wagon for a little two-seater Peugeot convertible. Soon the excitement of owning this vehicle made me dream romance could come into my life!

During the Spring of 1971, the movement for an independent Québec grew stronger in the school. The French students and teachers smoked in the hallways, with complete disdain for the English side of the school where smoking was not permitted. They threw garbage and cigarette butts all over the theatre floor. Worst of all, food fights broke out in the cafeteria between the two sides. Slowly but surely, I grew to hate my teaching environment.

Vive Montréal ! Vive le Québec !
Vive le Québec libre !
– Charles De Gaulle, Montréal, Québec, 24 July, 1967

Confident that Harry White, music coordinator for the Montreal Catholic School Commission, would find another job for me, I submitted my resignation in June.

That Summer of 1971, those teaching in Quebec without formal teaching certification were offered the opportunity – through three summer courses at McGill University – to gain a full teaching diploma. My major, of course, would be Music. Meanwhile, I was offered a job teaching music at Holy Names High School, an all-girls school in central Montreal.

I took a bachelor suite at Sutton Place, in Notre Dame de Grace, close to Montreal West and, on weekends, took trips into the Laurentians with chorus girls I met through the Arcadians and Lakeshore Players. We swam in the lakes and gathered at friends' cottages.

Nearly everyone talked about sex. And sex, of course, happened. I didn't date although – through my activities with the Lyric Theatre Society, the Lakeshore Players, and the Arcadians, I became infatuated with several gorgeous women and got involved in petting sessions – some "excruciatingly hot and heavy". Still, I never made the move across that invisible boundary.

I told myself I wanted the right girl, she whom I would marry in sacred union. When girls came up to see my etchings, I showed them my art work! And I explained the memorabilia on my walls from my years with the Hart Singers.

One snowy night, two of the girls from <u>My Fair Lady</u> had to stay overnight at my apartment. I gave them my bed while I slept in the living room on the couch. Knowing they lay naked in my queen size bed, I developed a strong desire to join them.

Well into the night, I heard them whispering and giggling. Maybe they wondered if I was gay. Or still a Brother. In my mind, certainly, I felt like a Brother.

The sexual revolution passed me by.

Often, during Sunday afternoons, I drove alone to the lookout on Mount Royal, where I parked the car and walked to the pond. When I watched happy couples strolling arm in arm or lying together on the grass necking, I was envious. I wished I had a girlfriend to love as my own.

Mount Royal was a busy place on Sundays when the sun shone. Children floated miniature sailboats on the pond. Other children clamoured around the old Italian with the bushy mustache as he ground his barrel organ, sending velvet strains of *Toselli's Serenade* floating across the green grass. Mothers with prams stood listening, or chatted in small groups.

On Mount Royal, the happier the day the lonelier I felt.

During the final two weeks of my first summer in the McGill Diploma in Secondary Education program, the professor paired off the students for a music assignment. He assigned me to work with a woman who sat shyly at the back of the class. Joanne and I had just two weeks to come up with a major paper.

Funny, I don't recall the nature of the assignment any more. I only remember walking with Joanne up Mount Royal that beautiful summer. When I hummed the major theme from Rachmaninoff's 2nd

Piano Concerto, Joanne hummed part of the melody with me. Immediately overcome with excitement and feelings of destiny, I told her, "I'm going to marry you, and we will make beautiful children together."

Poor Joanne. Who was this insane man? When she accepted my invitation to dinner at my apartment, I was so excited, I forgot to prepare a meal. While we laboured on the assignment, I gave her was a fruit cocktail topped with crème de café. Who needed food when here was a feast for the soul?[1]

Joanne told me she was seriously involved with a Dutch fellow named Willhelm, and that she would be going to Holland at the end of the summer to meet his parents. I replied, "Joanne, I love you. I'm going to marry you."

With ruthless logic, I introduced confusion into her otherwise ordered life.

"My father likes Willhelm. He works for the railway."

"But do you love him?"

"I don't know!"

"I love you."

Joanne lived in a small room near the university. During our first fortnight, I bought flowers and chocolates and left them at her door late at night.

Soon she moved to Montreal West to house-sit for some friends off on holidays.

We completed our assignment with an "A". All too soon, classes were over and the love of my life flew off to Holland with her Willhelm, still confused and overwhelmed. Not only did I ask her to write to me from Holland, I informed her I would await her return.

Not long after she departed, I drove alone, with few stops, until I reached Cape Cod. On Nanset Beach, Massachusetts, about as far east as I could go, I sat on the sand and gazed towards Holland. I wondered if Joanne was thinking of me.

The sea was lonely. And I felt lonely.

In front of me, breakers rolled in long crests and tumbled in silver showers. All about me, the low sand dunes rippled with the wind. In reverent response, the coarse, sharp grasses genuflected as my friend, the sun, bloodied the tide with his farewell to the day.

Fishing boats tugged at their moorings with smacks and

spanks. As the far shore settled in for a cozy evening of snuggles and hot drinks by family fires, the lights twinkled on.

Later, in the nearby town, I strolled the fishing wharves, and smelled the dead fish and seaweed. And felt dead myself – without the one who completed me.

Just one day after my arrival, I turned around and drove back towards Montreal. I stopped on the way, near Plattsburgh on Lake Champlain, where I visited overnight with vacationing friends. Then I continued nonstop to Montreal.

I couldn't enjoy myself until I received some kind of word from my love. And I got it! In the Monday mail was a card from Holland: "I miss you".

Now the rest of my holiday would be complete! Almost literally, I floated through the White Mountains and on to Virginia Beach. As Mother had piqued my interest in the books of Edgar Cayce, I visited the Institute constructed in his memory. Perhaps, I imagined, Joanne was the reincarnation of a long lost love of mine from another life. I rationalized that such beliefs did not contradict my Catholic Faith. After all, a mystical attraction drew us together.

I spent the next piece of forever patrolling the sandy beaches, perpetually gazing out to sea.

My return to Montreal became a pilgrimage of expectation. School would be in session. Joanne would be back. All I need do was see her, hold her, and never let her go.

Then the weather changed. Fog rolled in and rested there, thick as pigs' mud, choking my lungs. Freak weather in the midst of summer. Nothing for it; I had to wait for the road to clear. I pulled over to the side of the highway and slept.

Eventually the sun stopped sulking behind the mist. Rolling out from cover, it bathed me in its renewed smile. Nature, having paid its penance in the chilly morning, shouted out in joyful colours, with paint pots full of yellows and greens, reds and oranges, pinks and purples.

My heart turned into a rainbow of happiness.

Joanne taught Music in Ville La Salle; I had begun my new job at Holy Names. Every night my love and I spent hours on the telephone. Every weekend, we went for long drives in the country or walked up Mount Royal. Frequently, I asked Joanne to marry me. Occasionally, she visited Willhelm; how many times, I'll never know.

One night, while we drove out to Senneville, it got very late. All the house lights flicked out. On impulse, I stopped, picked a huge bouquet of hydrangeas from someone's estate garden, and presented them to Joanne. Fighting back tears, she said nothing; she only gazed in wonder at the blossoms in her lap.

About ten weeks after we first met, during one of our marathon telephone conversations, she remarked, "At this rate, we might as well get married." In excitement, I hung up, sped to her little room on the edge of Mount Royal, and presented her with the biggest diamond engagement ring I could afford. (I had set it aside shortly after we first met.) Joanne cried.

That night, we sat up making plans about meeting each other's parents. I told her I would ask her father formally for his daughter's hand. We agreed to get married at Christmas, then spend two weeks on a gorgeous honeymoon.

For the first time, I climbed into bed with a woman – and made love with her. The event was the most beautiful of my life. Here was the woman I wanted to marry. To my mind, her acceptance of my love sanctified the act of sex as the ultimate expression of our love.

The thought of "living in sin" was so far from my mind that I can't recall feeling anything but goodness in the act of lovemaking. I was gentle; she was soft and warm and receptive. This was love fulfilled.

Primitive peoples, the true children of nature and thus of God, accept physical desire as a natural appetite, to be satisfied honestly and fearlessly without any semblance of sin and sly shushings in the night.

Surely, if love is goodness and God is love, then loving another fully and unconditionally can be nothing but good. For the first time in my life, I felt whole and clean and right. I loved and I felt loved.

Joanne's parents lived, with their elder daughter, within walking distance from my apartment at Sutton Square. After Joanne introduced me to her mother and dad, I said, "Perhaps you should sit down." They sat. I held Joanne's hand, showed them the ring, and announced I was deeply in love with their daughter. "I have come to ask for your daughter's hand in marriage."

Smiles and shock followed. "Is this what you want Joanne?"

Joanne looked at me and whispered "Yes."

A confused conversation followed. "What about Willhelm? Marilyn's not married yet. Shouldn't you talk to her?"

I told them we'd like to be married at Christmas break.

"Why so soon? We need more time. ...The Church won't let you marry at Christmas."

Finally, grudgingly, I got the answer I wanted: "Well, you're not children any more."

We went to Senneville next. Everyone was delighted. Mother said she knew, as soon as we walked in, and welcomed Joanne like a daughter. While we drove off after our visit, we could see the girls jumping up and down and hugging.

When we visited Joanne's pastor at St. Ignatius of Loyola Church, he had other ideas. "A wedding at Christmas? Out of the question! Christmas Eve is a time of preparation." So we drove out to Lachine and spoke to my good friend at Resurrection Church, Father Gordon Harris.

For a long time, he spoke about the sacredness and permanence of marriage. Yes, we intended to have children very soon. No, Joanne was not pregnant. At the end, Father Gord decided to obtain permission for us from Joanne's pastor and to talk to us again soon, many times, in fact. He had to be sure we both understood fully what we were getting into. He would also help us prepare for the duties and privileges of married life.

Meantime, because I was in love, my days at Holy Name School were as a rose opening in early summer. Though Sister Superior was very stern [the girls went from class to class, in silence] I effectively began to change this mood. I taught Glee Club in the basement during lunch hour. At the end of our first practice, the girls climbed the stairs singing, "Did I fill the world with love? Did I fill..." One by one the voices stopped.

"Good morning sister!" I smiled and continued singing while I walked to my first class of the afternoon. Yes, I was a rabble-rouser. I also taught several of the Sisters to play guitar.

Every morning I greeted the Sister Superior with cheery greetings: "You look beautiful this morning, Sister." I was sincere. Soon, talking between classes was permitted, though no official pronouncement had been made to change the rule.

As Vatican II started taking effect, a few of the Sisters began wearing clothing other than their habits. The staff cheered up a great deal. Teachers exchanged presents. The Sisters gave me a beautiful Crucifix of the Risen Christ and wished me every happiness for my upcoming wedding.

December 24. Senneville. We drove to church in the family car – excruciatingly slowly. I fidgeted in the back seat. But I needn't have worried. We had to wait an eternity before Joanne's family arrived. Then Joanne came down the aisle to meet me. She was Juliet, with flowers in her hair.

Joanne and I had chosen our own songs and readings. At one point, we held hands and sang, "Make of our hands one hand" from West Side Story. A flamenco guitarist played accompaniment and other instrumental music throughout the appropriate moments of the Mass and Wedding.

During the love ballad, Joanne cried. With a voice quivering with emotion, I completed the last lines alone. "Only death can part us now."

Just a few people were present to witness our wedding, including my friends from Lachine. Afterwards, they showered us with tears and congratulations.

My sister, Louise, was in the hospital delivering a son. And my aunties from Quebec were not invited. (Both sets of parents laid down conditions for the wedding reception which was to be held at Joanne's family home. Because of space restrictions, our guest list was limited.) The wedding dinner was a beef Stroganoff cooked by Joanne's mom. Unfortunately, Joanne's sister threw a tantrum and locked herself in her room, after tossing off "We all know why you had to get married!" Joanne's attempts to placate her didn't work. Though she told her mother to give her bouquet to her sister, the bouquet remained wilting on the kitchen table a fortnight later.

Vic, Louise's husband, arranged a honeymoon in the Bahamas for us. Mother and Papa drove us to the airport.

On Christmas morning, we attended mass at a little church where little black altar boys stuck their tongues out at each other. During the first week, we took a variety of tours. A couple of times, we got dropped off on deserted beaches. On one such beach, I convinced Joanne to skinny dip with me. We were naked in the ocean, when a group of little black girls, accompanied by white-clad nuns, walked along the beach. Little fish nibbled at our privates. As soon as decorum allowed, I made a mad dash for shore and retrieved our swim suits. That night, suffering serious sunburn, I could only lie face down on top of the bed. Suddenly Joanne jumped up with a scream. A gecko was climbing up the wall. For the first time, I realized she was terrified of reptiles. All reptiles. So, in great pain, I picked up the little creature and carefully dropped it from the balcony into the bushes below.

We returned to teaching and enjoyed our happy new existence, cozy in our little apartment in Sutton Square, not far from Joanne's parents. Customarily, I drove Joanne to school, then headed to my own school, in the opposite direction.

During the 1970-71 school year, Harry White and I attended many meetings in Quebec City developing a music program for the Quebec secondary schools. I had also written a detailed paper on the use of creativity in the classroom which was published in part in an educational magazine.

Towards the end of the school year, Harry White approached me to develop and teach a special program for one of the inner-city schools. "Operation Renewal" involving a fusion of Drama, Music, and Art. The program would provide special help for new Canadians with mother tongues other than French or English. Classes would run at the new, open-area St. Patrick's Elementary School, in Montreal's inner city.

One of my projects at St. Patrick's was to get all the classes to contribute to a huge mural for the Department of Education in Quebec City. With my help, the children depicted some of their misconceptions learned in the Religion program. The children drew many pictures including "The flight into Egypt with Pontius the Pilot", "Our four bears in the desert", "John the blacksmith", and "Michael, the dark angel". A vicious-looking bird was labeled "Deliver us from Eagles". We also had "Blessed art thou a Monk Swimming", a ghostly Casper with a halo called "the Holy Ghost", and a bearded Father bearing the inscription "Harold be thy name". The art piece, labeled in both languages, was displayed in the Religious Education Office.

December 1972, Joanne was pregnant. We lived in a small upper duplex in Ville La Salle to be close to Joanne's school. Our landlady was an alcoholic single mother with a teen-age son. Over and over, she played "Please Release Me, Let Me Go". Desperate for beer, she broke the lock on our apartment door and claimed we had been broken into. Since only beer was missing, we suspected she was the culprit.

During my time at St. Pat's, the Front de Libération Québecois (F.L.Q.) trained openly in the street behind the school. A group of these ruffians, supported by students from a local junior college (known in Quebec as CEGEP), decided to block our noon-hour kindergarten changeover. Tiny children, just out of their cocoons, still fuzzy, moist, and squirmy, were being stopped from running to waiting mums and dads by a gang of screaming oafs. As a result. none of us could leave or enter the school. Soon the police arrived. When one child ran towards his father, a demonstrator came forward swinging a chain. The father grabbed the chain and a scuffle ensued. The father was arrested.

The Separatists demanded that all new Canadians, moving to Quebec, attend school in the French language only. In the suburb of Pierrefonds, marching demonstrators threw bricks through the windows of the homes of Anglophones and some new Canadians.

That December, because all my studies were from English language institutions, I was declassified and my salary cut. The fact that I was fluently bilingual and had taught in both languages had no bearing.

Joanne, on the other hand, did not speak French. However, her degree came from Marianappolis College, which was affiliated with l'Université de Montréal. She, therefore, was exempted from Bill 101. Since I taught in the Catholic schools, I was represented by the French teachers' union (the C.E.Q.) That union was anxious to see English teachers leave; thus they gave no protection to English Catholic teachers.

Many teachers moved to Ontario. I had fond remembrances of B.C. and Joanne had spent many happy years as a child in Nelson, B.C., so we decided to move to the West Coast, despite protestation from both our families.

I wrote letters of application to school districts on the B.C.

coast, including Vancouver Island, stating that I would be available for interviews during the Easter break. Joanne would take a leave from teaching.

On the last day of class , we flew to B.C. and stayed with Joanne's Uncle Walter and Aunt Thelma in Victoria. Walter was surprised I was not the "hippy bum" he had heard about.

We drove to schools all over Vancouver Island. Everybody was kind and welcoming, and the students especially polite. They opened doors for us and escorted us to sympathetic principals. Applying as a Music Specialist who also could teach French and Drama, I stated willingness to do anything to move to the West Coast. I determined to move to B.C. even if I had to pick fruit in the Okanagan.

The sun shone every day of our visit. We had come to a green paradise!

All too soon, we had to fly back to Dorval. The mercury had dropped, and a vengeful wind howled. Our Peugeot sat in the airport parking lot covered in ice. Though I managed to get the car started and chipped the ice from the windows, the frozen heater stubbornly refused to work. When we got to Ville La Salle, cold and miserable, the door to our apartment wouldn't open and "Madame" was not in. So I drove to Montreal West, left Joanne with her parents, and took the car to Sutton Place where I waited for it to thaw out in the garage.

Finally, when the ice blocking the heater ducts melted, I drove back to our apartment. Madame was home at last. She informed me that she had to replace the lock whilst we were away. She gave me a new key, I let myself in, and turned on the oil heater. Then I returned to pick up Joanne.

After our return, the weather wasn't all that was vengeful. Joanne's parents had spoken with my parents about our wish to get away, We were being very selfish. They wouldn't get to know their new grandchild. We placated them by promising to spend part of the summer with each family.

In late Spring, I was admitted to Jewish General Hospital with a ruptured hernia. While there, hospital support staff belonging to the powerful Quebec Labour Union, went on strike. At one point, the strikers cut part of the hospital's power supply. Patients spent several anxious hours in the dark, with no meals. Even some of the emergency power was cut. Doctors and nurses were blocked from entering or leaving and nurses unable to perform their duties. Visitors were neither permitted to enter nor to communicate with patients.

During this same strike, the school janitors went off the job.

Quebec was still smarting from the effects of F.L.Q. terrorism, including kidnapping and murder, and the subsequent War Measures Act of 1970. As a result, the English of Montreal were subjected to bitter resentment, even hatred, by many francophones.

As she did not yet drive, Joanne was dependent on buses while I was in hospital. Her bus stopped a short distance from her school in Ville La Salle where she was elbowed off the sidewalk by a picketing maintenance worker. The police did nothing but look on in amusement. We were increasingly anxious to leave Quebec.

On May 1st, moving day in Quebec, we gave up our apartment and moved to my parents' home in Senneville for the next six weeks of school. Mother had grown cold towards us both, and Joanne spent hours crying in our room.

I paid my parents for our room-and-board, and Joanne resented that, even though we also paid the same while staying with her parents. Meanwhile, Joanne needed special foods which she placed in the fridge with labels. This caused further tension.

I felt torn between mother and wife. Usually, Joanne won out. I was afraid of displeasing Mother. To move out at that time would have made matters worse as I had promised both my parents and Joanne's that we'd spend time with both families before moving to B.C.. Furthermore, we had already sold our few furnishings. We really were at the mercy of both angry families.

When the school term finished, we moved to Montreal West to live with Joanne's parents. Every day, we suffocated in summer school classes; every evening and on weekends, we wrote assignments and studied for exams.

At night, in the privacy of our bedroom, I wanted to share the last moments of the day in physical contact with Joanne. But the bed, with its protesting iron springs, would broadcast our every move. This terrified Joanne. We couldn't be intimate.

It was Sunday afternoon. The heat of the day had risen to a brick-red peak. Like a steady hum in the still air, a steaming sauna, it enveloped the house. Stubbornly refusing to find the open window, a fly buzzed angrily between the ceiling and the screen door.

I perched before my study notes, elbows glued to the sticky kitchen table, sweat trickling down my back to soak the elastic on my shorts. Joanne sat opposite, swollen and uncomfortable. The two of us struggled to complete our final assignment for the Summer Session at McGill and to prepare for the next day's exam. Joanne's sister, Marilyn, droned on at the phone in the hallway. I called out to her, "Marilyn, do you think we could all share that fan you've got going in you room? You're down here anyway." She didn't answer. Maybe she didn't hear me.

Ten minutes later, Marilyn entered the kitchen and pulled out the chair beside Joanne. "I've invited Aunt Evelyn to supper. You'll have to put that stuff away and start cooking."

"What?" I almost shouted. "You invited her. You bloody well cook the supper. We've got too much ..."

Marilyn faced me, nearly nose to nose, and growled through clenched teeth. "Mind your own business. I'm talking to my sister."

"Please, Marilyn," Joanne said calmly. "We've got to get this finished."

"No!" Marilyn shouted. "You have to cook supper. You know I'm not well." Her voice rose to a shrill whining crescendo, then shattered like slivers of glass in my ears.

"Well, then. You shouldn't have invited Aunty Evelyn. You certainly didn't check with me." Joanne was surprisingly calm.

Her face bloated with temper, Marilyn pushed the chair into the table. It squealed and thumped unhappily. "Get your junk off the kitchen table," she hissed, spittle flying everywhere. Then she pushed Joanne's papers onto the floor.

At this point, I jumped to my feet. "Oh, Marilyn, for Christ's sake, will you fuck off and leave us alone?"

Marilyn screamed as if sliced with a knife. She tore down the hall and out through the front door. Running pell-mell down the city street, she screamed again and again, long and piercing. Murder had been done. Blood spattered the kitchen walls.

"He told me to fuck off! He told me to fuck off!"

Neighbours opened their front doors and windows. "Poor Marilyn." Someone walked out and took her in.

When Joanne's parents returned from their bridge club, they told me what they thought of me. My mother-in-law, her voice cracking into splinters of indignation, opined, "You are absolutely disgusting, treating poor, sick Marilyn in such an unchristian way."

With a grimace of disgust, Joanne's father shook his head at me. "Filthy, filthy mouth." His voice sounded like a burnt, breaking twig, brittle and dry.

Though shaking, I was unrepentant.

Where did you come from, baby dear?
Out of the everywhere into here.
– George MacDonald

At last, Monday August 6th. It was time for our final exam. Though Joanne was due at any moment, she was not excused from writing if she wanted her certificate. Labour pains started in earnest while she was still plugging away. She had barely finished the last question before I rushed her to the hospital. Even then, I had to argue with the exam supervisor who said it was too early for us to leave the room. Often authority can be damned inflexible.

I had taken the prenatal classes with my wife. So I dressed in a hospital gown and got ready to assist. Joanne's labour was long and difficult, and I huffed and puffed with her for several exhausting hours. At last, a tiny head appeared, elongated from the process. In horror, I thought the baby was Mongoloid. But I kept my fear well hidden. As soon as I saw the baby, I told Joanne with tears of joy, "It's Heidi!" (Mindful of the Rocky Mountains, beyond which we would soon live, we had decided weeks ahead to call our first two by the Swiss names Hans and Heidi.)

I telephoned both families to tell them the good news. They had a granddaughter, Heidi Anne. Mother decided not to come to the hospital. "Why would I want to visit a baby I'll never get to hold?" I had difficulty understanding her bitterness. I took my little daughter, cradled her in my arms, and sang, "My little girl, soft and sweet, as peaches and cream is she..." Heidi smiled. Joanne's mother said it was gas pains. But I knew different.

From all my applications to teach in B.C., I received just one offer. I would have to report to the west coast and sign my contract prior to August 15th. This meant leaving before the end of the week and driving west, with whatever belongings remained. Joanne would fly out as soon as it was safe for the baby.

I drove out to my parents to say my good-byes and to ask sheepishly to borrow a few dollars until I could get settled in my new job. I was turned down. "We just do not have any money at present. But do enjoy your trip."

As I departed, I noticed the new dishwasher waiting to be installed. I felt cheated and angry. I hadn't asked for a gift, merely for a loan. But Mother was angry that we were leaving with her new granddaughter. The rift never healed.

* * * * * * * *

[1] *What was it about this one person that caused me to fall so insanely in love? Why was I so persistent, not giving her time to make up her own mind?*

Here was a beautiful woman so different from my mother. Joanne was shy, reserved, non threatening. She appeared to be neither aggressive nor domineering. I felt safe and comfortable.

At the same time, she was obviously an achiever. She loved music and dressed well. She was a teacher, therefore intelligent – educated.

Of all the women I'd met since leaving the Brothers, Joanne was the first I could envision spending the rest of my life with.

I would be the strong one. With my new positive self-image, I would protect her and help her develop her own self-confidence. Where I sensed sadness, I would make her happy. I longed for love. Here she was.

When Joanne didn't fall in love with me, I had to work desperately to convince her and make her love me. I couldn't let her go.

Chapter Eighteen
New Horizons

> *Home is a name, a word, it is a strong one;*
> *stronger than magician ever spoke, or spirit*
> *ever answered to, in the strongest conjuration.*
> *– Charles Dickens , Martin Chuzzlewit, ch. 35*

Early Friday morning, August 10th, I packed the little Peugeot two-seater until it resembled a Norris cartoon from The Vancouver Sun. After pushing and prodding some of our meager belongings into every imaginable niche and cranny around the driver's seat, I piled up the rest until I could no longer use the car's canvas top. To protect everything from the elements, I had to rely upon an ill-fitting tarp, one corner or another destined to flap at fellow motorists until Vancouver.

I had just four days to travel almost three thousand miles (4800 kilometers). I was leaving Mother once again. This time I would begin a new life with my new family. No longer Mama's boy but father, husband, lover. Perhaps.

Almost dusk on day two, hot and sweaty, I stopped for a dip in a warm, shallow pond just off the road. Dug around in my gear. No luck: Couldn't find my bathing suit. Trees masked much of the pond from the highway. I skinny dipped while a brace of geese winged their way across the flaming sky. Then the sound of young voices. Quickly, I dried off beside the car. A busload of campers pulled up, hooting and whistling.

In the clear night, I stopped to stretch. Gazing up at the expanse of stars, I allowed my imagination to float freely through time and space. The same stars that looked down upon me looked down upon the two loves of my life in Montreal West.

"Lord, keep them safe this night."
A dog barked "Amen!"

Day three. At the crest of a rolling hill, I watched the world gradually open up as light broke through, harbinger of another scorching day. A short distance ahead, a dusty road led to a small grove of trees and a couple of picnic tables. I pulled over, turned off the ignition, and got out to stretch. A few lights still twinkled in far-off farmhouses.

Body ached. Temples throbbed. Eyes burned for want of sleep. I got back into the car, drove to the grove of trees, yanked my sleeping bag out of the jumble of luggage, spread it out on the stubble beside the picnic table, and stretched out, face down. Immediately, I fell asleep.

Several hours later, I awoke, with the sun almost directly above my head. Nostrils dry with the heat; body hot, heavy, and stiff. If it weren't for the glare, I would've slept most of the day.

At the edge of the grove of trees, a deer glanced up from her grazing, watched me shake out my sleeping bag and fold it, and nonchalantly resumed its tugging at the tufts of low bush.

In Saskachewan, the sun turned the highway into a liquid, rippling mirage. My eyes burned – visual indigestion.

Then, "Thump, thump, thump."

To change a tire, I had to unload nearly everything while the sun beat down upon me with white hot blows. Huge trucks whizzed by. A colony of inquisitive gophers chattered at me from a nearby hillock.

Job done, dripping with perspiration, I pulled out a can of warm pop, leaned against the car, and contemplated the countryside. Lonely stands of scrubby trees panted for rain. The skies heaved. Flickers of lightning teased the parched prairie.

In the mountains at last, the little Peugeot puffed up steep inclines, summer traffic honking at her tail. She sang down precipitous stretches of open highway, only to join conga lines, bumper to bumper holiday campers. When I'd almost despaired, we reached Hope. Two hours to go. The weather had been perfect.

Oops! I'd forgotten Murphy's Law! Rain! And more rain. In the Frazer Valley, motorists flew past and drenched me in their spray.

Just before noon on Tuesday, August 14th, 1973, mere

hours before the deadline, I signed a teaching contract to teach at North Delta Secondary School. I was to report to my new principal, the following morning. As I departed, he observed, "You look as if you've just come in from the Klondike!" My face was scarlet, and my beard bushy and windblown.

A week later, Joanne arrived with tiny Heidi.

Until my first paycheque, Joanne and I couldn't look for a home of our own. I commuted from Richmond where we stayed with Joanne's Aunt Rose.

In early October, Joanne and I began looking at rental housing. We had no furniture, no curtains, nothing. Only a few eating utensils. On the strength of my teaching contract, I obtained a bank loan for furnishings.

Several teachers were discussing investments. Real estate was rapidly increasing in value. It would be advisable to buy rather than rent. All I needed was the down payment.

We had looked at several ugly rental properties. Then the agent showed us a house not far from the school, priced at forty-nine thousand. With a down payment of five thousand, it could be ours.

Back at the bank, I convinced the loans manager that I could manage both loan payments and a reasonable mortgage.

The house had no appliances. Worse, it needed cleaning, repairs, and a good paint job. Still, it gave us a roof. And it was ours!

After several days of scrubbing and carpet cleaning, we moved in mid October, taped newspaper to the windows, and slept on the floor in sleeping bags. Joanne cooked on a camp stove and stored perishables in our camping cooler. We cadged ice from our neighbours, and fruit and vegetables from Aunt Rose. And we bought Emphelac (baby formula) on credit. Heidi slept in a plastic bath tub until my principal provided a crib his grandchildren had outgrown.

In November, I bought a bed, fridge, stove, an unfinished table, and four chairs – second hand. Later, I bought a second hand clothes washer. Meanwhile, I laundered in the basement sink and hung rows of diapers on a clothesline, stretched across the muddy back yard.

Our back yard was solid clay with sparse patches of grass.

Undaunted, I bought a rake and garden spade. A neighbour gave me an old wheelbarrow. I collected bags of leaves which I spread over the entire ground surface and dug in row by row. The following spring, I marked off a couple of sunny areas for vegetable and flower gardens. In the rest of the yard, I raked, spread grass seed, and raked again.

Inside the house, I sanded, painted, and built an extra room in the basement.

The Delta School Board had built a "state of the Art" theatre auditorium in South Delta and was completing a similar facility at North Delta Senior Secondary School. The theatre would be available to the community when not in specific use by the school. My job was to organize Theatre classes and build up a Theatre Arts program.

After touring the South Delta Auditorium, I encountered potential problems. I suggested modifications which could still be made without adding to construction costs. First, I asked for a covered pit which could be opened for musicals. The principal told me the area under the stage was to be filled with sand. Second, the wing curtains "legs" at South Delta were fixed. I asked for moveable wings. That, too, was turned down.

My greatest concern regarded lighting. Stage lights were already being set to permanent positions, with reflective lamps containing bulbs of red, blue and yellow – primary colours for pigment. One of the teachers, an electrician in his spare time, was acting as lighting consultant.

It would take a couple of years to convince the authorities that we needed moveable lamps on bars that could be lowered and that frames could hold red, green, and amber gels to produce a multitude of interesting effects. As for front lighting, no allowance had been made to install them – ever. The administration was intransigent, so arguments got me nowhere. I was ordered to stay away from the auditorium until it was ready for use.

Good teaching is one-fourth preparation
and three-fourths theater.
- Gail Godwin

I taught my first semester drama class in a small room in the school basement. We built a puppet theatre and worked on voice, movement, and creative dramatics. We produced a series of puppet shows on traffic safety for elementary school children.

Using a hand-held camera, we produced a video, "This is Your School". The film, complete with sound-over, began as almost the entire staff appeared to arrive in one Volkswagen. A skeleton office staff was on hand as – you guessed it – skeletons. The principal, obliged by hiding in a cupboard, to be caught smoking a cigarette. The usual lunch room hubbub was accompanied by appropriate barnyard sound effects. The school band played "Twinkle, Twinkle Little Star", off-key of course. Most teachers and students were very cooperative when we asked to film them in ridiculous situations. We aired the tape in the school cafeteria during lunch for two days running.

Our first musical production, <u>Oklahoma</u>, was rehearsed and performed on the gymnasium stage. During rehearsals, we dodged basketballs, put up with the blare of piped music, and tolerated cheerleader practices.

Home was close enough that I could return for lunch most days. Joanne, pregnant with our second child, couldn't stand the smell of dirty diapers, so I'd change Heidi first thing in the morning and, when I could get home, just before lunch. Then I picked her up right after school and took her to rehearsals, giving Joanne a chance to rest. The girls, and some boys in my Drama club, were fantastic baby-sitters.

During that first semester, I also taught French 11. The vice principal, whose mother tongue was French, attended one of my classes. During his forty-minute visit, not one word of English was spoken. We sang French-Canadian folk songs and conversed in small groups about hockey and parties. I went from group to group, helping in pronunciation, and suggesting words where needed.

We covered the required curriculum, but in French only. Any translation needed was done as homework, from the required text. Although mine was the only French class conducted entirely in that language, it was the only French that I ever taught at N.D.S.S. As often happened throughout my career as a teacher, there were two ways to do things: my way and the "correct" way. I stubbornly did things my way and paid the penalty, not because I taught French as French only, but for my "free and easy" approach to discipline.

I enjoyed my classes immensely. The head of the Art Department was a super teacher who believed in experimentation. My students and I painted with melted wax crayon applied with old electric irons. Some days, when the class occurred during fourth period, we took paints and sketch pads to the river to draw and paint boats and old buildings. Other times, we scattered about the school to observe perspective, tone, and shade. Those who chose to skip class still had to find ways to complete their portfolios.

Some, who initially had taken Art 11 as an easy elective, developed an appreciation for drawing and painting as their own skills developed. Of course, there were always a few who were just about impossible to win over. Not everyone got a passing grade.

With the success of <u>Oklahoma</u>, I had full Stagecraft 11, Acting 11, and Acting 12 classes in the second semester. My fourth class was Art 11. I felt fulfilled on every front.

By the beginning of the second year, the demand rose enough to allow me to teach full time Theatre. I began to integrate Writing and Directing students with Acting 11 and 12 classes as well as with Stagecraft 11 and 12. As a body, we worked on main stage productions, student scenes, student productions, fashion shows, classical plays, and musicals.

On the eve of Thanksgiving Day, 1974, I rushed next door to ask our neighbour to baby-sit Heidi. She came over in her dressing gown. Then I drove Joanne, emergency flashers blinking, through red lights, pausing every so often for her contractions. After accidentally missing the Emergency Entrance twice, we finally arrived at the Maternity Ward at Surrey Memorial Hospital.

I parked the car, scrubbed up, donned the green gown and mask, and assisted in the delivery of our second child. The nurse was so nervous she dropped the bottle of intravenous fluid. The doctor arrived just in time to deliver Christopher Ben, named to honour the patron of travellers who had kept me safe during my drive across Canada

Christopher led the chorus amongst the newborns. What a

fine voice! Aunt Rose came over to help with Heidi while I telephoned Montreal and Senneville to announce the good news.

Each day, as soon as classes ended, I dashed home, changed diapers, picked up two babies, and brought them with me to rehearsals. Heidi and Chris became "stage brats" from their earliest moments. I had no end of willing and capable sitters. My children were brought up with literary classics, Shakespeare, Broadway musicals, and children's theatre. They got to take part in productions when toddlers and young children were required.

Students and I scrounged lumber from school building sites and built enormous sets. The stage was a giant canvas, ready to be filled with form and colour. I taught future directors and actors to use every area and level possible. We planned with miniature models of balsa and cardboard. Often learning as I taught, I helped young thespians to perform magic with lights and make-up and to gain experience in making their own decisions about costume colours and stage movement.

The set for <u>A Midsummer Night's Dream</u> comprised a huge discarded fishing net, obtained from the fisherman father of one of the students. We stretched that net to fill the entire proscenium. Another student provided plastic flowers and greenery from a Zellers where she worked part time. Lighting helped make the set magical. Characters entered and exited, seeming to appear from nowhere.

Two years later, we used the same netting and plastic flowers for <u>Romeo and Juliet</u>. Romeo climbed confidently amongst greenery and roses.

For <u>Man of LaMancha</u>, we built a full-size dungeon with steps leading up to a clanging gate that fell shut with a heavy roll of chains, as a prisoner tumbled down to the convicts below. Rats scurried as lights came up on the opening scene while inmates scratched for lice or tussled over bits of rag and crusts of bread.

We made all sets and costumes with scrounged materials and rampant imagination. Stagecraft became an exciting part of the school's Theatre Arts program.

To raise money for our productions, we showed Disney movies on Saturday afternoons, having to split proceeds with the Physical Education Department. This kept me on the good side of the

Phys. Ed. teachers and scored brownie points with school administration. Sports always took pride of place. In one school Annual, I had the Drama Club pose as a soccer team; the picture was included with school sports teams.

Shortly after Christopher was born, I taught Joanne to drive. When she had developed enough confidence to drive on her own, she became a teacher on call for Delta and Surrey. Not only did her work get her out of her doldrums, she regained self-esteem at being back among professionals.

Joanne taught French in junior high schools. But she liked teaching Home Economics best, so she began taking Home Economics courses at U. B. C. during summer sessions. She took a room on campus while I stayed at home with the children. She hoped for a full time teaching job.

We became involved with St. Bernadette's Parish in Surrey, taking on a children's choir and the parish youth group. For both groups, we used our basement rumpus room.

In 1980, we found a larger house, a ten minute drive from North Delta, in Sunshine Hills, a much more upscale neighbourhood. After clearing a number of overshadowing alder trees, I built a shallow pond and waterfalls in what was to become the back garden and play area. When Joanne's parents came to visit, her dad helped me construct a playhouse. A little later, I built a large sandbox. We had enough alder firewood to keep us warm for years to come.

Life was beautiful. My past was packed carefully away; childhood trauma banished to the deepest recesses of my subconscious. I could live on, forever basking in my successes. Teacher, father, husband.

Chapter Nineteen
Poems From the Past

And I will make thee beds of roses
And a thousand fragrant posies
– Christopher Marlowe

The demands of the Church upon our lives grew. Of those, the most significant turned out to be Marriage Encounter.

One day in 1974, a couple, whose children were members of our Youth Group, invited us to a Marriage Encounter Weekend. Baby sitting was arranged free of charge.

The "weekend" was presented by three team couples and a priest. The lead couple were a dynamic husband and wife from Seattle. I liked the content of their presentations, their deep introspection, and their ability to find out how the various marriage partners felt.

Emotions out in the open, I got swept away with enthusiastic participation and freely shared my feelings with the entire group. On Sunday night, the team couples invited Joanne and me to join the organization as another team couple.

At this point, a little background is needed. A few months before, I had been diagnosed with skin cancer which required two weeks of radiation treatment on both shoulders. Since my weight had gone down to about 115 pounds, Joanne was convinced my days were numbered. I was more optimistic. We kept the news to ourselves – not to upset my mother.[1]

Marriage Encounter is a crash course in communications for married couples. The weekend, because of its strong Roman Catholic perspective, also renews the faith for many.

When Joanne and I started working as team members, we wrote and rewrote presentations. Many nights, I stayed up typing until it was almost time to leave for school. Not only did I act as typist, I did much of Joanne's writing as well. Joanne had been a shy person. Marriage Encounter began to bring out her leadership qualities. Before long, we became a lead team couple. We also looked after scheduling for B.C and Alberta.

Within two years, we had helped to present twenty-one

"Weekends". Frequently, we rewrote our talks, always keeping the presentations fresh. We work shopped other couple's talks, too. While we spent weekends away, Heidi and Chris became part of many families.

Beautiful things happened in Marriage Encounter. The most outstanding occurred one Friday afternoon, while we were driving in our Peugeot to Seattle with Father Tom Nicholson. Our engine blew a gasket, and we had to pull over to the side of the highway. "Grab your bags!" said Father Tom. Immediately, he stuck out his thumb, and a car stopped. Our Good Samaritan helped push the Peugeot further onto the side of the I-5 and drove us to his farm. With no more than a few words, he asked for the key to our car and told us to take his vehicle until Sunday night. We arrived in good time to present the Weekend.

On Sunday night, when we returned to the man's farm near Bellingham, the replacement gasket had not yet been found. Again, the Good Samaritan stepped in to help: "Take my car and call me at this number midweek. We'll see what we can do." It turned out the man who helped us – and his wife – had "made" (attended) the Marriage Encounter weekend and felt its healing power.

On another occasion, Joanne and I were invited to a Marriage Encounter Convention in Los Angeles. While we were there, we met a couple who lived in Beverly Hills. They invited us to fly down with our children during the 1980 spring break. We did – and had a wonderful five days with them. Not only did we attend every attraction at Disneyland, our host drove Joanne and me around Los Angeles, over a maze of twisting five-lane highways, to Hugh Heffner's Playboy Club and other adult attractions. He was a professional gambler. Broke on one occasion, he took twenty dollars and left us in his car for under half an hour, while he turned the twenty into several hundred.

Apart from air pollution and horrendous traffic, I enjoyed our visit.

Since my sojourn there in the early fifties, Los Angeles had changed. We arrived by air, poisoned air. As the plane began its approach for landing, I saw a straight line of thick, grey fog ... no, smog. One huge blanket of it.

In many places in the downtown core, because the acid air

had killed trees, flowers, and grass, plastic imitations had been put in. When we stopped for lunch we sat in plastic chairs at a plastic table, ate cardboard sandwiches tightly enshrouded in plastic wrap, and drank plastic coffee from styrofoam mugs.

Like zombies in oversized sunglasses, plastic people in plastic shirts, shoes, and slacks killed their feet on concrete slabs beneath plastic palm trees. Even our host's teenage daughter wore a plastic see-through dress – the latest adolescent rage in Beverly Hills.

Huge sunglasses. And so little sun. Angeleños wear sunglasses not to avoid the glare of the sun but to avoid the plague of the smog, which makes the eyes water copiously.

Broken hearts and hangovers may also be reasons for watery eyes, of course. But in Los Angeles, what with all the sunglasses, how was one to know?

Despite the love all around us, especially with the Marriage Encounter community, our own relationship was strained. Without consciously acknowledging the implications of what I was doing, I desperately attempted to make things right, in many different ways.

It was frustrating. Though I redoubled my endeavours to keep the house clean, though I increased my efforts in the kitchen, though I did all the laundry, Joanne seldom expressed satisfaction.

Invariably, she found dust and dirt I'd missed. Worse, I shrank sweaters, washed the spring out of elastic waist bands, left streaks on newly washed drinking glasses, and overlooked grease in hidden corners of the kitchen.

I took to buying flowers for no particular reason, but to say "I love you". Almost daily, I made it a point to tell my wife, "I love you". But now she no longer returned my endearments. Instead, she only said a dreary, "I know". This drove me to renewed, near-desperate efforts to please her, to rekindle the fire of her affections.

Surely, I hoped – prayed – since we helped so many other couples, God would not permit our own marriage to wither and die.[2]

Meanwhile, Joanne had been supply teaching. In September, 1984, she received a full-time position, teaching Foods and French in our friend Tom's secondary school in Surrey.

Eventually, the time came for a checkup of my skin condition. Doctors were amazed. I had been too busy to think about being ill. My weight had come back up to about 155 lbs. I felt healthy. Apart from the occasional bit of light surgery – and with my new awareness the dangers of being out in the sun without full protection – cancer became the furthest thing from my mind.

In 1982, our priest friend from Marriage Encounter, Father Tom, planned to combine a trip to Rome with a visit to his sister in Northern Ireland. As he had been a lawyer before entering the priesthood in Vancouver, he knew how to access documents and investigate legal matters. So, when he asked if he could do anything for us during his trip, Joanne replied, "Father Tom, could you locate Ben's dad?"

"Of course", he replied. "Jot down his address and phone number for me."

I explained that my father had been "killed" in North Africa, that the British Red Cross had been unable to find any trace of him, and that he had worked at <u>The London Times</u> before going to Africa in the early thirties. That's all I knew. As far as I was concerned, he was buried somewhere in the deserts of North Africa and long forgotten. Yet I felt a slight glimmer. Maybe, just maybe...

Six weeks later, Father Tom returned to Vancouver. When he telephoned me, he asked me if I were sitting down. In London, he looked up the name Nuttall-Smith in the telephone directory and found one John Nuttall-Smith, Jr., living in London. He telephoned and left several messages. Then, receiving no reply, he travelled on to Rome. On his way to Ireland, he tried again. Still, no reply. Finally, with one day left before returning to Canada, he called once more – and was successful. My cousin, John Nuttall-Smith, answered the phone! When Father Tom asked him about my father, his response was immediate: "Poor Uncle Freddie! He's a Franciscan Friar in East London."

Father Tom got the number from my cousin, telephoned the friary, and was told: "Brother Frederick is in bed. Could I take a message?"

Father Tom explained the situation and promised to telephone back the next morning, just before his trip to Heathrow

Airport.

The next morning he talked to my father! The chat was friendly and emotional. "Ben, his voice is identical to yours. I thought I was talking to you."

Father Tom had called me from Vancouver International Airport.

He told me the most amazing news of my life! Tears streamed down my cheeks. My heart beat so fast I thought it'd explode. Joanne put her hand on my shoulder. It couldn't be. It just couldn't be. The many lost years streamed back. Where had he been? What had kept us apart so long? Why had he stayed away?

Almost in a whisper, I asked Father Tom, "Could you please come over?" Within the hour, our good friend knocked on our door. We had a long, wonderful talk.

I wrote my father a lengthy letter. Almost right away, he replied. His handwriting was shaky and hard to decipher.

We made plans to visit the following summer. We were invited to stay at my Uncle John's estate in Essex. Meanwhile, I sent poetry and pictures of Joanne and the two children, told him about my years with the Christian Brothers, that Naomi had died of cancer, and about his grandson, Naomi's child, Fred.

We were excited about the coming trip. Having rediscovered a piece of myself, and after conferring with Joanne, I applied to have our names officially changed to Nuttall-Smith.

We met my cousin Jan, who lived a Bohemian lifestyle near Parksville on Vancouver Island. Jan's father, my Uncle John, had been a pediatrician in Nanaimo for years. In all the time I served at Naden, I never had the wildest idea that an uncle lived so close to me. In fact, not only did I have a cousin Jan living in Parksville, I had six uncles, one aunt, and many cousins. But the greatest surprise of all was that I had a sister, Anna, only a year and two thirds older than myself.

Anna is both my sister and my cousin. Her father was my uncle George Alexander in New Zealand and Mother's first husband. Her mother – my mother – had run off to Africa with my father, Freddie, while Anna Marie Louise remained with granny and grandpa Nuttall-Smith, nurse Nollie Holk, from Denmark, and her father, my Uncle George Alexander, in a large house in Oxford.

Mother once told me how, in her late teens, she got permission to attend art school in London. There she met Anna's father, my uncle George Alexander. Nine boys vied for the attention of this newfound beauty. But George Alexander (Alex) caught her eye.

The couple were wed at St. Ansgar's Church in Copenhagen in September, 1929. But, unfortunately for him, George had a withered leg. Since young Alice found this repulsive, (so she told me) she soon began to dislike the leg's owner.

Uncles in England told me the rest.

Shortly after Anna was born, in fact, while she was being nursed by Nollie Holk, George's younger brother, a reporter for _The London Times_, took a shine to his sister-in-law. In short order, my mother and father ran off to Africa. (Freddie had been newly assigned to the British diplomatic corps in Tanganyika Territory.)

Quite literally, I was born on safari. My birth was registered in the town of Tabora, only shortly before Naomi was due. Consequent to my mother's second pregnancy, Freddie was reassigned back to London. In January, 1934, George divorced my mother. As for Anna, my grandparents held on to her. Mother told me she was only permitted to see her daughter on occasion and that she was never permitted to hold her. What a terrible thing to happen to a mother!

Yet my parents weren't the only sinners. When I dug into the matter, it soon became apparent that several of the boys in the Nuttall-Smith family had run off with one another's wives.

To sum it all up, my grandfather, the Reverend George Nuttall-Smith, B.A., was the grandson of another Reverend George Nuttall Smith (no hyphen), all originally High Anglicans from Glasshouse, just outside Dublin in Ireland. The family, descended from Puritans, were awarded Glasshouse for their service to Cromwell during the suppression of the Irish rebellion in 1649-1650.

Although the Puritans were typified by moral severity, the actual Puritans of history were the radicals and revolutionaries of their era, not conservatives or fundamentalists. Throughout their early history, in fact, they offered hatred and destruction, and very little peace, love, wisdom, and humility. Under the rule of Oliver Cromwell, this proved to be especially true.

My Uncle Pat told me that their father was severe and that my father was afraid of him. Having fathered seven sons and one daughter, my grandfather was quoted as having declared that God's one mistake was having allowed humankind to take part in creation. Perhaps he had to be severe to control so many boys. Whether or not his severity came from Puritan roots, I wasn't told.

More Catholic than Anglican, my grandfather wrote and published _The Chronicles of a Puritan Family in Ireland_ as well as a book of religious poetry. [3]

Our official change of name came through just before Christmas, 1982; immediately we applied for passports. We arranged to leave as soon as school let out at the end of June.

My cousin Jan suggested that we take toilet paper, since English toilet paper was very coarse. The customs inspectors laughed uproariously when they opened our suitcases. It proved even funnier when we presented our "gifts". English toilet paper is just as soft as ours.

Cousin Cecilia met us at Heathrow Airport. We boarded a train for London. At Paddington Station, we transferred to another train for the final leg of our journey. From the train, I saw the odd pillbox, left over from the war. The sky was low. Suddenly I experienced terrifying flashbacks of planes diving from clouds. I had to pull myself to the present and hold on to my emotions.

Uncle John met us at the railway station, accompanied by a man, just over five feet tall, who looked a lot like me, even to the smallest detail: For a year or so previously, I had sported a short beard – not a goatee, just a short beard. This man wore the exact same beard! Uncle John repeated, over and over, "Oh, my God! Oh, my God!" I couldn't even manage that. I hugged my father right there, on the open railway platform, and wept openly. In the drizzling rain.

Uncle John's wife had inherited a massive Mansion, with a costume room in the tower. Here Heidi and Chris spent hours dressing up. The house was filled with ancient paintings, sculptured busts, and suits of armour. We were shown an original charter from King Henry VIII! The grounds consisted of acres of well-kept lawns, fish ponds, and great sculptures done by family members.

The atmosphere was formal. We visited my father in the main house, and occasionally took tea with everyone. Apart from those visits, Joanne, the children, and I were given a basement suite. We did our own housekeeping and cooking, and shopped at a greengrocer nearby. I felt like an outsider.

Uncle John showed me a photograph of my grandfather. Of all the family members, I was his double, and the double of my great-grandfather, too. I learned about another Christopher, my cousin in Africa. Another cousin had a son named Ben, the same age as our Christopher.

When my sister Anna came for a visit, we planned a trip to stay with her in Oxford. Anna looked like my mother and had identical mannerisms. She favoured the same brand of cigarettes and held them the same way. She even told the same stories and jokes. Joanne remarked that many of my sister's jokes and songs were already familiar to her; having heard them from me over the years.

Anna was married to a Palestinian named Amin. Both taught in Jordan. Anna had taken leave in order to be with us in England. She had a permanent home in Oxford; while she was absent, she rented a suite to friends from the Middle East.

Dad, Joanne, and I rented a car and drove to Finchingfield. We managed to get ourselves invited inside Willets' Cottage. I remembered a thatch roof, but that, long since, I speculated, had been replaced with a tile roof.[4]

Naturally, electricity and indoor plumbing had been installed. But the low doorways hadn't changed; I remembered the many times my father had bumped his head. (In my memory he had been so tall.) We climbed up to the tiny room where Naomi and I had danced with the little people.

The farm where we visited the "piggies" was still there, but now the yard was filled with chickens. The old witch's house looked all too ordinary. The church on the hill and the graveyard looked the same. The windmill still stood in the field behind the house. We were told that Willets' Cottage had been featured in a This England magazine. I couldn't find Mrs. Turner's greengrocer shop.

I wanted to find the house where we had lived after Dad went off to war. But Dad – everyone but I called him Freddie – was getting tired at this point and did not wish to visit "that evil place". Nor would he show us where the ack-ack gun placement had been. In fact, my father behaved in a grumpy manner all the way back to Uncle John's home; he even complained I was a terrible driver.[5]

We enjoyed a beautiful stay at Aunt Penny's and Uncle Pat's home at Cadgwith, Cornwall. We spent time, high on a hill overlooking the Atlantic. I had suggested renting another car, but Dad insisted we go by rail.

I heard Uncle Pat calling my dad Fritz. He told me that most of the uncles called him Fritz because they had a German governess before the First World War – Fraulein Zoll. The endearment stuck since then.[6]

Aunt Penny produced short films for BBC Television. Uncle

Pat worked with ceramics. Heidi and Chris were more interested in Aunt Penny's ponies!

For me, one of the greatest thrills of the trip occurred in a village pub in Cadgwith. Sailors sang in beautiful four and five-part harmonies. Many of the songs were identical to those sung in Newfoundland, but with the original Cornish references.

Their harmonies wove a multicolor tapestry of sound, sometimes soft and gentle as lamb's wool, at other times, like wind in the trees, rising and falling in volume.

We borrowed Uncle Pat's car and drove to Land's End and Saint Ives where we saw more palm trees and more warm, sandy beaches. Who'd have thought there'd be palm trees in England?

During our stay at Uncle John's, I asked my father what he thought of the poems I sent him. I was shocked by his answer: "I burned those poems when I was in the Novitiate. I had a terrible Novice Master named Father Francis." About my poems, he had nothing to say. I was referring to the poems I'd written in the Christian Brothers' Novitiate. He was referring to poems he'd written in the Franciscan Novitiate and, under orders of his novice master, had destroyed. I had hidden mine. The parallels were astounding.

When I told him how I had wanted to commit suicide by falling through the ice, Dad was quick to reply, "There was never a day that I did not pray for you and your sister Naomi." Was that angel on the ice sent in answer to my father's prayers?

On July 15th, the Brother Superior of the Anglican Franciscans in England came to visit. I asked him if it was by intention that he had come on the feast day of St. Bonaventure. Of course, my question had to do with my name – Brother Bonaventure. Another amazing coincidence. I saw all of these events as truly mystical. My life has been full of miracles.

The Brother Superior told me how Freddie had returned from the war in North Africa and, after searching everywhere for his wife and children, had entered the Franciscan friary and asked to work with the blacks on the London docks. For many years, he lived as a man without hope. He said that our reunion had awakened "dear old Freddie", brought him back to life but I witnessed only an embittered man who showed no warmth about our reunion – the most painful disappointment of my life.[7]

We left Freddie with Uncle John and went off to visit Anna in Oxford, where we stayed with Aunt Katie in King's Mill, an ancient mill on the River Cherwell (a tributary of the River Thames). King's Mill was listed in the "Doomsday Book" (a census of the whole of England commissioned in December 1085 by William the Conqueror). For the last three or four hundred years, King's Mill has been owned by Magdalen College, one of the more famous colleges of Oxford University.

When we were there, King's Mill comprised a living room with a low-beamed ceiling, a huge open fire, a tiny passageway of a dining-room, and a jerrybuilt kitchen and bathroom, added on when Katie and Ralph moved in. Because of the war, they had to use all sorts of second hand building materials - plumbing, bricks, flooring, wooden window-frames and doors, none matching, and all cobbled together hastily! Up a narrow, steep wooden flight of stairs was the big bedroom, overlooking the River Cherwell and the mill race. Up one more floor, two tiny attic bedrooms could be found. That was all, apart from numerous outhouses and sheds, including an old generator that they once used before they were connected to municipal electricity.

The house is down a muddy lane, far from neighbours, and at one of the entrances to the University Parks. The murmur of the mill race flowing incessantly over the sluice-gates rises to a roar in winter when the rains have swollen the stream; it offers a constant, soothing background to everything that happens at King's Mill, relaxing and soporific.

We had a wonderful visit in Oxford – apart from visiting Katie, where Heidi and Chris fished from the bridge over the sluice-gates of the mill. We went punting on the Cherwell and ate at The Trout Inn up the River Thames just outside Oxford, where a ruined convent called Godstow Nunnery stands, about which romantic historical legends have sprung up. Then, in the evenings, we all visited with Aunt Katie, who told humorous stories and jokes and related anecdotes about the Nuttall-Smith family. The conversations with Aunt Katie and Anna were entertaining indeed.

On one of our day excursions, we went to Stratford-on-Avon, where we visited Ann Hathaway's Cottage and the schoolroom where Shakespeare studied. Unfortunately, we couldn't attend a play; bookings had to be made too far in advance. But I did enjoy walking through the many buildings and walkways where the Bard spent his youth.

On still another visit, we went to the house in Oxford where the Nuttall-Smith family had been raised. Anna showed us an idyllic, tiny cottage, just down the lane from the Nuttall-Smith home where her father, my Uncle Alex, and our mother had lived the two brief years of their marriage. We looked at my grandparents' grave sites in an overgrown churchyard. We wandered through churches in the Cotswalds where my grandfather had been pastor. Every day brought new surprises.

All too soon, the time came to return to Canada. I could have spent weeks, even months more, exploring old haunts and rediscovering my childhood.

In the end, I wrote a long letter to Mother. I told her I loved her and that I accepted the life she had led. I even asked her to forgive and love me as her son.[8]

In later correspondence, I learned how Papa François was disappointed that I had changed my name. I hadn't explained to him, nor to Mom, why this was so important to me. All I knew was that I now understood who I was! My life had been transformed. I had an identity. One gigantic miracle!

Not long after our return home, Anna wrote to ask if we would sponsor her and her husband, Amin, to come to Canada, where they would seek landed immigrant status and apply for Canadian citizenship. Joanne and I agreed.

When they arrived, we gave them a bed and some basic furniture. They lived in our basement in Sunshine Hills until they were able to rent an apartment in New Westminster. While Anna went to work as an editor for the British Columbia Teachers' Federation, Amin took courses at Simon Fraser University to obtain a degree in Economics.

* * * * * * * *

[1]   I had already lost two sisters from cancer. The pattern seems obvious. Was my cancer hereditary, or a result of poor diet or overexposure to sun? I believe, above all other factors, cancer is caused by stress. Stress weakens the immune system, leaving us susceptible to cancers. Naomi, Nicky, and I all suffered high degrees of stress in our childhood. Ergo, cancer.

[2]   When was "the defining moment" – the point at which Joanne stopped loving me? When she was constantly crying, while living at my parents' home in Senneville, was that prenatal blues, as I suspected, or did she not feel sufficiently secure and adequately protected and defended by me? I was not able to stand up to my mother when my wife complained that she was under constant, although subtle attack by her.
    To me, everything was going so blissfully dandy; then Joanne, right out of left field, arbitrarily moved to end the marriage. She caught me by surprise. In retrospect, the true reason she did not want more than two children was that she did not want me any more, and had not for a long time. Was she just waiting for the children to grow up and finish school? Why did I not see the writing on the wall?

[3]   see **Nuttall-Smith**, G.N., M.A., T.C.D.; *The Chronicles of a Puritan Family in Ireland* (Oxford: Oxford University Press, 1923)
    Nuttall-Smith, G.N., M.A., T.C.D.; *Light - A Poem in Eight Cantos;* (Oxford: Basil Blackwell Broad Street, 1939)

[4]   Actually, the roof had always been tile, despite childhood memories and early photographs show a tile roof. Maybe I just remembered all the other thatched cottages in Finchingfield.

[5]   When we were alone together, my father sometimes appeared sullen and incommunicative. (Perhaps he felt guilt for having run from our lives.) And when he tried to relate to his two grandchildren, he didn't quite know what to do. Was it difficult for my dad to emotionally handle Joanne's and my relationship with our two children? Naomi and I had been nearly their age when he went off to war.
    I think my father was bitter about what had happened to him. At one point, he even told me to break off all contact with "that evil woman", my mother.
    I'm sure the memories of life with my mother were hard for him to take. Not to mention the fact that my mother took me and Naomi away from him, without telling him of our whereabouts. No wonder he was angry!

[6]   As for me, I didn't know what to call my father. I never had been able to call him "Dad". Certainly, I no longer could call him "Daddy". When speaking to other members of the family, I referred to my father as "Freddie". And when I spoke directly to him, I just did so without naming him.

[7]   *Both my father and I had wanted to serve our black brothers and sisters. So many parallels...*

[8]   *Yes, I asked my mother to forgive me. For what?*
    Here I had a mother who lied to me consistently, for years, about my own father and who acted deliberately to keep me away from him. Where was my anger about all of this? Did I really want my mother's forgiveness for having found my father? Did I need Papa's forgiveness for having reclaimed my birthright?
    Any rage I might have felt at this point was so deeply buried, it was almost indefinitely postponed. In fact, it didn't surface, where I could feel it, until the time when Mother and Papa cut me out of their wills.

Chapter Twenty
Fly Away Little Bird

Once I knew a fine song,
—It is true, believe me,—
It was all of birds,
And I held them in a basket;
When I opened the wicket,
Heavens! they all flew away.
I cried, "Come back, Little Thoughts!"
But they only laughed.
They flew on
Until they were as sand
Thrown between me and the sky.
– Stephen Crane, 'Scaped

The summer following our trip to England, we all flew to Montreal to visit Joanne's parents, her relatives on her mother's side who lived in Glen Robertson, and my mother and Papa François who now had a cottage overlooking beautiful St. John's Lake near Lachute, Quebec. Although I assured Mother of my love and understanding, she and I still had great difficulty communicating. But she and Joanne had several long conversations.

Joanne later told me that there would never be another love like that between my mother and Freddie, my father. Mother was in the early stages of Alzheimer's. Several times she called police to report she was being attacked by a strange man in the house – Papa François. My sister Louise spent many days and weeks helping her father look after Mother.

The following summer, Mother was admitted to hospital in Lachute. Joanne and I visited her. We also spent several days with Joanne's cousin in Glen Robertson, about a forty-five minute drive past Hawksbury, across the Ontario border.

I barely recognized Mother. She sat upright in her wheelchair, shriveled, a tiny bird with its feathers plucked. Beneath her blue-tinged skin, I almost could see her thin, brittle bones.

While she folded and refolded an imaginary serviette on her lap, Mother's silver hair seemed to float, like little downy feathers. She always had prided herself on her flowing red hair. When I visited her just a couple of years earlier, she had managed to keep this rich colour.

No more.[1]

"Send those lawyers home. I'm sick of lawyers. No more questions. No more questions." Her eyes lit up. "Thank God you're here! "Thank God you've come."

Wow! She recognized me.

"Enough of those damn lawyers!"

"Hello, Mom."

"Did you come to feed my birds?"

"We came to see you."

"Who are you?"

"I'm Ben. Your ... son." The word choked in my throat.

"Did you come to feed my birds?" She puckered her lips and made calling sounds. Maybe she thought I were a parakeet.

I tried to be cheerful. "Would you like to go for a walk? I'll take you."

Mother narrowed her eyes. "Who are you?" She spoke sentences and phrases but made no sense.

Other patients sat, babbling. Some drooled, open mouthed. One woman beckoned to me. "Allo. Allo. Allo." She was tiny, sweet, and appeared very old. Repeatedly, she tried to brush away imaginary cobwebs over her face. Another woman gazed at me, glowing like a dim bulb with a fine, weak filament. "Quel heure est il?" (What time is it?) Her tongue slipped, thickly, as she slid from one bit of nonsense to another.

"You know me, Mom. I'm Ben, your son."

She sounded annoyed. "Of course I know who you are. I'm not ... I'm not ..." She lost her train of thought. And gazed off into space.

"I know, Mom. I know. Let's go for a walk."

I pushed her out into the sunny courtyard. All around her, Mother saw flowers. And a robin on the path. For years she'd kept a budgie and fed the wild birds that came to her garden feeders. "Allo bébé. Pretty bird." Some of her memories remained.

I looked at my mother's knees. Tucked over sideways beneath the blanket, they looked all bone and wrinkled flesh. She used to have such beautiful legs.

The egg shell skin on Mother's bird-boned wrist glistened with large, blue veins. Her body's hunger signals no longer connecting with her brain, she slowly was starving herself to death.

Mother had gone. Soon her tired old body would catch up. There in the sunshine, I spoke to the Mother I knew, the Mother I loved and hated and loved again.

"Goodbye, Mom."

She gazed past me into space, farted with a groan, and smiled. Like a baby relieved of her discomfort.[2]

At this moment, Louise and Jackie arrived and wheeled Mother inside, where a nurse put her to bed for her afternoon rest. After visiting with my sisters for a while, I drove back to Glen Robertson, confused and unhappy.

The next day, I again visited Mother. This time she seemed sedated. While folding and refolding the imaginary serviette on her lap, she blurted more than her usual amount of gibberish.

"Get out of that puddle!"

"What are you doing here? You're supposed to be in school."

"Talk about your rocky road to ... to ... to ..."

"Hello, sweetheart."

"There's no milk. The cow is dead."

"You'd better get ready. They'll be here soon."

"I think you'd better go now. You'll be late."

"Mustn't be late."

"Hello sweetheart."

Then, after gazing up at a painting on the wall – "Why did they send him to spy?" – she made a sensible request. She asked to go to the toilet. No nurse was available. So I helped her into the bathroom, helped her get seated, and stood by. When she finished, I wiped her shrunken bottom.

Truly, we had come full cycle.

REVERSED

'tis three score ten gone by
you cleansed
with cotton wool my wrinkled folds
held tiny feet with care
and patted and
powdered me
do I recall young legs spread wide
and so proud

my duty done on potty seat?
you served me likewise then
with gentle words "Good boy!"
my bottom was a happy place
there in that nursery room
and then
not long ago
in septic halls
I did the same for you
roles reversed
gentle hands
a wrinkled,
bed sore, nether part.
"Good girl!"
a week before you left to start
again

A few weeks later, I flew to Montreal and then boarded the train to Saint Anne de Bellevue.

Time to attend Mother's funeral.

She lay in a coffin in the funeral home. I gazed at the wrinkles at the sides of her eyes and remembered the love I sought and seldom found. Then I closed my eyes and smelled her perfume and lipstick, from the days when I loved her, in Finchingfield. I tasted her mashed potatoes and mushroom gravy and heard her singing old farmer songs.

At the church, I asked permission to sing from the choir loft. My request was granted.

No one saw the soloist who sang Cesar Franck's <u>Panis Angelicus.</u>

This was my final, emotional goodbye to Mother.[3]

After the burial, we all went to a restaurant in Ste. Anne de Bellevue. Aunties Pat and Madeleine were there as well as Uncle Emilien and his wife Laurette. The following day, I flew back to Vancouver and returned to my job at school.

The next summer we vowed to fly to England to visit my dad. We bought plane tickets for the two of us as well as a Brit-Rail Pass. By then, Joanne's parents lived nearby, in Delta; they agreed to look after Heidi and Chris. We planned to leave for one month, as soon as school let out, and agreed to combine a visit with my dad with an overdue holiday of our own. But after hearing that my stepfather, Papa Boucher, was in hospital, we felt it would be a good idea to stop over in Montreal.

Meantime, my own father died two weeks prior to the date we were scheduled to leave Canada. His body was cremated. After we called them, the Brothers agreed to postpone the burial of the ashes until we arrived.

When we arrived in Montreal, it was obvious that Papa would not last long. He was in much pain and had difficulty breathing. I talked the matter over with my sister, Louise, and her husband Vic, and asked if we should stay.

Our visit clearly upset Papa François. He waved me off. "Leave! We don't want you here."

After Vic promised to contact us, should Papa's health situation worsen, we took off to London.

From Heathrow, we traveled to the Brothers' house in East London. The Brothers there told us that my father's remains were at the Mother House in Dorset. We were invited to stay at the retreat center and catch a train to Dorset next day. The following morning, we attended prayer services, after which I spoke with several Brothers who had known my Dad well. They all mentioned how he had changed since we found him.

Late the following night, Vic phoned the Dorset Mother House. Papa Boucher had died. Despite that, Vic suggested we remain in England and continue with our plans. But Joanne wanted us to contact the airline and return right after my father's burial. I agreed to follow her advice.

Following a brief prayer service, we tagged behind the procession of monks as they carried my father's small casket down a gravel path to the cemetery. I heard the birds sing in the trees. I saw the Brothers in their bare feet. I had an overwhelming feeling of déjà-vu.

The return flight to Canada was silent. My emotional cup was brimming, and I didn't know how I'd react to my step-father's funeral. The recent rejection had stung me deeply. However, I pulled myself together to support Louise, Jackie, and my aunts. In the same church where we'd had Mother's funeral, I again sang from the choir loft. This time Mozart's <u>Ave Verum</u>. (As before, no one knew I was the soloist.)

Then I eulogized Papa François in French and English. I said he always had wanted a son and that I had tried my best to fulfill that role. Speaking of his devotion and good example, I asserted that my life had been blessed by having known him. I couched everything I said in diplomatic phrases which, I convinced myself, were as truthful as I could make them.

Thus ended the most eventful, emotional chapter of my life. Until now, at least.[4]

* * * * * * * *

[1] *For most of my life, I had been unable unable to face Mother as an equal member of the human race. Rather, I had carved her in false mythic proportions, installed her on a pedestal, and propitiated the goddess in all her volatile moods – even the unloving and the wrathful.*

Now, here she was, meek and unthreatening. Just a frail human being. The mother I had known was gone. No more did I have to sing for her.

I should have felt emancipated. Yet I felt only great sadness and terrible loss.

[2] *I once read something to the effect that, in cases of incurable, degenerative brain disease, such as Alzheimer's and other forms of dementia, the spirit may depart from the body prior to actual bodily death.*

Since we are spirits in possession of bodies – not the reverse – it should be obvious that our spirits can depart whenever they wish.

[3] *My mother's death presented me with the sadness of reconciliation never achieved. With questions never asked. With questions never answered.*

How did I honestly feel about my stepfather? His parting words to me, as we left to bury my own father, said it all. He rejected me. And probably, in his mind, I had rejected him by reclaiming my own father's name. Never, in the years I'd known him, had he shown me any love. So how could I feel any love for him? Perhaps he sensed the burden of guilt I had always carried. And most likely he was not able to identify what it was he saw in me. Thus, I believe, my childhood shame poisoned our relationship. Now I felt guilty for my lack of love.

As for my own father, at first I regretted the years I had been deprived of him. Then, when I met him once again, a bitter old man, I was disappointed .

In Dorset, I mainly buried the "Daddy" I knew at Willet's Cottage. With him, I also buried the only happy part of my childhood. At my father's burial service, though I felt sad and cheated, I kept my silence. Truly, I wanted to say a great deal. Diplomatically, I elected not to. I could only think of all the things I wanted to say to my father, but didn't or couldn't.

I had yet to experience two other emotions about my dad: devastation and emptiness. These didn't rise to the surface until much, much later – when I was able to deal with them better.

Chapter Twenty-One
In-laws and Outlaws

Unless one pretends to be stupid and deaf,
it is difficult to be a mother-in-law or father-in-law.
– Chinese proverb

Shortly after our return from England in 1982, Joanne's father retired. At our suggestion, El and Terry came to join us on the west coast. They bought a house in North Delta and added a basement suite, complete with kitchen, so that Marilyn could live with them yet be independent.

We spent a lot of time together right from the start. Almost every Sunday, we either had dinner with them at our home or we at their home.

I'm sure it was good for Joanne to have her mother close by although I occasionally felt tense around her parents. The problem was they had never really accepted me as part of the family and told me so. When Joanne and I disagreed, she invariably had her mother and dad to take her side disallowing us to work things out on our own.

Sometimes, I attempted to win over Joanne's parents with my "good humour". When her dad became chairman of his local neighbourhood watch committee, I asked if that made him a "blockhead". Joanne's mother, Terry, thought I was being disrespectful but she smiled anyway. All things considered, I think we managed to get along most of the time.

Marilyn's multiple sclerosis worsened until she was admitted to extended care at Surrey Memorial Hospital. Her parents moved closer to the hospital but within a few months, Marilyn was transferred o a Salvation Army group home in New Westminster. Joanne, the children, and I visited her often, picking up El and Terry on the way. Often, I brought my guitar and entertained patients and staff both. This made me feel special and that I was making amends to my sister-in-law.[1]

Often, we picked up Marilyn and drove her either to our home or to her parents' home. Having been a hospital orderly, I knew how to lift a paraplegic to and from the car. I was able to empty her colostomy bags, change her, and clean her up when accidents occurred. "Close your eyes, Marilyn. I'm going to change you". When her parents objected to my performing this service, I suggested one of them do it, but the task was too great for them. Marilyn was heavy to lift. I prided myself in my hospital know-how and in being so "broadminded".

Discipline must come through liberty.
– Maria Montessori (1870-1952) *The Montessori Method* [2]

One task I found difficult was disciplining my children. My own father had never spanked me. He left that task to my mother who used a hairbrush.

From my earliest years, I felt that Mother loved me only when she spanked me. Since she applied a hairbrush to my bare behind, her spankings were painful. As time went on, I learned to cry and sob until I received hugs, even if the wait took forever. Quite simply, the cuddling made the paddlings worthwhile; at last I received the love and attention I craved. Pain and love went hand in hand for me; I didn't know one without the other.

When my sister also got spanked, that proved much worse for me. I'd have to wait outside the bedroom and hear her screaming as the slaps of the hairbrush turned my legs to jelly. Then it would be my turn. The waiting was a greater torture than the paddling. Sometimes she'd spank, then hold me across her knee for a few moments and remind me why I was being punished. Then she'd spank some more. I don't think I heard her explanations because I was too unhappy holding on for the next onslaught.

I never associated caning with love. The cane was always cruel. The cane blistered. Straps and rulers used by teachers all through my primary and elementary school years, hurt the hands so much they made writing difficult. Yet often we were too proud to cry. Sometimes, we didn't dare cry. Sometimes we couldn't help ourselves.

The threat of the pointer at the blackboard inhibited my thinking. Oftentimes, I remember my mind going numb when a pointer slapped at the board in front of me.

Hairbrush, paddle, hand. These stung but somehow said to me: "I care!" I don't believe that anymore, of course. These weapons terrorized my childhood.

When we grew older, Mother switched her focus from our bums to our faces – and we got slapped hard. To that act, no love was attached, only frustration. When I ducked her smacks, she got angrier. It seems I lived in constant terror.

So here I was, forty years later, with my own children. Since my father never spanked me, I loved and respected him. I obeyed him because I loved him. It was that simple. Or was it?

As I loved my children, I did not want to behave like my mother or my father. Often, in frustration, Joanne shouted, "When will you spank that child?" "Be a father!"

I could hug my children. I could change their diapers. I could bathe them. I could love them in countless other ways. But not by spanking them. There was no love in spanking.

I pleaded with my children to behave for the sake of their mother. But I could not spank. I would not.

"You have no backbone. Are you afraid to be a real father?"

Though these words hurt, they didn't change me.... All right, I admit it: Once in a while, I did spank my children.

Did I do it in frustration and anger? Yes, I did get angry at Joanne. Yes, I did get angry at her parents for interfering. And yes, I did get upset at the increased demand for me to do something I did not want to do. Inevitably, I didn't agree with the reasons given and judged them petty. Frustration grew. When in anger, I caved in and whacked my children, I felt terrible shame for weeks afterwards.

Of course, I sometimes felt anger towards my kids when they misbehaved or were disrespectful, but I hated punishing them.

Chris was the one, according to Joanne, whom I consistently failed to discipline. When Chris rebelled, I rebelled at Joanne's pressuring. "You are too old to be a father. The damage you do in spoiling your son will never be undone.[4][3]

Today, I'd never spank a child. The thought makes my stomach turn. I feel a shuddering in my back and a weakness in my legs.

In the fall of 1982, I registered to complete a Master's program in Theatre at Western Washington University. We sold the old Peugeot and bought a new Sprint Chevrolet and a Honda Passport mini-bike which I drove in all weather, healthy and happy. At school, I parked in the theatre storage room. On Saturdays and some evenings, I drove from Sunshine Hills to the University campus in Bellingham, about seventy kilometers. The trip took almost two hours each way allowing for delays at the border. The following summer, I attended seminars, took part in productions, and drove home late at night.

In 1983, Joanne and I saw a beautiful two-and-a-half acre hobby farm with a Tudor style house on a hill in South Langley. Sunshine Hills was becoming increasingly rough, with young bullies ruling the streets and parks. I didn't want Heidi and Chris subjected to bullying. Country living would be good for the children. We presented a successful offer, sold our house in Sunshine Hills, and moved to the country.

Though we already had a Siamese cat, I also wanted a dog to help look after the property. We selected a Doberman pup and named her Esther after the heroine in the Old Testament who guarded her people. Ester was a gentle dog, but Joanne didn't want her in the house. So I built a sturdy dog house on the side of of the tool shed close to the house. In winter, I gave Esther plenty of straw and old blankets. She was a good guard dog, and accompanied me through all my farm chores.

The property was covered in weeds, thistles, and brambles. So I hired a farmer friend to plow the front field down to the bottom of the hill. Then I got him to bring in a back-hoe and dig out a pond, with an island for ducks in the middle. For several weeks, Heidi, Chris, and I raked from top to bottom, carrying rocks and debris to the sides in a wheelbarrow. Then we planted a mixture of grass and clover. Soon we had the greenest acreage for miles around.

Tommy was the son of Joanne's principal, a boy we had known since he had been a member of our church youth group. I hired him to help fence the entire two-and-a -half acres. He had learned how to install sheep fencing by helping his dad on their five acres. Between us, we pounded in every post with a two-by-four and a sledge hammer, and stretched and stapled a four-foot sheep fence, placing rocks along the bottom to keep coyotes out. Then we dug a ditch for electric cable and ran electricity down to the barn, where we raised a yard light. At the front entrance, I built stone light posts and installed a set of big iron gates.

Finally, I winterized the barn with insulation and plywood and picked up several bales of hay from a hay and feed supplier in the Fraser Valley. Everything was ready. I bought three young doe lambs from a farmer friend, a dozen Golden Comet chicks, and six ducklings from Buckerfields. I was a hobby farmer in my glory.

Soon we had fresh brown eggs to eat and sell to fellow teachers at school. One year I raised plump meat chickens. They were the best I'd ever eaten. Our deep freeze was full. I was less successful with turkey chicks. They grew to be stupid, messy, and hard to contain. They pooped all over our front patio, getting me into constant trouble with Joanne. Though the meat was worth the time and effort, I would have to think twice before attempting turkeys again.

One dark and stormy night, one of our favourite sheep, Blackie, slipped into the pond at the bottom of our property and drowned. The next day, Chris and I had to pull her out and bury her. The children and I had grown fond of Blackie. Later, we borrowed a ram from our friend, Tom. A few months later, the other two sheep produced lambs.

For a while, we had a pony. I was remembering my own pony in Finchingfield and wanted to share that joy with Heidi and Chris. However, without a saddle she was difficult to ride and Joanne didn't share my enthusiasm so I sold the horse.

In winter, Chris and I cleared the driveway with a plow loaded on the front end of our tractor lawn mower. I always had an eager driver in Chris, both for snow clearance in winter and grass cutting in summer.

One summer, Louise and Vic, Jackie and Bill, and all the nieces and nephews came to visit. They found us living in Paradise. Later, we all toured Gastown and North Vancouver. We threw weenie roasts on our hill. My brother-in-law was so enthusiastic, I think he would have sold his airline and moved to the West Coast. The following Thanksgiving, I sent them a homegrown turkey.

Meanwhile, I continued my courses and wrote a double thesis on Creative Dramatics as well as a play, which I directed as "Involvement Theatre". My Stagecraft students and I built a huge, workable ship's deck with wheel and sails.

The play was a musical adaptation of "Treasure Island". As youngsters arrived, they were permitted to sign on to the ship's crew. Others were secretly recruited as pirates by Long John Silver and given "the mark" which was secretly stamped on the palm of the hand to be shown when the secret signal was given. The entire audience got involved with singing, making thunderous ocean waves and scary jungle noises, and shouting warnings.

With children in the play, we never could be sure which side would win. At the end, whatever the outcome, we provided buried treasure for one group and emergency supplies for the other – small bags of candy for all.

Graduation Day arrived. I went up for my diploma and a little voice called out: "Way to go, grandpa!" It was Chris with my sense of humour. As for me, the boy who had dropped out of high school in the middle of grade nine had finally made it, thirty-six years later, in 1985. (I was fifty-two – old enough to be a grandpa.)

No matter how involved I got with schoolwork and university studies, I made sure to take Heidi and Chris to school concerts, music and ballet lessons, and birthday parties. Both loved their school and made good friends. I lined up before dawn to register first Heidi, then Chris, in the French Immersion school. In those days, children were accepted on a first come, first served basis. For the second year, some parents even camped overnight. Before long, my kids became fluently bilingual.

Langley offered string classes, so we bought a violin for Heidi and a cello for Chris. Eventually, with government cutbacks to education, instruction became available only through private lessons. Our children continued.

We enjoyed St. Joseph's Parish, with Father Jim Comey. Joanne and I got involved with the parish youth group. I directed a parish production of Godspell, enlarging the cast to accommodate all wishing to take part. The rehearsal process brought me closer to those young people that any other activity I had ever done in the Church. We hosted bonfires on our hill and toboggan parties. And we still were involved with Marriage Encounter, taking part in occasional "Weekends" and team meetings, but without the extra hours of organizing.

Belonging to such a large parish family was one of the greatest benefits of living in Langley. We had many friends.

There was an active prayer group in the parish. I went to a couple of meetings but that was no longer my style. Instead, I requested to become a member of the Third Order Of St. Francis, a lay organization that met once a week and prayed. I felt I needed to honour my father's memory by joining a spiritual group with the same name as his own order. Unhappily, I didn't get along with all the members, especially since some of them had demonstrated the strongest objection to my production of <u>Godspell</u>. They judged that the show mocked Christ, although it did the opposite. What really annoyed several people was when members of the parish prayer group voiced their strong opposition to the production, it caused more people to attend than might otherwise have come. So, despite overwhelming approval from the pastor and most parishioners, I made enemies and could not convince those in charge to accept me as a full fledged member of the lay Franciscans.

Clearly, not everything was rosy.

At school, especially, things did not go well. For several weeks, the auditorium was broken into, expensive equipment stolen or damaged. Prophylactics and sex toys were left on the stage for my students to find. Someone was playing a terrible practical joke. The administration accused me of inadequate supervision. When I suggested people were gaining access from the roof, the vice-principal said that was impossible.

I discovered several grade twelve students painting a "Grad" slogan on the roof "that was impossible to reach". Investigation by a school board maintenance man revealed workmen had left a roof hatch unlocked. The hatch got locked and incidents ceased.

Some weekends, the principal asked me to supervise rallies and other gatherings in the auditorium. Usually I agreed to do this. And usually I experienced no problems.

There was one occasion, though, when militant and moderate Sikhs held a rally in the auditorium to resolve their differences. Their disagreement had to do with whether or not chairs should be used in their Scott Road temple.

Some men began punching one another. Others jumped onto the stage to attack the speakers. I gave my student assistant a quarter and sent him to a pay-phone to call the police. (I did not have a telephone in the auditorium although I'd requested one since the beginning.)

Fearing accusations of racism, the police decided their

involvement could only make matters worse. Not only did they decline to show up, they sent my assistant home.

I was on my own!

When several men struggled to get at the microphones on the stage, I cut the sound. One of the organizers came to the sound booth. I told him the problem had to do with the main power box and that I would fix it right away. Then I locked the booth door, walked down to the power room [with a veneer of calm], locked the door behind me, and flipped the main breaker. I stood in the dark room, knees shaking, until everything fell silent. After what felt like hours of waiting, I opened the power room door and peered out. I felt sick to my stomach; my legs shook.

All was quiet. Everyone had left.

I turned the lights back on, tucked the microphones away, and locked up. Then I drove home and went to bed.

When I described the incident to the school administrators the next day, they accused me of exaggeration – and dismissed my concerns. Later the same day, a radio report stated that a Sikh man, following arguments at a meeting the previous night, had been killed by an ax in a nearby restaurant.

Despite this, no one gave me any support.[4]

* * * * * * * *

[1]   *Marilyn began exhibiting signs of MS when I first knew her in Montreal West. As far as I was concerned, she was self-centered and spoiled by her parents.*

According to Joanne, her sister had always been spoiled. As a girl, she was sent to a hairdresser; Joanne had to wash and set her own hair. Marilyn got braces; her parents couldn't afford them for Joanne. Marilyn often teased her little sister; when Joanne retaliated, she got punished.

I found my sister-in-law hard to deal with. Were her unpleasant behaviour and disposition early signs of MS? I don't know. Of course, I'd already had my run-ins with her from the beginning.

257

[2]   **Montessori,** Maria; *The Montessori Method*; George, Anne E., trans.; (New York: Frederick A. Stokes Co., 1912), ch. 5

[3]   *When my mother spanked me, my father left the house. He didn't try to stop her. He didn't protect me. I don't believe I deserved the kind of punishment I received.*

Was my father too weak to stand up to my mother?

My mother and father danced a not unusual dance. She behaved brutally toward her own children. By not stopping her, he enabled her violence, allowed it to continue. The Queen of Hearts and the King of Hearts.

[4]   *I was victimized by political correctness. No one, not even the Delta municipal police, not even the school administration, wanted to be accused of "racism". So they said and did nothing. And left me hung out to dry.*

"piggies"

Willets' Cottage, Finchingfield

behind Willets' Cottage
with our dog, Buller

Naomi and Bendt

The organ grinder
sharpens knives and scissors

Old Bessie and our caravan

King-of-the-castle

me

my dad

peering over the fence

Naomi

My father at Cambridge 1920's

Grandpa Nuttall-Smith with Anna - 1930's

Mother circa late 1920's

The wedding party
bottom row Siegvard, Mother, Major François Boucher, ...

My uncle and me circa 1941

SIGVARD LEO WEBER
PRESIDENT
THE WEBER STUDIOS ENTERPRISES
MOTION PICTURE PRODUCERS
HOLLYWOOD. CALIFORNIA

Broadbridge Heath, Sussex
with Louise and Nicole, 1944

Strathmore
Quebec 1949

Nurse Nickie

Hitchhiking U.S.A.

Naomi circa 1950
Paul Robeson in Oils

Teaching at N.D.S.S. Mother circa 1950

Christmas in Sechelt
with Heidi & Chris - 1996

Brother Frederick S.S.F.
(my dad)   Brother Bonaventure F.S.C.

Chapter Twenty-Two
Essays, Basic English, and Dead Poets.

> *For every person wishing to teach,*
> *there are thirty not wanting to be taught.*
> – Robert Yeatman, *1897 - 1968, And Now All This*

In September, 1989, I had just become fully qualified with an M.A. in Theatre when, once more, cutbacks threatened the arts in education. My Chorus class, with more than fifty students, was awarded to a young lady recently transferred to our school. I was also to share my Drama classes with an English teacher moving up from a junior high school. He would teach the Grade 12 classes and I could retain Acting 11 and Stagecraft 11 and teach two English classes.

I judged the other teacher had less experience than I – and no degree in Theatre – I deemed this unfair and felt I was being pushed out. When I couldn't agree to the new situation, I ended up teaching English 11 and 12 and Communications 11 and 12.

The new drama teacher had experience acting in professional theatre and television productions. Most of the students knew him from junior high school. When they stopped to speak with him in the hallways, he called them all by their first names. He was younger, more popular, and seemed more in touch than I.

I resented the man all the more since he failed to acknowledge me in any way. Worse, contrary to my own experience, the new man never lacked support from the school administration. Within weeks, he had a telephone in his Theatre office.

To add insult to injury, all the photographs and posters of my past productions disappeared from their display cases, seemingly overnight, to be replaced by materials from those junior high school productions that many of the new grade eleven students "could identify with".[1]

No longer was I recognized for my successes. Except when I absolutely had to be there, I avoided the school auditorium. It was no comfort to me to hear that the same was happening to other Drama teachers. One woman teacher I admired in particular also ended up teaching full-time English. I sank into a deep depression. My classroom became my hermit's cell.

Communications 11 and 12 were designed for kids who had difficulty with the regular curriculum. The idea was to provide them with such skills as writing resumes and letters of application. Those students were often anything but "students" and tended to be restless. It's hard to share one's enthusiasm for poetry and good writing with youngsters who hate school and find any topic boring before it has begun. Still, I vowed to accept the challenge and make the best of the situation.

For English 11, I shared my dramatic ability by trying to bring Shakespeare to life. <u>Macbeth</u> was on the curriculum. I read many of the parts of that play with my classes. Sometimes, we shouted out scenes such as the final sword fight between MacBeth and MacDuff: "Lead on MacDuff, and damned be he who first cry hold, enough!" Once in a while, my noisy sessions disturbed other classes or elicited the attention of roving administrators, and I was instructed to quieten down and get back to work. "You're supposed to be teaching English, not Drama." I was incorrigible. Before long, my classes returned to just as noisy and undisciplined a state as before. Maybe I was learning the first step to assertiveness: knowing when you're right.

Volume was often necessary, such as when the whole class read the chorus to the witches' cauldron scene, in high-pitched, cackling voices: "Double, double, toil and trouble / Fire burn and cauldron bubble." Students prepared at home and presented the individual ingredients for the potion. "Fillet of a fenny snake / in the cauldron boil and bake." "Eye of newt and toe of frog." I awarded extra marks for enthusiastic delivery.

I enjoyed teaching poetry, especially reading dramatic poems aloud. For example, I closed the blinds and lit candles to read Edgar Allan Poe's "The Raven", as a man going mad. I preceded such poems with vocabulary exercises so that students knew the meanings or backgrounds of such words as "Lenore", "nepenthe", "quaff", etc.

I also read modern poems that speak of the environment, such as "And the Seagulls Were Dying" by Gary Dunford, or poems by Lawrence Ferlinghetti, such as "The World Is a Beautiful Place".

I also motivated my students to write poetry. Once I asked them to translate Lewis Caroll's "Jabberwocky" into their own words.

To illustrate, I gave them my own version, which I wrote on the board as they pondered the assignment.

FRIDAY

"Twas Friday, and the restless youth
     Did squirm and fidget at their desks;
All sunny was the great outdoors
     And the weekend did invite.
"Beware the idle mind, my son!
The tongue that wags, the gum that snaps!
     Beware distracting chatterbox
And get that essay done!"

He took his trusty pen in hand
     Long time elusive thesis sought –
So wracked his brain and yearned to find
     The order he'd been taught.

And, as in foggy thought he sat,
     But still no inspiration came;
The topics offered left him flat;
     His eyes were all aflame.

With sudden surge of savoire faire,
     He caused his pen to fill the page.
With brainstorm notes and many thoughts,
     The essay did engage.

"The hour is up! Assignments in!"
     A loud voice echoed loud and clear.
Our young lad checked his final draft
     And cried a silent cheer.

"Twas Friday, and the restless youth
     Did squirm and fidget at their desks:
All sunny was the great outdoors
     And the weekend did invite.
     – With apologies to Lewis Caroll

Students frequently worked in groups; projects accomplished by teamwork. Tests and quizzes usually got corrected, upon completion, by the students themselves, so that correct answers could be reinforced.

In most cases, an atmosphere of trust prevailed, even though some cheating did occur. But then, who was the cheater fooling? Himself, obviously. Still, my methods were criticized. I lacked discipline in my classes.

One day, several of my students urged me to see a film, starring Robin Williams, entitled <u>The Dead Poet's Society</u>. They said I would see myself. When I did, I felt vindicated.

When I hear about continued strife between teachers and government and about cutbacks that end up enlarging class sizes and increasing work loads, I remember the late nights and long weekends spent on school work, while teaching a full semester of English. With four classes, averaging thirty students in each, and one essay per week, requiring at least seven to ten minutes of marking apiece, a teacher would have to spend a minimum of sixteen hours correcting essays alone. Then there are tests to correct, lessons to prepare, reports to fill out, students to give extra help to, extra supervisions to do, and school clubs to supervise.
Good teachers, of course, are accustomed to burning the midnight oil. One either must love teaching or go crazy. Or both.

Whenever I needed to let off steam and relax, I worked in my garden. I pulled weeds and tossed rocks against the fence. My love of plants extended to the classroom; most times the window ledge sported a pot of mums or aloe vera.

One year, right after the Christmas break, boys in my Communications 12 class presented me with a leafy plant. My plant grew bushy and tall. Then, one day, it disappeared. One of the quiet girls in the class told me I had nursed a marijuana plant while students ran a betting pool as to when I or the school administration would discover the joke. What a contradiction! For quite some time, I had tried, unsuccessfully, to convince the school's administrators that several students came to class stoned and smelling of pot. Yet I couldn't identify a marijuana plant when I saw one!

During the summer of 1986, Heidi, Chris, and I spent many days at Expo in Vancouver. Joanne had been struck with a flu bug – that later turned out to be full-blown pneumonia. She spent most of her time in bed. Joanne sent me off with Heidi and Chris, thus assuring her peace and quiet to rest. Friends visited regularly; always within reach, should she need them.[2]

Joanne's parents, however, proved less supportive. Her mother found the farm "dirty". A twenty-minute drive from their Surrey home was too far to drive. They had come to the West Coast to be close to their daughter and grandchildren, yet we had moved "into the wilderness". Joanne, they said, should be more readily available to her sister and parents. Their insistence mounted: we had to move to Surrey.

Heidi, Chris, and I were happy in Langley and didn't want to move. But Joanne felt we had no friends because we were so far away but failed to count the numerous friends we both had in our church and the many good friends Heidi and Chris enjoyed.

In the summer of 1988, I capitulated. We put the house up for sale. It was soon gone, at considerable financial loss. While deciding where we would live next, we rented a house in White Rock. On our first Sunday at church there, Chris pointed out how old everyone was. (White Rock is a retirement community.) The pastor was old and rambled on and on about golf and terrible teens. There were very few young people at church.

We took Esther for walks on a lead, and she tripped Joanne. Too big for the city, the dog had to go. We gave her to a lonely old man in the country. A few weeks later, the cat was gone as well.

I felt cheated, overruled by Joanne and her parents. More than that, I felt that I had capitulated much too much.

In an attempt to make Joanne happy, I suggested we have a new house built to her specifications. We chose a builder and bought a lot in one of the new subdivisions near White Rock. Then we drew up a plan and presented it to the builder. Architect and builder helped us choose a plan similar to our specifications, although much larger.

Since we couldn't afford landscaping, I took my wheelbarrow, spade, and rake to the mounds of earth and created a lawn, dug flower beds, and built rockeries. The house looked beautiful. But we had bitten off far more than we could chew.

I suggested we sell the house without an agent and recoup our losses. Then I made up sales contracts on the computer and placed a "For Sale" sign on the front lawn.

I told Joanne that St. Joseph, my patron saint, would help me sell the house and began a novena – nine days of special prayers. It would be a tough job; we were asking top dollar. Joanne was not willing to budge one penny.

On Sunday, the ninth day of my novena, I attended Mass

with Heidi and Chris. Joanne didn't feel well and stayed home. After Mass, I lit a candle at St. Joseph's statue and said a silent prayer. St. Joseph gave up his home to move with Mary and the infant Jesus to Egypt. While I was in church, Joanne received a call from people who had driven by and wanted to view the house. She told them we wouldn't be ready for viewers until later in the afternoon.

Shortly after I got home, another couple phoned to say they liked the house from the outside, and asked to visit right away. I suggested Joanne take Heidi and Chris out and offered to show the house myself. Instead, Joanne stayed and put cinnamon buns in the oven. She was happy that we might sell the house after all!

The couple walked through, then left. I waited in agony; I couldn't sit down. About an hour later, they phoned to say they wanted to make an offer. A few minutes later, the couple, who had telephoned earlier, went through the house. After spending a few minutes alone in the back garden, they said they wanted to make an offer. Now we had two couples interested! Both had sold homes in Vancouver and wanted to move to the suburbs. As each couple presented an offer, I told them about the other party. Eventually, the people who telephoned while I attended church offered full asking price.

Many people don't believe in miracles or help from patron saints, but I thank St. Joseph. He always helps when asked.

Not far from where we had been living, we found a beautiful English-style house on a quiet street. I loved the house right away. Joanne wasn't so sure. Finally, she agreed we should make our offer and we bought the house.

Again, I created a garden, built a back deck, and surrounded it with roses.[3] Inside, I sanded, painted, and put up wallpaper and moulding. After several frustrating weeks, Joanne was happy. The house looked beautiful.

When Joanne invited her parents to come and see, they approved. All was well again.

For a little while.

Since we had recouped our real estate losses, Joanne told me I should trade in my scooter in for a new car. We bought an Oldsmobile Cutlass Cierra and a camper trailer. I felt compensated for the loss of our Langley farm and dared to hope that we would draw closer once more. Joanne told me she was happy to be living in a more civilized world, away from animals, farmers, and loneliness. I accepted that. At last, I thought, we were back to smooth sailing.

With beautiful summer weather, we all went camping at Silver Lake in Manning Park. Heidi met a boy from Ireland who played guitar. They went canoeing together. We could hear our daughter's laughter from far across the lake.

The following summer, we drove through the mountains to Saskatchewan and visited Joanne's cousins. We saw old abandoned homesteads and walked the farm where Joanne's dad had grown up. In Regina, we walked around Joanne's high school and drove up and down streets where her girlhood friends had lived. This was her summer.

On the way back through the Rockies, we stopped in Nelson, and drove to the house where Joanne had spent the happiest part of her childhood. We visited her old school and the cathedral where she had made her First Holy Communion and talked to the monsignor who had been her pastor.

The summer after that, we drove through the midwestern United States to Salt Lake City. We visited the Mormon Temple where I especially enjoyed the music. Then we continued southeast through New Mexico, Texas, and Louisiana, to New Orleans, where we parked the trailer and stayed at a small hotel. Oysters in the half shell in News Orleans taste unlike anything one could eat anywhere else. We took a short boat trip on the Mississippi and toured some of the sites I remembered so well from my navy visit.

In the French Quarter, a shoeshine boy stopped Chris and made a wager. "I bet I can tell you where you got your shoes. If I guess right, you pay me for a shine." Chris was sure the boy wouldn't have even heard of Surrey, British Columbia, Canada. "You're on!" he said.

Then the boy told him, "You got your shoes on your feet - on Bourbon Street - in New Orleans. Pay up!"

In the evening, we walked through the narrow streets of the French Quarter. Everywhere – marvellous music. When naked girls swung out from bars on trapezes, Joanne was shocked. We went to bed early, to the sounds of a jazz trombone.

Next morning, we returned to our car and trailer and headed

away from that sinful, but exciting city and travelled along the Gulf of Mexico. We skipped Florida. Joanne was terrified of snakes. We drove directly north from Mobile, Alabama, up the Atlantic seaboard. How much the South had changed since my last visit! Blacks had a new dignity, and people behaved politely and very hospitably. Still, I felt an old, inward terror, but said nothing to Joanne about it. I had never told her about my misadventure in Mississippi.

An unusually dry summer, snakes crawled about campsite washrooms seeking water. When we parked for the night Joanne had to visit the facilities and asked Chris to go with her while I set up the trailer. When she walked out of the washroom, Chris pointed out a warning sign about snakes being drawn to the washroom areas in dry weather. Joanne panicked. She insisted we raise the camper and block every possible entry area. In our hothouse quarters, I tossed and turned all night.

Farther up the coast, a terrible storm struck. About midnight, Chris and I walked outside, hauled in towels and swim gear, and tied our trailer to the surrounding trees.

A blinding shaft of pure white light zigzagged across the bay and backlit the boats anchored in the harbour. The powerful clap of thunder heralded a downpour. Wind howled; trees swayed.

Throughout the night, we tossed and turned, slapped at mosquitoes, and said very little. In the din, conversation was impossible.

Two days sightseeing in Washington D.C. impressed and saddened me. At the long black Vietnam Veterans' Memorial and the Kennedy Memorial Flame many paid tribute with flowers and mementos. Some, full of emotion, traced names on the stone with their fingers. Many were veterans with missing limbs.

We walked through endless cemeteries and visited the Lincoln, Washington, and Jefferson Memorials. Then we browsed the Smithsonian. I could have spent several days in Washington. But we only had so much time. How wonderful it would be to spend a lot of time in one place and just explore. We were running – hurry, hurry, hurry.

The highway in New Jersey was rough and the sun blazed down. We blew a tire on the trailer and replaced it with the spare. The rim was damaged, but we were unable to replace it. Then, while bypassing New York City, we blew the spare, too. All we could do was park at the side of the highway. A couple of Spanish-speaking men stopped and offered to take us to a repair shop. A police cruiser pulled over, and the Spanish men took off. The two officers advised us to trust nobody. They called a tow truck for our trailer. We ended up in a repair shop where the mechanic said he would have to send to Quebec for a new rim. As that would take a couple of days, we stayed at a hotel room, paying one night at a time – in advance.

Two days later, we received a phone call that our trailer was ready. The bill for repair: $500 U.S., included storage fees. This was preposterous! When I protested, a big man walked out with a crowbar in his hand. I had no choice but to pay in full, Visa was accepted.[4] Joanne was disappointed that I hadn't been more of a man and stood up for my rights.

We spent several days with Joanne's brother, Ted, and his wife, Jean, in Pointe Claire just outside Montreal, then drove to Toronto to visit my sister Louise's family.   Joanne expressed her concern that I had been left out of my mother's will. She thought I should at least have one of her paintings. I knew she was right but didn't want to press the issue. In the end, Louise, gave me several pieces of Mother's pottery, including a couple of lamps Mother had made. I was happy with the ceramics.

In Northern Ontario,stopping for gas, I ran into one of my old companions from the Christian Brothers. Joanne was amazed to see two men hugging, right there in the middle of nowhere. Dan introduced his wife, Anne-Lynn, and their children. They were a Marriage Encounter team couple, too; they saw our sticker on the car before Dan even recognized me.

We all went for lunch together, and Dan and I shared old times. Dan's wife had been a nun before leaving her convent – and meeting her husband. Like so many who left religious communities, we all retained our devotion and our desire to continue as lay apostles.

At Thunder Bay, we stopped to see the Terry Fox Memorial. Then we crossed to the States, where gas was less expensive and the roads in better condition than the Trans-Canada Highway. From Grand Forks, Minnesota, we detoured north to visit my sister, Jackie, and her family in Winnipeg.

Jackie offered me a ceramic tile collage of St. Francis, made by Mother. Both she and I believed Mother had made it as a way to remember my father. Since Jackie had several of Mom's paintings, Joanne asked my sister if we could have one of them. Once more, Joanne was upset at my inability to stand up for myself.

After Winnipeg, we returned to the States and drove, without further sightseeing, through North Dakota and Montana, seeing the Badlands from a distance. The holiday was over.

The following spring, we sold the camper.

Joanne returned to U.B.C., this time for a Master's in Counseling Psychology. Again she spent her summers living on campus. I remained at home with the children. Sometimes, I went to her residence to type papers.

One Christmas, Heidi and I took part in a White Rock pantomime – "Jack and the Beanstalk". Since I had to drive my daughter to rehearsals and pick her up, it was a good idea for me to take part. I auditioned – and got the role of the Wicked Wizard.

Joanne and I ran the parish youth group, but the pastor showed only minimal support. When we used the parish school bus to attend a youth rally, the pastor scolded us publicly for rowdiness. For a long time, we had to hold our meetings in the church basement, on the same night smoky meetings of Alcoholics Anonymous were held. We had to keep "the noise level" down so there were no games. After much haggling, we got to use the school gym, – but under heavy restrictions. Too often frustrated, we finally gave up.

Joanne and I were involved with church music. Joanne played the organ and I directed choir. Frequently, especially at Christmas, practices were held in our home. Often, I served alone with Heidi, Chris, a few other voices, and my guitar.

Most of our music ministry took place at the little church near Crescent Beach. Many younger families attended Mass there while older parishioners attended the main church in White Rock.

Chris joined his School Band program. Just before a band trip to Disneyland, Joanne confiscated his trombone. I failed to make a stand that I thought the punishment far too severe for whatever it was Chris had or had not done, so our son missed the band trip. Undaunted, he joined vocal jazz – and won a prize for solo vocals! Though he also got involved with student government, the school

Music program was really what held his interest.

It was time for Joanne to complete her thesis at U.B.C. It was a busy time for both of us. She borrowed a computer from her school. I left Heidi and Chris with neighbours keeping an eye out while Joanne showed me to an empty study room in her residence where I could type. Since I thought success would make her happy, I was pleased to help. A benefit for me was I also learned a great deal of Psychology, especially regarding the middle child and reconstituted families.[5]

Joanne's graduation was a full-family affair. Her family, at last seemed proud of their daughter. We had copies of her thesis printed for parents and relatives. Through the help of our good friend, Tom, Joanne was offered a position as District Counsellor for the Surrey School District.

As for Joanne's sister, when the Salvation Army converted their MS facility in New Westminster to a larger Seniors' Home, Marilyn had to move to White Rock Hospital. Daily visits from both of us together soon became the norm. Though we were allowed to take Marilyn home for visits, she was getting so much weaker that it became too much of a chore for her and us.

The day in July, 1987, when Marilyn died, we all had been to see her. Later, Joanne returned to the hospital alone – and witnessed her sister's last moments. Death terrified Joanne and with grieving, she fell into a bad depression.

I plunged deeper into school work. One year, my Christmas gift to myself was a computer. At school, I became enthusiastic about recording class marks and projects on computer. I volunteered to make English Departmental Exams computer friendly for easy marking. I assembled dozens of quizzes with multiple answer keys and devised crossword quizzes, based on the English Literature program.

At home, I kept track of all accounts. I learned early on to back up files on floppy disks.[6] Since I got lost for hours on my new toy, I escaped much increasing tension at home.

I obtained permission to introduce my English classes to the school's computer lab; in that way, the students could more easily work on essays and do research. Despite problems of plagiarism and other forms of cheating, I wanted them to have every opportunity to experience the new technology. In this way, I, too, could learn with – and often from – my students.

I marked papers and planned new projects and spent more and more time alone. Since I even ate my lunch in the classroom, I alienated myself from my teaching colleagues.

In an effort to get my English students more interested in poetry, I read interesting works to my classes. Then I asked them to find a poem to share with the class. One boy chose to read St. Paul's First Letter to the Corinthians, Chapter 13, "Though I speak with the tongues of angels and of men...". Lickety split, a parent complained to the school principal that I had allowed Bible reading in an English class. I argued that The Bible is an essential part of English Literature and that the charge was malicious and ill-founded. The principal ordered me not to use The Bible in school.

Then, another boy in the same class wanted to write a book report on The Satanic Bible, by Anton Szandor LaVey. I said, "No!" If religion is banned in classrooms, I reasoned, Satanism must be banned too. This time, I was told I was not permitting my students freedom of choice. Nevertheless, I refused to mark the paper. So the principal marked the report – in my view a worthless piece of writing – and awarded an "A".

Several on staff openly stood by their religious convictions. One was a Protestant fundamentalist who spoke well of everyone. Another was a Jehovah's Witness who taught electronics. He and I often spent our lunch hours talking. Just prior to an Easter long weekend, which coincided with the start of spring break, he hanged himself in the electronics storage room. Like me, he felt isolated and alone. And like me, he had marital problems.[7]

Soon I became increasingly critical of what I saw as anti-Catholic bias. The English department head taught a class of Social Studies, in which she covered the wicked popes, the Spanish Inquisition, and the English martyrs under "Bloody Mary". She spoke about problems of overpopulation in priest-dominated countries. I heard about these lessons from students who were also in my English classes. I felt angry that, in a school where "religion was not permitted", anti-Catholic sentiment was acceptable. A fundamentalist organization called <u>Campus Life</u> held a rally in the school, recruiting students to join a Spring Break crusade to Mexico "to help bring the Mexicans to Christ". A teacher ran the lunch time Bible Club that sponsored this recruitment.[8]

Sometimes, Joanne and I drove out to Abbotsford to visit our good friends Tom and AnneMarie. Tom was one of a number of Catholic principals in the Surrey School District. AnneMarie was a registered nurse at the Surrey Memorial Hospital. Once in a while, conversation turned to our perception of anti-Catholicism in B.C. schools and hospitals. But at school, I avoided all discussion of religion, whether negative or positive. I felt the sting of anti-Catholic barbs, especially from those who once had been Catholic themselves. One ex-Catholic member of the staff in particular loved to tell Virgin Mary jokes just to watch my reaction. Though by no means sanctimonious, I usually got up and left the room.

A reason for my timidity was the following: the media had begun to cover the news at Mount Cashel. Several members on staff knew that I had been a Christian Brother. Suddenly, of all those dedicated and caring men, every one was branded a pervert.

The Brothers at Mount Cashel had been members of the Irish Christian Brothers. My order had been the De La Salle Brothers. That didn't matter; we were branded "all the same". I felt "guilt by association" and became increasingly angry about it.[9]

My turn came to be inspected by the principal, to make sure I was still effective as a teacher. This was a process every teacher underwent, once every five years. Usually the visits were brief and simple, with follow-up notes and suggestions. The trouble was, my visits came toward the beginning of the semester, when I barely knew my students.

For the visit, I chose to teach lessons on "Macbeth". Since this was my area of expertise, I felt quite confident. And since I had not yet reached that part of the curriculum, this would be an introductory lesson. I informed the principal of my intentions.

Rather than announcing to the class that we were now going to study Shakespeare – which I knew would produce groans – I tried to recreate that scene as an introduction to the play for my English 11 classes. With the principal sitting at the back of the class, I began with sounds of wind and rain, then I cackled like three old hags as I presented, from memory, my dramatization of the two main witches' scenes. Then, I instigated an animated discussion of witchcraft – past and present. I asked the students to consider the following:

Are there witches' covens in the Langley woods?

What do witches do?

Do they really steal babies from maternity wards at Halloween?

I wanted the students to get some idea of the real fear people had of witches in the age of King James. Finally, I gave a brief description of the politics of James of Scotland, as well as of life in Shakespeare's England. I explained that women were not permitted on stage. Therefore, men played women's parts and rough characters, possibly sailors, played witches.

Following the lecture and discussion, I handed out the text with a home reading assignment, clearly indicating questions that would be posed on a quiz at the following class. This had been my normal procedure. The method always sparked interest.

A couple of days later, the principal handed me a negative report. In his verbal explanation, he told me he found me too "artsy-fartsy" and off topic. He "encouraged" me to learn the U.B.C. method of lesson planning and presentation. "Tell the students what you are going to teach. Teach the lesson. Ask questions." I argued that my teacher training had been at McGill and that I always had been innovative. "And besides," I said, "what's the matter with using a bit of imagination in the learning process?" (Here we go again: my way versus the "right" way.)[10]

The principal offered to return for another class, taught according to his instructions. He was not happy with my second presentation, even though he acknowledged that I had improved. The negative report remained.

Since I judged the report to be unfair, I sought consultation with the president of the Delta Teachers' Association. We met for breakfast one day before school. On her advice, I returned the paper unsigned.

The following year, I was again inspected by the same principal. This time I taught a lesson in grammar which, under normal circumstances, would be very straightforward. Although couched in softer language than my previous report, this one made reference to my age and my "apparent lack of organization". I shared this with Joanne and with our principal friend. Both found the wording inappropriate; however, I felt compelled to sign, "to get my principal off my back".

The Vice-Principal at that time proved encouraging to me. In May, 1989, he told me about a position of helping teacher in Fine and Performing Arts being advertised in the district. He was aware of my qualifications and experience in Drama, Music, Art, and French at all levels and encouraged me to apply.

My application was not even acknowledged.

A few weeks later, I applied for a transfer to teach Drama, Music, Art, or Elementary school. Soon my principal friend offered me a Drama and French position in his school. I saw my chance to escape. Immediately, I requested leave of absence from Delta for one year. Request granted. But when I arrived at the Surrey School Board office, I discovered that someone had opposed my hiring. The Superintendent wouldn't see me. Disappointed, discouraged, and terrified that I might find myself without a job, I scurried back to the Delta School Board to rescind my request.

As time went on, our vice principal went on to become the principal of a junior secondary school and his position at our school was filled by a new man. One of the new vice principal's responsibilities was to monitor supplies. Paper was becoming increasingly expensive and in short supply. Every department in the school used reams for class assignments, quizzes, and tests. Though I also ran off my share of tests and notes, I recycled as much as possible by having students put answers on their own paper and copy notes for homework.

When interim report card time came, I used a new computer reporting program and printed a set on the staff computer printer. The new vice-principal told me I was using far too much paper, and my reports were too long. Most teachers still used the short (1/3 page), handwritten comment sheets, attached in triplicate. I had composed a bank of computer comments and included all assignment and test marks.

Because of the vice-principal's comment, I printed only one copy of each report, asked each student to read and sign,   The counsellors then had to check the parents' copies before distribution.

Counsellors asked why they had not received copies. I told them what the vice-principal had said and suggested they either see him or make photocopies. My rebellion was reported to the administration.

A boy who had behaved disruptively with another teacher, was transferred to one of my classes. Upon arrival, I placed him in a front seat. He waved to some friends in the back, put his feet up, and farted loudly.

I said, "Excuse me, sir, would you kindly leave the room."

He responded by mimicking me. Then he said, "make me".

I shouted "Out!"

He stood, waved to everyone, lifted his middle finger and walked out, slamming the door.

A short time later, he returned with the vice-principal with whom I was having a bad time. The VP said "Mr. Nuttall-Smith, this gentleman tells me you swore at him."

I smiled and shook my head. "I'll come and see you both after school."

The boy interjected, "I can't stay after school, I have to work."

"Go back in and sit down." the vice-principal said to the boy, indicating him into my classroom.

"You might like to ask the class what happened," I suggested angrily.

"Oh, I couldn't do that. That would embarrass the child."

So upset and angry I was shaking, I told the class to continue with quiet study or homework for the remaining few moments of the school day.

As soon as I closed up, I attempted to compose myself. Then I went down to the office. The boy did not show up. I waited for about fifteen minutes, then the principal ushered me into a small storage room adjacent to the office where he and the vice-principal stood facing me. After telling me me to sit down on a stool, the VP gave me a stern lecture on the evils of "child abuse". "Yes," the principal told me, "swearing at children is child abuse."

Confused, angry, and in tears, I protested that I did not swear at my students and certainly not at that boy. The vice-principal responded, "I have known this student for years and I

274

know his parents. He is not the kind of child who would lie."

I was outnumbered. I no longer could protect myself. "I don't think I swore... I don't remember swearing." ... I wavered. In tears I rushed from the office. I sat in my car for nearly an hour before I was able to drive home.

That evening, in despair, I sat alone in my back study. I didn't know how much longer I could hold on.

* * * * * * * *

[1] *Months later, a box of photographs and posters was found in the staff room. I took them home.*

[2] *Now I wonder if that bout of pneumonia was also a sign of deep emotional stress and depression. Unfortunately for both of us, I had not yet recognized my own underlying emotional baggage, so I was unable to help Joanne in that regard. Instead, I kept myself busy on the farm, with the kids, and at school. My wife was left to sort herself out.*

[3] *Every time we moved, I talked myself into believing it would be the last time. I remodelled and redecorated, broke my back in the garden, and planted trees that would take ten or more years to mature.*

[4] *We fell victim to a common scam. The police send for a tow truck that takes your vehicle to a rip-off garage, where you are overcharged for "repairs". Later, the police take their cut from what the mark pays the garage. Actually, in a police-supported racket like that, the mark is helpless. If he protests vehemently, he loses his vehicle, under the state's Mechanics Lien Act — all, of course, enforced "legally" by the cops themselves.*

[5] *Like a middle child, Joanne told me she had been considered "a nuisance since the day she was born". She had grown up second to her elder sister Marilyn in everything and I perceived that she felt resentful of her younger brother Ted. When Ted married and he and his wife Jean produced babies, Joanne's parents declared "At last we have grandchildren". Didn't they consider Heidi and Chris grandchildren?*

[6] *This habit paid off later when I needed to produce those very records in court.*

[7] *Jehovah's Witnesses have an exceedingly high suicide and divorce rate, much greater than society's norm. Their core problem lies with their own fanaticism. They spend huge amounts of time in proselytizing, more often than not at the expense of family, friends, careers, and even their own good health.*
I didn't know this at the time of course. I simply identified with his marital problems and apparent alienation in the school – which I experienced in common with him – and didn't think about any other problems he might have had.

[8] *Of the people of Mexico, eighty-nine percent identify themselves as Roman Catholic. In many areas, their Catholicism includes various combinations of indigenous practices.*
In recent years, Protestantism has grown more popular, particularly amongst Native Mexicans in rural areas. The Mormons and various evangelical sects have benefited the most. Protestant religions now account for three percent of Mexico's population.

[9] *In 1995, Darcy Henton, a Toronto Star reporter, and David McCann published a book entitled Boys Don't Cry. McCann told of abuse by the French DeLaSalle Brothers. Then, in 1995, charges were laid against eight English speaking brothers who had served at St. John's Training School in Uxbridge, Ontario. I had known some of those brothers.*
See **Henton**, Darcy and **McCann**, David; *Boys Don't Cry* (Toronto: McClelland & Stewart, Inc.; 1995)

[10] *Some people actually believe that imagination and fantasy are one and the same and that creativity is a deceptive ornament we don't need for earning a living. "Mens sana in corpore sano" is loosely translated to say "Clean minds clean bodies". Under this motto, sports are given priority over all else, "straight thinking" is promoted as far more intelligent than creativity, and the Arts are dropped with impunity from school curriculums.*

Chapter Twenty-Three
Thorns Among the Roses

I loved a Love once, fairest among women:
Closed are her doors on me, I must not see her-
All, all are gone, the old familiar faces.
– Charles Lamb, (1775 - 1834)[1]

On Wednesday, December 6th, 1989, Marc Lepine entered the University of Montréal's School of Engineering building and shot fourteen women. A year later, Thursday, December 6th, 1990, as I sat at the back of my class listening to student presentations, a young man entered the classroom dressed in army boots and fatigues and wearing a balaclava over his head. He pointed a black submachine gun and shouted, "I want the women!" Pandemonium broke out as he shot several girls sitting at the front of the class with water from his gun. Angry and shouting "stop!", I darted after him, amidst screams. Bright lights flashed before my eyes; my head swam as I chased the boy down the stairs and past the vice-principal.

The vice-principal called after me, stopped me, and ushered me into his office to "cool down".

"Who's looking after your class?"

I told him the best I could what had just happened.

"Why are you making such a fuss over a silly prank?"

"He had a gun."

"You were yelling in the hallway."

"I tried to stop him."

"You were disturbing classes."

The next morning, I went to school early enough to see the principal. But he was busy. When I did get to see him at the morning break, he told me to take it easy over the weekend and talk to him on Monday. On the Monday, nothing was done. The gun incident was not important. I was making a "big thing out of nothing". "Forget about it. These things just don't happen".

Nobody ever found out who the young "terrorist" was. My memory became a confused nightmare. The following weekend, I related the incident to my friend the Surrey principal. He advised me to report the episode, in writing, with a copy to the School Board and one to the Delta Police Department. But I was too frozen in fear to act. I'd allowed too much time to pass. Worse, I got to the point where I couldn't recall the date of the occurrence. Soon, the entire incident became a blur in my memory. And then I forgot it altogether until I remembered it, with horror, a few years later.

In the weeks and months to come, I became increasingly confused, until I could no longer identify my students. In October, l991, on the recommendation of my family doctor, I was given a battery of tests at the U.B.C. Hospital Alzheimer Clinic. A follow-up examination was scheduled for January, l992. The doctors found no specific organic cause for memory loss which was getting steadily worse. Noise was increasingly troublesome. A soft drink machine in the hall outside my door irritated me with its constant jangle. I had dizzy spells. Doors slamming made me jump. Tinnitus caused constant hissing. A hearing specialist prescribed hearing aids. In class, they amplified surrounding noise, causing further discomfort and confusion. Pranksters dropped books behind my back.

Keeping attendance records became almost impossible in one Communications class. Students exchanged seats so that seating plans were ineffective. One by one students disappeared until there were but a handful in class. I gave spot quizzes, hoping to use the results for my attendance register but signatures were often missing or illegible.

One lunch hour, I fell in a school hallway and broke my ankle. While students gathered around, I got up and hobbled into the staff lounge, then stubbornly returned to class for the afternoon sessions. After school, I visited my doctor, who sent me for x-rays. Sure enough, my ankle was broken. I returned to school the next day with crutches and wearing a cast.

On a Saturday in January or February, 1992, Joanne and I went shopping in Bellingham and ended the day with dinner and a movie, The Prince of Tides [This starred Nick Nolte as a trauma patient and Barbara Streisand as his psychiatrist.] At the point where Tom Wingo [the protagonist as a boy], his mother, and his twin sister Savannah are violently raped by three armed ex-convicts, I experienced such a vivid flashback I sank down in my seat. I did not see, thus I did not recall the remainder of the movie. I simply sat in shock and cried, audibly.

278

When the lights came on in the theatre, Joanne got up alone and walked to the lobby. I was the last to leave.

I controlled myself enough to begin the drive home. Joanne said nothing. So I said nothing. Just north of Bellingham, I could contain myself no longer. I pulled over to the shoulder of the highway and cried, uncontrollably.

"I was the boy in the movie." I whispered again, "I was the boy in the movie."

Without a word, Joanne got out of the car, walked around to my side, and motioned for me to shift over. Then she drove us home. Later that night, she told me to see a psychiatrist.

I slept alone on the downstairs couch.

The next day, Sunday, Joanne and the kids attended church and visited friends for the day. I remained at home. On Monday morning, I phoned in sick, called our family doctor, and asked for an emergency appointment. In turn, he arranged for me to see a Vancouver psychiatrist.

Joanne and I discussed the matter no further.[2]

In April, 1992, I started regular appointments with a psychiatrist. As in so many recovery scenarios, I had to feel the worst before I experienced anything better. I had nightmares of burning schools, bombings, snipers, and lost classes.[3]

On May 6th, 1992, I talked to one of the school counsellors about two students in a Communications 11 class who were being very disruptive. She suggested I talk to the vice-principal. In turn, he called in the principal who, instead of offering support, asked me if I'd considered retiring. I broke down. That was my last day at school. I didn't even retrieve my personal belongings; I couldn't return to class.

For a long time, I couldn't read. My mind was so overloaded, I'd read a passage and not remember what I'd read. I spent much time sitting in silence, watched little television, unable to listen to the radio, and only skimming the newspapers. Sometimes, I'd pick up a video only to realize, upon viewing it, that I already had seen the film weeks earlier.

For no apparent reason, I'd burst into tears and sob audibly.

In the end, I had to get Joanne to drive whenever we went anywhere. After church one Sunday morning, I blacked out and was disoriented when I came to. Panic attacks and blackouts increased. Joanne became more and more frustrated.

When the disability insurance company asked for a letter from my psychiatrist, he told me that the charge for such a letter was a little more than one hundred dollars. Joanne said I should no longer see that doctor. Furthermore, she didn't believe in Post Traumatic Stress Disorder. I paid the doctor.

Then, a boisterous family bought the house next door and erected a basketball hoop on the edge of their driveway, almost right under our living room and bedroom windows. Stray balls pounded against our wall and windows. Since our new neighbours refused to stop, Joanne insisted we go to the police.

Basketball is a popular sport. We had no business denying children the right to play, especially on their own property.

When the situation became unbearable, I stood on the neighbours' driveway and made an ass of myself, begging the kids and their mother to stop banging balls against our house. The father came out and threatened to have me reported to "his friend", the attorney-general. "They have places for people like you".

The battle escalated. Our front lamps were broken repeatedly. Eggs were thrown against our house. I found bits of copper piping poisoning our cedar bushes. Once, while Chris helped me remove a dead bush from our front hedge and replace it with another, the mother from next door came out and confronted him. She charged that he had threatened her with his spade. I knew this wasn't true. I had been pulling at the shrub at the same time Chris had dug the spade beneath its roots. Once again, the father came out. We picked up our tools and went into the house. Then, two police constables arrived to check on the "attempted assault". Next followed a series of police visits back and forth between the two houses. In the end, one of the constables told us we would have to keep the peace with our neighbours and allow the children to play without harassment.

Feeling under constant attack, I hid in the back study, listening to the drip, drip, drip of the kitchen faucet while I waited for the troubles to go away. No matter where I sought refuge, basketballs resounded – thump! thump! thump! The sound terrified me. An enemy pounded mercilessly at my walls. There was no escape.

It is said an Eastern monarch once charged his wise men to invent him a sentence to be ever in view, and which should be true and appropriate in all times and situations. They presented him the words: 'And this, too, shall pass away.' How much it expresses! How chastening in the hour of pride! How consoling in the depths of affliction! [4]

Clatter! Bing! Bang! Boom!
Spring pounds on city sidewalks
skateboards scrape
hot tires squeal
shouts and laughter echo off the buildings
basket balls bound on post and fence
and dribble past and back and 'round the old man
lost
in his past

Clatter! Bing! Bang! Boom!
battle screams in the night sky
engines roar
ack-acks pound
shouts and curses fearfully sound
big bombs whistle as the walls resound
shrapnel whines past his head

"Bloody kids!"

"Get a life, grandpa!"

Chris, the only one who appeared to understand me, hugged me when I broke down. Joanne grew increasingly frustrated and suggested one of us had to leave. Sometimes she stayed with her parents for the evening and left me alone in the house. The phone would ring, but when I answered, there was nobody there. Heidi and Chris spent more time with their friends. When Chris stayed out past curfew (ten or eleven o'clock), Joanne locked the door and our son had to spend the night at a neighbour's house.

I joined my wife for brisk evening walks but couldn't keep up. Joanne arrived home well ahead of me. Then the boy from next door would be standing in my way just before I reached home. "Hey, mother-fucker! I'm goin' to beat the shit out of you." His father stood at his front door, watching. While I ran into the house, father and son laughed loudly. Deeper, ever deeper, I slipped into the whirlpool. I couldn't claw my way out. My chest ached. I couldn't breathe.

I had frightening nightmares that the school was on fire. I couldn't find my classroom. Snipers in the hall were shooting at me. I dreamed of jungles and little men with sharp jagged teeth.

Between horrific nightmares and apparent and imagined threats, I sat day after day through the month of June, praying for peace, and waiting for my troubles to go away. Time dragged on.

One weekend in July, 1992, Joanne and I took a ferry and drove up the coast to Sechelt to visit a couple we had known since our days at St. Bernadette's in Surrey. Mike and Maureen had been on one of our Marriage Encounter Weekends and their boys baby-sat our two when they were little. Though Mike still worked in town, the couple had bought a new house on Porpoise Bay, just outside Sechelt,two hours beyond Vancouver, accessible only by ferry. They both told us how much they enjoyed the community, the nature walks and the fresh air. They showed us around Sechelt and as far as Tuwanek, a tiny fishing village, north of where they lived. I fell in love with the area and suggested to Joanne that Sechelt would be a wonderful area for our retirement.

After some thought, Joanne agreed to permit a realtor to show us around. When we viewed an old house on a hill in West Sechelt with a fantastic view of the ocean, I pictured a home I could renovate and paint, and a garden with endless possibilities. The house, occupied by an elderly couple in poor health, needed repair and and a paint job. I told Joanne I could spend some of the time I now spent lost at home, fixing up the house and property. "If nothing else, it would make an excellent investment for our retirement. We could rent out most of the house to cover the mortgage. And it would be fun to fix a small suite for us in the basement until we'd be ready to move in."

We drove around looking at other houses for sale – many in areas too remote for Joanne's liking. Then we returned to West Sechelt to make an offer.

The following day, Joanne's parents came back with us to Sechelt to see what we were buying. Her father was enthusiastic.

But her mother refused even to get out of the car. When Joanne's dad suggested looking around Sechelt for a place for them, too, her mother hissed, "Don't you even think it."

They never returned to the Sunshine Coast.

Joanne and Heidi had been taking singing lessons for a couple of years. I decided it would now be a good time for me to learn piano. But Joanne told me she needed to excel at something without me. "Furthermore," she said, "I want to open a bank account in my name alone. What if something happened to you? How would I manage?"

So I said "okay", and Joanne transferred the balance of our savings to a savings account in her name alone. From then on, we would live solely on my medical insurance payments. Her salary would be saved for our retirement when she reached sixty.

From September 1st, when we took possession, to October 31st, I decided to live in Sechelt while advertising the place as available for rent from November 1st. I packed my car with tools, a sleeping bag, a cooler, and plenty of food. And prepared to set to work.

I hardly knew where to start. Mice and larger rodents had taken up residence everywhere. The one-time garden ran amok with tall hay, poppies, lavender, thistles, dandelions, and tangled blackberry vines. The ditch contained pages from old newspapers, cigarette packages, Coca-Cola cans, and broken beer bottles. I had thought the place had potentiality, but ...

I walked up the rotting wooden steps of the rockery to the kitchen door. A pair of pigeons protested my intrusion. They fluttered uncomfortably, made small complaining sounds, and sat there on their perch above the door. A snail drew its albuminous trail across the dusty path. A silent line of ants climbed the one cement step to a crack at the base of the wall. I made a mental note to pour hot water along their trail, and to block their access to the house.

I walked to the gazebo at the top of the tumbling rockery. Wood bugs scuttled from rotting steps. Toward the ocean, a flock of starlings dive-bombed a crow above the arbutus. Everywhere, plants climbed. Roses grew wild – luscious pink, crispy white, silky yellow, and long-stemmed, hardy red – and other flowers rioted in profusion.

I almost stepped on something. Just a short time before hatching, a baby bird had plunged to its death, leaving scattered bits of shell, a shapeless smudge of feathers, and bluish-red flesh.

Beyond the ragged palm tree, I viewed the ocean, the islands, and the distant mountains of Vancouver Island. Suddenly, I felt new hope.

I took a deep breath and rolled up my sleeves.

Quickly, I cleaned the upper level, then set to work clearing drains, repairing the front deck, cleaning an old oven and refrigerator, and building a suite in the basement with a separate entrance from the laundry room. As soon as the house was rented, I knew I'd be able to spend weekends in Sechelt, gardening and painting the exterior of the house.

On the day my advertisement appeared in the local paper, a young mother-to-be contacted me. Her husband was a roofer. She told me they both intended to quit smoking and promised they'd keep their big shaggy dog outdoors at all times. (The ad stipulated: No smokers, No pets.) With a baby on the way, I believed her. The arrangement seemed perfect. I continued patching and painting the upstairs and preparing my basement suite so that they could move in November 1st.

It wasn't long before I started attending Holy Family Catholic Church in Sechelt. One day, a group of men were gathered by the church with paint brushes and ladders. They were painting the exterior of the church a pale blue with white trim. When one of the men asked who would climb up to paint the cross, I said I would. I climbed the long ladder onto the roof and then scaled another ladder to the spire.[5]

From the spire, I looked down – and discovered my fear of heights had gone. When the church painting was finished, I returned to the house in West Sechelt and painted all the white areas under the eaves that previously I had been unable to reach.

Once the renters moved in, I returned to South Surrey and visited Sechelt every two to three weeks to keep the winter garden under control and spend quiet time in my basement hideaway. On one of my visits, the lady upstairs complained of rats in the attic, so I climbed up with wire netting and a staple gun to block entry holes. I set a number of rat traps, baited with cheese and peanut butter. About a week later, I returned to the attic with a green garbage bag and collected dead rodents.

One weekend just before Christmas, Joanne came to see the improvements I had made and to inspect the basement suite. Mike and Maureen came over. Maureen saw a huge rat in our basement flat and screamed. While Joanne and Maureen stood on the far side of the lawn, I seized a shovel and killed it. I had to convince Joanne that the rat had run in from the outside because the door had been left open. Rodents indoors and snakes in the garden were sufficient reason to convince my wife that country living was not her cup of tea. Still, she did agree to come up with me once in a while, if only to see what I was doing with our investment. She didn't think she'd want to stay overnight. But over time, when no more incidents occurred, she changed her mind.

For the balance of the winter, we visited our new home the occasional weekend and met several neighbours, whom we invited to visit our tiny flat. When summer arrived, a second hand hide-a-bed, a small refrigerator, a two ring stove, and a microwave turned out to be sufficient to help furnish our summer place by the sea. Joanne and I renewed plans for eventual retirement. We picked a colour for the house's exterior, and I began painting. Already, I had chipped and repainted the white trim and was labouring hard to pull the grounds out of chaos.

During the week in South Surrey, I wrote poetry, cleaned house, and began to feel much happier, despite the noise from next door.

That summer, Heidi and Chris took restaurant jobs to help pay for college. Heidi would enter her second year at Douglas College. Chris won a first-year scholarship for Journalism School at Carleton University in Ottawa. I planned to spend more time during the week on the Sunshine Coast, and join Joanne and Heidi in South Surrey on weekends.

My first job outdoors, after a general cleanup, was to rebuild and enlarge a shattered rock garden. I cemented stone steps and walls, rebuilt a lawn, and cultivated berry bushes and fruit trees on the far side of the house. The ditch and banks were smothered in blackberry vines, which I cut and pulled until the entire property began to look civilized. The neighbours were delighted and brought me pies and soups.

Remembering my own homesickness as a child, I sent Chris fare to fly home for Christmas. Joanne was angry that I'd done so at a time when we had decided to be more frugal. Then she suggested we sell the big house and move into something smaller. I saw this as a possible escape from the problem of the next door neighbours. Enthusiastically, I put the house up for "sale by owner" and, despite constant vandalism from next door, managed to keep the place presentable.

While all this was going on, we looked at many smaller houses. I suggested we look for a condominium, where the two of us could live. Joanne agreed. I would spend part of my time in Sechelt, and we would alternate weekends between Sechelt and South Surrey. The arrangement seemed perfect to me.

After much searching, Joanne agreed to a brand new double-suite condominium being built in White Rock. After the sale of our South Surrey house, we would rent storage for the good furniture and take temporary lodging until the new condominium was ready. Naturally, the older furniture would serve our country home.

On June 11th, 1994, Joanne and I joined a friend for a symphony concert at the Orpheum in Vancouver. As we left the theatre, the great Vancouver hockey riot was in progress.

We made our way to our regular bus stop near Eaton's. No buses were running. Worse, the rioters approached closer and closer. I asked Joanne if we could please walk towards the Skytrain, but she saw no need. Meanwhile, I became increasingly agitated. Joanne and her friend moved away from me. Then, a bus did arrive, but I couldn't move. Joanne's friend got off the bus to help me. My wife felt so ashamed that she told me to sit by myself, "I don't want to know you."

* * * * * * * *

[1]   **Lamb**, Charles; "The Old Familiar Faces" in *The golden treasury of the best songs and lyrical poems in the English language*; Palgrave, Francis T., ed., [London: Macmillan, 1875] p. CCX

[2]   *This proved to be another defining moment. As soon as I spoke out loudly and passionately about my vampires, about my pain, about my emotional needs, my wife fled in fear. She grew cold, impersonal.*
      The trouble was, I had withdrawn too far to see the obvious, to realize that, once more, my loved one had abandoned me.
      My world fell apart.

[3]   *Memory of the school gun incident did not return until early January, 1995, shortly after I separated from Joanne.*

[4]   – **Lincoln**, Abraham; "Address to the Wisconsin State Agricultural Society Milwaukee, WI, September 30, 1859", in *The Morris Dictionary of Word and Phrase Origins* (New York: Harper Collins Publishers, 1988)

[5]   *I was always terrified of heights. I had the feeling that someone or something would push me over the edge.*

Chapter Twenty-Four
Broken Promises – Shattered Dreams

> When I promised you a rose garden
> I forgot to mention the thorns. Sorry.

While I stayed in Sechelt, Joanne's parents helped their daughter pack our belongings into boxes. She would sort photographs and albums later. Joanne said her dad would look after all accounts and that the bills I had kept in file folders would be better off in his care. I was no longer to worry about such things.

Joanne said the quiet of living alone in Sechelt would help me recover; furthermore, the temporary flat would be too small for two.

On moving day, a van took Joanne's furniture to a rental apartment. Chris and his friend helped me move the balance.[1]

I had given the tenants the customary thirty-day notice and returned their deposit with interest. We deposited my belongings in the basement. I needed to clean the upstairs and paint before moving in.

It took me a while to realize that the entire upstairs was damp, moldy, and smelled of dead skunk. With increasing trepidation, I saw the house would require a drastic overhaul.[2]

For those first few weeks, I sat in the basement at night and listened to the scurrying of rats in the walls. I heard rats in and around the furnace, which had been turned off for the summer, and in the space between the downstairs ceiling and the upper floor. I sat in silence, absolutely alone. Peace took some getting used to. Often, I tried to telephone Joanne. But she said she was busier than ever and had no time at all to see me. Or talk to me.

My wife informed me that she would spend Christmas with her parents and would not see me. Heidi came up to Sechelt for a visit. I drove her back for Christmas Eve, to be with her mother. On the way, I bought two large bouquets of flowers. When we arrived at the condominium, I asked Heidi to take in the flowers while I waited in the car. I hadn't seen Joanne for a long time – hell, I hadn't even seen the new condominium – so I prayed that my wife would invite me in. I waited and waited and waited, but Joanne didn't come out. Neither did Heidi. Of course, I should have, at least, dropped in with my daughter but lacked the courage.

I drove back to Sechelt, so lonely I cried all the way. Unable to get out on the ferry because I didn't want to bump into anyone on Christmas eve, I huddled in my car.

Christmas day, Chris joined me to cook dinner. But I couldn't eat. Patient and loving, my son spent several days with me. To help me get out of the house for a while, he drove with me to several points of interest further up coast. When he left for a skiing trip, before returning to school, I just sat, silent and lonely in my living room.

Before long, I got busy renovating the upstairs. I wanted to forget my loneliness. I removed heavy drapes and sent them to the Salvation Army, leaving only sheers, which I washed three times before they were ready to rehang. I pulled up shag carpet to discover part of the floor was damp and beginning to rot. One by one, I called in help where needed, to change plumbing and update wiring. I pulled out the old, cracked bathtub and completely redid the bathroom with a deeper tub and shower enclosure. The weather turned cold and the electric furnace burned out. I phoned a heating contractor and arranged for natural gas. With a new furnace and hot water tank, I installed a gas fireplace in the living room.

Gaining momentum, I hired a carpenter and together we pulled down and moved walls, enlarged the kitchen, and opened up the house to the bright southern view of the ocean. I covered the front of the living room fireplace with gyp roc. Joanne had not liked the brick facing; I was sure she'd approve.[3]

I built a large mantel and installed marble facing. Then I found matching material, in a composite, for the kitchen countertops, and, with the help of a plumber, replaced sink and piping.

With fresh paint, vertical venetian window coverings, carpeting, and paintings on the walls, I was finally ready to return outside and complete the rockery with a grotto, waterfall, and fish pond.

In the evenings I wrote:

DEER IN MY GARDEN

Down in the garden, on all fours,

I'm pulling weeds, a frequent chore
When summer sun is not too high.
Suddenly, I chance to spy
A pair of hoofs and legs, and then
Another two, the very same.

"Hello!" say I, "And what's your name?
Not Bambi, surely, standing, lunching,
Unperturbed 'midst roses, munching.

Slowly I rise, not to fright
A deer in my garden, what delight!
A sudden movement from behind;
I turn to face another friend,
Bambi's brother, standing tall.
My raspberries! "Don't eat them all."
And then, beneath the apple tree,
With antlers great, stands number three,
Chewing at leaves contentedly.
"If you kindly will stay right there,
I'll fetch my camera, so's to share
How privileged I am to stand
With Nature's creatures close at hand."

My next step was to have the house blessed by the parish priest. I invited several new friends from Holy Family Parish. One lady baked and decorated a cake.

A week after the house blessing, Joanne paid a brief visit. She was not happy with what I had done. The grotto had to go as well as the fish pond. The stone steps were too rough, and the statue of Mary did not belong in the garden. I had used granite gathered along the highway. Joanne preferred smooth beach rocks and commercial cement rounds.

While she stood by, I moved the statue into the house and took a pickaxe to the grotto, fish pond, and to the steps. I was angry. I did not destroy my work because I agreed with Joanne, or even because I wanted to please her. I didn't stop to think.

Never did I question, disagree, or even try to tell my side. So Joanne dished out more. She informed me she was not happy in the condominium. I must sign it over to her so she could sell it and buy a house.

That was her last visit for a long time.

What a fool I was! What a blind, submissive fool!

Shortly after Joanne went back to White Rock, I wrote to her that I thought I understood her reactions and pleaded to find a way to get us back together. I begged her to forgive me for the many hurts and suggested we sell the Sechelt house and the condo, and buy a house in Surrey for the two of us.

I received no answer. A few weeks later, Chris came up. He expressed shock and anger that I had destroyed so much of my work in the garden. Then he helped me to start rebuilding pond, grotto, and steps. [4]

When the second Christmas approached, I determined we should all be together, at least for Christmas dinner. Joanne agreed to have dinner at "her place".

I felt nervous as we parked in the guest parking lot. Chris carried in two bottles of wine. I carried our wrapped gifts for Heidi, Joanne, and her parents.

The apartment was stunning, very up-to-date. Joanne's parents were already there, as were Heidi and her boyfriend. Joanne received the wine and gifts without a word. Her mother said she was sorry they had "forgotten cards" for Chris and me. As dinner wasn't served for quite a while, we all sat uncomfortably, making polite conversation with the grandparents, while Joanne continued in the kitchen.

Following the traditional turkey, Joanne told us dessert would take a while, too, as it was not quite ready. Joanne's mother reminded us, "We should always wait awhile, to allow our first course to digest." I was worried about the time. Chris needed to return to Sechelt on the last ferry. I wanted to remain and try to find healing with Joanne, so I told Chris to take my car.

Since he would have to leave within the next few minutes, I asked if Chris could have dessert ahead of us. Joanne told Chris to be polite and wait, like everyone else. I suggested he take some plum pudding on a paper plate. Grandma replied, "Those who do not have the good manners to wait should go without!"

In the end, Chris left without plum pudding. Heidi and her friend left soon after. Joanne's parents remarked that children today have neither the respect nor the morals of the children of their day. I sat in silence.

Finally, the parents left. Joanne put a blanket on the couch. She told me the other bedroom was full of boxes and I couldn't use the shower in the second bathroom since she had no guest towels. The couch was too small for me to sleep on so I stretched out on the floor in front of the gas fireplace, fully dressed, and pulled the blanket over me. I lay there, listening to the faint sounds of music coming from a nearby apartment. Perry Como was crooning "Oh, there's no place like home for the holidays." Oh, sure! Eventually, I got up and undressed. Folding my clothes neatly beside me on the floor, I got into my pajamas and tried to sleep. I regretted not having left with Chris. Tomorrow, surely, I'll have a chance to talk one on one with Joanne.

Much, much later, I drifted off.

The following morning, I awoke to sad reality. I slipped into my clothes and folded the blanket. Joanne's parents arrived just before she got out of the shower. I helped my mother-in-law clean up the dinner dishes. Joanne came to the kitchen and made coffee and toast.

After breakfast, we all went for a walk. Joanne walked with her mom and dad, I followed, alone like a bedraggled puppy. Later, we ate cold turkey and went out in the evening to see the lights in the park. Again, I slept on the floor, this time with a small cushion in a pillowcase. The next morning, I walked to the bus and made my way back to Sechelt.[5]

After the holiday season, I arranged to give a benefit performance at the Raven's Cry Theatre, in Sechelt, ostensibly to help get the Management Society out of the red. An old friend, Dorla from Langley, and her two friends, formed the "Aldorio Trio". They agreed to come up from White Rock where they usually rehearsed and join me in a program of music and poetry. Dorla played the cello, Celia played violin, and Alicia played piano. I read poetry. The program combined excerpts from classical and old favourite musical compositions, with a variety of poetic readings, presented in the style of the Palm Court Trio. This style recalls the elegant hotels and restaurants of late 19th and early 20th century Europe, where such groups popularized the themes of classical music for the general public and where young poets often introduced their writings.

Two weeks before the concert, I wrote Joanne, with hopes she would attend. Then, with my wife in the audience, I aimed love poems directly at her.

> *I love thee with a love I seemed to lose with my lost saints,*
> *I love thee with the breath, smiles, tears, of all my life!*
> *and, If God choose,*
> *I shall but love thee better after death.*
> – Elizabeth Barrett Browning.

Joanne was unimpressed. Immediately after the concert, she informed me she wanted to sell the condominium as well as the house in Sechelt.

I replied, "We should be able to do that without much difficulty and find a really nice house together."

"Not with you, I won't."

"Where will I live?"

"I really don't give a damn. There must be an apartment you could rent in Sechelt."

"I can't do that!"

Well-wishers gathered around me, Joanne disappeared to catch her ferry. I stood there, heart pounding, devastated and embarrassed.

The next time I saw my wife was at the wedding of Tom's younger son, Nelson. As we had known the family for years, all of us were invited. During the service, the priest's homily stressed the indissolubility of marriage.

At the reception, Chris and I sat together. Heidi sat with Joanne at another table. When the music began to play, Heidi asked me for the first dance. I asked if she would mind if I asked her mother instead. Joanne accepted, stiffly and at arm's length.

She asked me, "Why do I never hear from Christopher?"

As I could not speak, she broke off the dance and walked away.

I stood alone on the dance floor. It seemed all eyes were on me.

I hurried outside and took a walk, away from the hall. Tommy and his wife Cathy, caught up to me, held me between them, and tried to comfort me. When they told me I had a right to happiness, I broke down in tears.

Again, I wrote to Joanne: October 9, 1996

Dearest Joanne:

You asked me at the wedding if I knew why you had not heard from Chris for such a long time. That question has been eating at me ever since. I knew that, eventually, I would have to write you about it on the off chance you really do not understand what has happened with our son.

I wish Chris would call you or go to visit you. But his hurt is too deep.

Chris and I never discuss these things, as he just refuses to talk about the relationship. I can only tell you what I have gathered from my own observations.

I believe Chris feels you have spurned his attempts to share himself with you. He wanted to share how excited he was about his journalism experiences, and he very much wanted you to look at and admire his photography portfolio. The pictures were laid out on the table. When you said "not now", or something to that effect, Chris felt slighted and put the material aside. Then you added insult to injury by telling him what a wonderful photographer someone else's son was. You ignored your own son's work.

Rejection is hard to bear, especially in close relationships. Believe it or not, your relationship could have been much closer. However, for quite some time, a battle royal has raged between the two of you, and I frequently felt stuck in the middle. Chris has cried out for you to love him. Remember, he always has been the home boy. He loves to cook. He loves pets and the things that are home. The situation at home before I left, was very volatile, and yes, I was ineffective as a father. Some of the situations were really petty. They got blown out of proportion. I don't think Chris was able to handle that.

Joanne, you too have suffered childhood emotional abuse, so you must understand the turmoil. Now that I've had time to stand back, I can see the picture more clearly. My greatest pain today is that I still love you. I yearn for us to be a family again, but I don't know if that will ever happen. So I shield myself by keeping busy.

Chris is doing well. His marks are A's and B's. He writes for the U.B.C. paper and even for <u>The Georgia Strait</u>. I believe it was our son's effort which cleaned up <u>The Ubyssey</u> and got it reestablished. Chris' skill as a photographer is also helping him to prepare for a future as a journalist.

If there is any way you could begin to reach out to Chris, to accept him as he is, without judgments, to even acknowledge that you have hurt him, though unintentionally, and that you do not want to lose him, then do so as soon as possible. It won't be easy. You cannot throw religion at him; he sees that as "self-righteous". When you reach out, hope and pray, too – that he will come back to you.

I hope you are doing well. I still love you and want you to know that. Your suggestion that I live alone in some small apartment in Sechelt scared the living daylights out of me. I have to hang onto something. I do not want to lose this house – it is all I have.

If you've read this far, bravo! And thanks. We should get together some time and talk quietly. I could come over to Surrey or Vancouver and meet you, if you like.

Love, Ben.

Joanne once urged me to join the Royal Canadian Legion. So finally I did. When the executive learned I could write, I was asked to publish a monthly newsletter. Before long, I wrote a weekly column for the local press. Each week I wrote about one of the Coast veterans or about an historical event of interest to the Legion.

Another activity that gave me satisfaction was acting and singing with the Sunshine Coast Music Society. I played parts in productions, including Tevye in <u>Fiddler on the Roof</u>. I also made time to sing with the Soundwaves Chorus and to participate with Nicki Weber's 69ers, an all-male chorus. A couple of times I acted as Master of Ceremonies for the Coast Music Festival.

Soon, I had many friends. Volunteers are always in demand. I entertained for "Over Eighties" teas and for the White Cane Society. One year, I wrote and directed four short folk tales for the White Cane Society. The visually impaired players enjoyed entertaining at luncheon, during the local Story Festival.

On another occasion, Chris took photos in the two high schools, on behalf of a Legion program I wrote for Remembrance Day, "Then and Now". As the production was televised, a copy of the tape was sent to Legion Headquarters in Ottawa.

One of the constant visitors to the Legion was Jimmy Paul, a Native Canadian veteran who had been wounded during World War Two. He had received no recognition from the Department of Veterans Affairs and no government pension. Like so many Native veterans, he lost his Native status. Jimmy wasn't bitter about that; in fact, he was an active volunteer at the Legion.

I wrote a feature story on his plight. A copy of my article was sent to the Senate Committee on Native Affairs in Ottawa. Some time later, Jimmy was given back his Native status and provided with a small house on the Sechelt Band Land. More than fifty years after he had lost part of his right hand in Germany, Jimmy Paul received a lump sum payment amounting to just five years of the pension that had been denied him so long. The following November

11th, Chris spent a day with Jimmy Paul and helped to produce a special edition of <u>The Ubyssey</u> on Veterans and Remembrance Day.

Years later, I wrote the following in remembrance:

to Jimmy Paul

they was callin' guys up
I'm as good as the rest
I'm a shíshálh
proud canadian too
ready to fight for king and country
red white and blue
my country
my nation
so I go
wear the tartan
and the rifle
and march to sicily in worn-out boots
in germany
this kraut shoots through
my hand and
my arm

still got three good fingers
still can shoot a rifle
and lift a pint
or two
or three
but
I can't lift a pint
when I ain't allowed in
then they kick me off the reserve
and say
you not status indian
an' people look at me and say
hey, jimmy paul, where the hell ya bin

hell of a lot they know
government kept my pension too
most of it
hell, yes, i love my country
do it all again
god damn ottawa
let me buy you a beer
this one's on me

Pat Carey, a member of the White Cane Society, asked me

to write a book for him. Pat, who had worked as a bush pilot in the Northwest, was one of aviation history's earliest pioneers. Many a day I sat at his kitchen table, jotting down stories and notes and drinking homemade rhubarb wine. We titled the book "Flying With White Eagle".

When I completed the final draft, I asked Pat's son, Robert, to read it and to identify a set of photographs. Since Robert was busy building a plane of his own, the book was put on hold.

Still, I wanted to see the story published while Pat was still alive and able to sign copies. To make matters even more urgent, The owner of Harbour Publishing expressed interest in the story. Unfortunately, Pat died on Thanksgiving Day that year. When I informed the publisher about this, he advised me to obtain a copyright from Ottawa and then bide my time.

The book never got published.

Not long after Pat's death, I telephoned Joanne and asked her if she would ever consider making a "Retrouvaille Weekend". This is a weekend based on Marriage Encounter, aimed at marriages in trouble. She replied, "With you? Never!"

A few days later, I received a letter from her, stating that she wanted a divorce and an annulment from the Church. Once more, my life became a whirl of chaos.

My friends on the Sunshine Coast urged me to see a lawyer in order to protect myself. I resisted this action for a long time. Maureen, the friend who first encouraged a move to Sechelt, advised me to see someone she knew, a lawyer who came to Sechelt two days each week. According to her, a financial settlement would resolve any arguments over money matters and clear the air for both of us. Reluctantly – I did not want a divorce or even a long term separation from Joanne – I went to see the lawyer.

The Sechelt lawyer told me I should pay my wife the money she would be awarded by the courts anyway, and save myself the expense of a dispute. The Sechelt home would have to be sold and the condominium. She said I had no choice in the matter. I would not win in court, I would be lucky to keep my pension. I was desperate.

Someone put me in touch with a lawyer in West Vancouver. Then, I rediscovered my old Quicken back-up disks and ran off the same records Joanne had presented. My records were more inclusive.

With my new lawyer's help, I discovered how easily I had been led around by the nose. I would not have to lose my home. With renewed hope, I added an art studio to the ground floor and bought a hot tub for the back deck.

By early Summer, Chris had won the National Student Journalist Award for his coverage of the Vancouver A.P.E.C. conference. He had also been accepted to complete the prestigious Masters' in Journalism program at Columbia University in New York. He attended Columbia and proved his worth, made the Dean's Honor Roll, and published his thesis in New York Magazine.

After graduation, he became a reporter for The Toronto Star. Before long, he received an invitation to join the staff at The Vancouver Sun.

Both Heidi and Chris had successfully embarked on their paths to happy careers and lives.

> *One who represents himself in court*
> *has a fool for a lawyer.*
> – Blackstone.

Divorce proceedings turned out to be lengthy and bitter. Joanne dismissed her first two lawyers and chose to represent herself. In the end, she won none of her demands. I not only retained my Sechelt home and my pension, I was awarded a fair portion of the family savings too. Joanne got her divorce.

Vindicated and relieved, I was free to live my life.

Months later, I received a letter from the Archdiocesan Marriage Tribunal granting Joanne a Church annulment. By Pauline Privilege, our marriage was declared invalid.

The Catholic Church does not recognize Civil Divorce.
The Pauline Privilege is based on I Cor. 7: 12-15. In canonical law, St. Paul's words have been expanded to apply to the marriage of two persons, one a practicing Christian, the other either a non-Christian or a Christian who fails to live up to the faith in some specified, essential way. If the unbelieving spouse abandons the believing partner – physically, emotionally, or spiritually – then, in a sense, the believing partner is deemed to have been abandoned in

the marriage. Thus he/she is free to remarry.

I had listed several members of the clergy as witnesses on my behalf, but no one informed me that clergy are not allowed to testify in annulment cases. It was only when I visited the Chancellery Office in Vancouver, a few days after being interviewed by my own pastor, that I met the Church advocate assigned "to act on my behalf". She had failed to contact me at all. I had been betrayed by my own church. And I felt angry.

Joanne received her annulment.

And – ironically – set me free.

* * * * * * * *

[1] *This was obviously intended to be a complete separation, yet, I seemed to be totally unaware of what was going on. I still loved my wife, and could see nothing wrong in her actions. If I did suspect anything, I obviously chose to overlook it.*

[2] *Once more, I'd allowed others to take advantage of me. The tenant was a burly man, so I trod gingerly. I'd had enough conflict in Surrey. His was to be a fresh start.*

[3] *Yes, I still was trying to please my wife. If I made everything beautiful, she would come back to me and love me. I continued a lifelong pattern.*

[4] *Poor Chris!! He had been forced into manhood way ahead of his time by having to support his wounded father, especially in the realms of firmness, decisiveness, and emotional maturity. Would growing up too quickly one day come back to haunt him? Pray God, no.*

But without his support in those rough times, would I have survived? Perhaps not.

[5] *Joanne's parents had denied me any chance to talk to my wife alone. Either this was prearranged with their daughter, or they wanted to make sure I remained out of her life as well as theirs.*

I was so crushed , not only by the apparent ending of the relationship, but also by Joanne's coldness. I was unable, in every instance, to stand up for myself or my children. I grovelled.

Chapter Twenty-Five
The Healing Process

That which hath been is now;
and that which is to be hath already been;
and God requireth that which is past.
– Ecclesiastes 3: 15.[1]

Did my life fall apart in some sort of defining moment? Or did it gradually disintegrate?

For certain, I mourned the loss of my teaching position. Teaching Theatre and Voice had kept me so involved that I didn't hear my demon voices. For certain, while I struggled with recalcitrant English students, I felt unappreciated for those creative forces of mine that previously had kept me afloat.

The gun incident didn't help me either. It triggered memories of the sudden violence of my childhood – especially of air raids and attacking male figures.

Worst of all, I awakened to the fact that my wife probably didn't love me. Whether she ever had or not was another matter I was not yet ready to deal with. We are so often in love with our own image and definition of our spouse. I was still in love with that dream.

Though I held on for a while, inexorably, inevitably my fingers slipped from the oily ring buoy. Inside, I felt I was going to drown in the icy waters of Lake St. Louis and the North Atlantic. Threatening fingers reached up to pull me down.

Throughout the years, while I struggled to be heroic, – as a sailor, missionary, monk, teacher, husband, and father, I had held my childhood nightmares tight to my chest. As Happy Ben, I had joked whenever the smallest unhappy thought or anxiety came my way. I had swung my jester's stick to beat the boogiemen down – until I could breathe again. I had laughed whenever it hurt too much to cry.

At last, my trapped demons had their way with me. No longer could I swallow them down or spit them out. They restricted my breathing. They kicked at my chest until my tears proved stronger than my laughter. They leaped onto my shaking hands to embarrass me before my wife, children, and before my friends.

Music gone, magic ended, comedy over, my pretenses lay

whimpering and trembling, impotent.

At long last, the hour had arrived to pay for my sins, to face the guilt and shame of my youth.

Memories flooded over me. I recalled Mother's crying, complaining words: "I have sacrificed the best years of my life for you children. And where has it got me?"

So I blamed myself for her unhappiness.

Only when I spun away from Mother's orbit did I begin painting, singing and acting with any degree of satisfaction. Even then, I lived to please a new "mother". In my wife's view, my paintings had no place on the walls of our home. My vocal efforts were "off key". My poems were okay, but "Not now!".

I longed for approval and applause, for unconditional love. I found such affirmation with my Hart Singers and with my Drama students. Yet I couldn't find affirmation from those who counted the most, my mother and my wife. It seemed, as far as they were concerned, I failed. No matter how hard I tried.

No longer could I contain my anger, resentment, grief, and feelings of worthlessness. When I lay down to sleep, they stirred around in my head and kept me awake.

It was the gun incident that tipped my tentative mental equilibrium. I could have laughed it off as a stupid prank; after all, no one else made any fuss about it. No parents stormed the school seeking redress. None of the girls in my class seemed upset. Only I detected sinister overtones.

To exacerbate matters, I acquired tinnitus. Louder, ever louder, noises screamed and hissed through my ears. Sounds of skateboards, basketballs, and slamming doors overwhelmed me. Noticing my hearing aids, pranksters dropped books behind my chair. When I jumped in alarm, they laughed.

I suffered dizzy spells. During one such spell, I fell in the school hallway and broke my ankle.

But the pivotal moment was yet to come when I viewed the film The Prince of Tides. Here, the darkest secrets of my life were being ripped into the open. I was not ready to face them. Anything but that!

I am sure that there are some wives, who after being told what I told Joanne, would not respond positively. I recognize this now. They would wonder why their husbands didn't tell them this sort of thing long, long before.

Especially for women, the sharing of secrets is synonymous with intimacy. One theory would be that Joanne thought I didn't love her and trust her enough to tell her my deepest feelings and experiences right at the beginning of my relationship with her. Her resentment about this would have been certain to distance her further from me. More truthfully, I look back and see that Joanne's ability to be supportive was limited by her own fears and insecurities.

In April, 1992, I started to attend regular appointments with a psychiatrist. I had bottled up so much for so long. Like an exploding volcano, I burst forth at every visit. Among many other topics, I talked about my nightmares of burning schools, snipers, and lost classes. Despite antidepressants, my panic attacks and blackouts steadily increased.

Then, there were the nightmares. Stated in present tense, here's a typical such dream. I'm standing in a steamy, muddy jungle before a rock wall. In the middle of the wall is an immense black iron door. Darkness billows out from behind the door. The room on the other side is filled with snakes and scorpions; I hear them hissing in alien tongues. Suddenly the door shrieks, as though in pain; as it slowly opens, a river of bubbling blood oozes out. From this, a large black bird flaps out, dripping blood, and flies menacingly towards me. I turn to run. But I'm slowed down by the mire.

I climb a slippery bank towards a row of twisted houses. I glance through their windows. Inside, I see ghostly fat men in long white robes. One of them is my Uncle Sigvard. After whispering to one another about me, they depart from their houses and advance against me, carrying spears and emitting horrible, half gurgling sounds. I leap into the air and try to fly above them. The effort feels like swimming in molasses. I'm caught in silvery webs, spun by huge, grey spiders. While I struggle, native drums beat in the air all about me.

In another nightmare, I'm lost in a large city. Aimlessly, day and night, I drive through streets choked with traffic. While cars and trucks and buses roar all about me, my car routinely strikes potholes; the experience never fails to be bone shattering. Alongside the streets, I see condominiums that look like barnacles and used car lots with loudspeakers. The loudspeakers call out, "Larry to line one." I also see shopping plazas, flashing neon signs, Macdonald's restaurants, KFC restaurants, screaming drunks, and squalling babies. The babies just sit there, on the side of the streets; their parents seem nowhere around.

Sechelt turned out, in the manner of Thoreau's <u>Walden</u>,[2] to be a closed, silent retreat – and the venue for my healing. Manual labour and the sorting out of memories and emotions dominated my waking hours. I ate sparingly, slept briefly. I heard no radio, watched no television, and read no newspapers.

Past, present, and future coalesced into ever-present Now.

A little black thing among the snow,
Crying "weep! weep!" in notes of woe!
"Where are thy father & mother? say?"
They are both gone up to the church to pray."
–William Blake, The Chimney-Sweeper

Western culture permits little silence. We are constantly bombarded by voices, music, traffic – noises that surround us even when we sleep. In losing silence, we lose the opportunity to face our inner selves, to find out who we really are. We float along in the general hubbub, afraid to be alone, happy to be "part of" something, yet unable to define what that "something" is.

Even with sound all about us, we seek distractions – television, movies, games, parties, recreational drugs of all sorts. We are afraid to face the silence, in which our spirits may commune with our minds and bodies. We are afraid to face ourselves.

At some level, I needed to hear God's voice in the silence. Only then, I knew, could I work through my inner turmoil and find peace – and healing.

I filled my days with prayer. But not prayer in words. No "Our Fathers". No "Hail Marys". My garden was my chapel. I looked around at God's beautiful nature. I saw Him in the flowers, in the many birds by my waterfall, in the deer that came freely into my garden.

My two pigeons are back again this year. They've moved to the top of the gazebo where they perch in the sun, no longer complaining when I approach. I guess they've decided to let me stay. The same flock of starlings still strafe the same crow above the arbutus.

..... Uncle Sigvard threw a party for some friends. My sister, Naomi and I slept in the same room. She was six. I was seven. We were supposed to be asleep, but I lay awake listening to the chatter.

When I got up to go to the bathroom, my uncle saw me and invited me in to meet his friends. Somebody handed me a drink. I was thirsty and drained the tall glass. Everyone laughed. My uncle picked me up and set me on the fireplace mantle. I sat there for a moment, happy to be the centre of attention. ....

A pair of barn swallows have built their nest of mud and straw beneath the highest eaves above my bedroom window. In graceful flight, they twist and turn in search of flies and wasps then swoop back to their home then out again. They're feeding nestlings bluebottles and horseflies. I'm so glad.

I hear the chirping from three hungry mouths as parents come and go from before dawn until well after sunset. What devotion to their young. I wonder if the parents ever rest.

So far the ground below the nest is clean but soon I'll need to quietly place a box of soil to catch the droppings as the baby birds back up and defecate over the edge of the nest. Last year I collected quite a pile of fertilizer before the second brood had fledged.

Other swallows have also nested nearby. Like neighbourhood watch, they appear to work together and look out for one another's young. One morning, I watched a flock of angry birds mob a neighbour's cat with aerial acrobatics to make an air ace envious. The attack sent the old hunter running for cover behind my patio flower pots. Oliver has learned in seasons past to stay well clear of swallows while they feed their babies.

Then my uncle directed me to lie flat on my stomach on the mantle. But I turned my face to the wall when he pulled down my pajama bottoms. Someone ran a hand over my bottom. Eyes shut tight, I froze up and wouldn't move. I couldn't move. Hands tried to turn me onto my back. I was cold and began to tremble. My uncle smacked my behind and lifted me to the floor. Everyone laughed.

I pulled up my pyjama bottoms and ran to my bed confused and embarrassed. Naomi cried. Uncle Sigvard came in. With my face to the wall, I heard him spanking Naomi. Then he came to me, pulled down the covers, thrashed me and muttered "Bloody nuisance". I cried quietly, rocking my head from side to side. I couldn't sleep. .....

Like children at recess, spring flowers and shrubs tumble about in laughing chaos from every nook and cranny. Reds and pinks, blues and yellows giggle in bunches. Beneath a stem of Bleeding Heart, purple crocuses caress the garden fern with water droplets, crisp, fresh, clean.   Here and there, the odd weed sneaks in and tries to masquerade as something sweet I'll dare not pull. Their roots are deep and they cry out to be left to live in peace. I feel their pain. I once was ugly and rejected but held on. With so much beauty all around, how can I cast them out? They too have tiny buds. I'll let them stay.

..... Much later, Uncle Sigvard came in and picked me up. He hugged me and kissed me. He smelled of gin and stale tobacco. My uncle carried me into his bed. He said he was sorry he had to spank me. I didn't understand. He didn't explain.

I was sad like thick grey cobwebs. Uncle Sigvard kissed me. He put his tongue in my mouth. Hugging me under my pajamas, he rubbed his hand between my legs and over my bottom. My eyes were closed but I heard him reaching under the bed. Vaseline! He put Vaseline into my bottom with his finger. The sensation wasn't foreign to me. Mother used to put pieces of soap in our behinds when we were constipated. ....

Striped prince of the underworld slithers past my shoe. Vivid stripes of almost blue blend with the leaning lavender. Poor creature so maligned. Surely, it was Eve who tempted you. I know you've snatched a goldfish now and then. You've surely earned the prize. You also swallow snails that eat my water plants. Pass in peace. Enjoy the evening shade. You'll not be banished from this garden of plenty.

... The next move was lightning!

305

Covering my mouth with his hand, Uncle Sigvard pushed his body against my backside. Burning! Pain as my anus tore. Pain in my stomach. Pain in my head. He groaned. I was exploding. I couldn't breathe. I grabbed frantically at his hand and arm. I bit his finger. He removed his hand from my mouth. I threw up all over the bed.

"Pig!" My uncle leaped out of bed and slapped me hard across the face.

My bag of bird seed feeds Stellar's jays, finches, Oregon juncos, rufous-sided towhees, starlings, chickadees, yellow warblers, crows, and red-winged blackbirds. They even feed racoons, squirrels, and various other rodents. I'll happily feed whoever comes.

I was on fire. My bottom burnt, my insides churned, my lip bled. I was going to die.

"What would your mother say if she knew what you've done all over my bed? Look at what you've done! You pig!"

I couldn't bear the thought. I stood beside the bed, shaking and crying.

"I should have thrown you out the first time you came crawling here."

Uncle Sigvard dressed and stormed out, slamming the door.

I wanted to leave, too. Maybe I could get lost and nobody would ever find me. .....

While the birds take turns at the bird feeder, and bees tease the rhododendrons, my cat Oliver and his feline friends frolic around the grotto rocks and roll in the catnip at the Virgin's feet. Now I gaze at the grotto – a work of love built from beautiful chunks of blue and green rock.

Between 1990 and 1998, sections of the Coast Highway from Halfmoon Bay to Pender Harbour were blasted from some of the most beautiful granite on Canada's west coast. Day after day, I drove that highway picking up treasures – rocks formed in the dawn of time then buried, pressed and pushed beneath mile thick ice and finally covered with moss, Douglas Fir and Arbutus. Western Sword Fern, Sorrel, Salmon Berry, Thimbleberry and Wood Rose with large fragrant pink flowers spread out beneath the trees. Then, that beautiful piece of coastline, home to deer and racoons and bald eagles and owls was stripped, blasted and broken so that commuters and tourists could speed to their destinations without

pausing to see the beauty by the roadside.   Here,
along that scar, were pieces of rock in all sizes, shapes and colours,
jagged gems in shades of blue, white, pale yellow, dark green, light
green. Here were boulders to be wrestled from the bottoms of
ditches, pried out, rocked out, rolled out end over end and lifted into
and out of the trunk of my poor old car.

All one spring, I hoisted and carried, rolled and pushed small
mountains and monuments into place. Pieces with clean cut edges I
positioned just so to contain fish ponds and steps. Jagged edges
were perfect for waterfalls, for the Virgin's grotto and for highlights
between rhododendron and azalea.

My back may never forgive me but my spirit rejoices in the
Creator's materials and in my own handiwork.

*..... I picked up the stinking sheets, wiped myself off, and
shoved them and my pajamas under my uncle's bed.*
*I went to the bathroom and tried to wash myself in the sink. I
couldn't get clean. I poured water into the bathtub and washed away
blood, semen and vomit. After I dried off, I crawled naked into the far
corner of my bed and curled up small. Rocking back and forth, I wept
silently. I didn't want anyone to hear me.*
*The stink of sour vomit and musty sweat caught in my throat.
My stomach churned. Shaking with chills and fever, I dashed to the
bathroom and puked green bile. ....*

Nature's dream catcher hangs suspended between
grapevine and garden shed. A rainbow shines through each
dewdrop – a million diamonds sparkling in the morning sun. Plump
spider vibrates her web as I draw near but pass with care.

Just below the garden shed, a colony of ants scurry back
and forth with eggs so big I'm reminded of the weight of the slab of
rock beneath which they've built their home. Just as I carried and
placed that hunk of granite near the top of my garden, so do these
ants carry enormous weights far greater distances and perhaps far
heavier in their perspective. Oh, how sorry and ashamed I am for
once having poured scalding water on their homes and on their
babies. Now I apologise in deep respect to these oldest residents of
our biologically diverse planet. I've read that ants have colonised
and mined almost every land mass on earth for almost sixty million
years and constitute 15 to 25% of the total animal biomass. Now I

stand in awe of this colossus.

.... I listened for sounds of my uncle. All was quiet. He must have gone out. My legs and arms felt like lead; my head was pounding.

After a while, I went back to bed. Sleep did not come. It never would come again; this I knew. Naomi stirred but stayed asleep. Through the window, the moon, eye of an avenging god, glared down upon me. He was not pleased.

I cried. For my dead father. For my terrible sins. I cried because I felt so dirty and miserable.

I wanted to die. .....

My garden contains the graves of one stray cat, a friend's small dog, several birds and a hamster. Three young friends, and I celebrated a beautiful funeral for Charlie, the hamster. I don't recall the cause of Charlie's demise but I do remember the ceremony when we laid him to rest with full honours in the little flower bed at the foot of the Virgin's grotto. The deceased was laid out in a handsome shoe box coffin suitably painted mahogany brown with my best acrylic paint and lined with Kleenex tissues. Following a homily of suitable words proclaimed by Jamie, closest to the deceased, three children sang *"All things bright and beautiful, all creatures great and small ..."*. I, the organist, played accompaniment on the harmonica. Either I or the choir was slightly off key but no one in the congregation seemed to mind. Following the interment and planting of a small head stone of plain description, we all retired to the vicarage (my patio) for chocolate chip cookies and lemonade.

..... What seemed like hours later, and after a very long air raid, Uncle Sigvard sat on my bed. "Well, if you can just try to be good," he whispered, "we won't need to say anything about this to anyone." Nodding, I agreed.

"We'll just keep this little secret between the two of us. You must promise."

"I promise", I whispered. Curled further into my little corner, I couldn't look at him. He would never look the same.

For hours, I rocked back and forth. I still couldn't sleep. .....

My cat spends most of the day sleeping. But then, he spends the long night hunting and carousing with other night hunters in the neighbourhood. Only occasionally do I hear his night songs although another tom sometimes comes to howl outside my bedroom window. Oliver doesn't howl, he's been neutred. Non-neutered and non-spayed younger cats howl. It's part of the mating ritual.

No need of mouse control in my garden. Oliver catches one or more each week to supplement his diet of pet store food. I'm glad he's such a good hunter when it comes to rodents. They burrow nests beneath the clematis and chew the roots. I'm not so happy when he catches birds. I've managed to rescue quite a few this year. Oliver forgives my interference. He knows I encourage his mousing skills.

..... The next day, Uncle Sigvard forgave me with a shilling. I went for a long walk by myself and cried as I walked. I couldn't spend the shilling. The money was dirty. If I were caught spending it, people would find out what I'd done. I didn't want to see anyone; I felt too ashamed. I hoped there would be an air raid, and I'd be killed.

That night Uncle Sigvard took me back to his bed. This time, despite the agony, I accepted in silence. This time I managed not to be sick. I closed my eyes tight and let him do what he wanted.

But the pain was ... unbearable.

"You'll soon learn to like it," he said. "It will feel good. I promise. You're my special boy now."....

Snails still draw albuminous trails across garden paths. Ants run conga lines near the kitchen door. I've asked them to stay outside and they obey. We made peace years ago. Wood bugs scuttle where wood bugs must scuttle. Roses, luscious pink, climb the kitchen wall. Wild flowers riot in profusion before the compost boxes which sprout new potatoes grown from last year's peelings. I'll harvest white and red gems before the fall turning onto this year's lawn clippings, kitchen peelings and coffee grinds. On the front bank by the driveway, my palm tree, no longer ragged, announces the sparkling bay.

.... He made me do other things I didn't like. But I didn't dare tell him, or I'd no longer be his special boy. Maybe he'd go out and find someone else, and Naomi and I would have to live with the homeless people in the London tubes. .....[3]

With cats, cleanliness is next to godliness. What better place to groom than perched atop the grotto in the noonday sun. There, paying little attention to the stone Virgin below, Oliver licks paw and fur, fur and paw, until his coat befits his perch.

Oliver is fastideous, but there are some cleaning tasks he can not perform himself. So I'm there from time to time to clip his claws and clean inside his ears. He loves to be brushed with a stiff cat brush at least once a week. I place the brushings neatly in a corner of the garden for birds and squirrels and surely mice to line their nests.

..... *When my uncle forced his penis into my mouth, I tried to keep my tongue from touching it. When I choked and cried, he got angry and spanked me until I felt a sticky mess shooting onto my stomach and chest.*

I felt dirty all the time. Even the money, going to films and the feeling of being special were accompanied by feelings of dread and loathing. Uncle Sigvard promised me such wonderful things. I would be in movies and ".... get to sail all over the world in a yacht as soon as this bloody war is over. But you must never tell a soul. If you tell anyone, you and I will both be put in prison, where they will do terrible things to us." .....

A bright orange monarch with black wing veins flits and settles on a yellow rose to drink and sun and then to flit again. He lands to share the space where my cat lies. Oliver looks up but does not pounce. He knows a butterfly will make him sick with milkweed toxin. Butterfly knows the orange cat and flutters in the sun.

..... *I never told anyone, not even Naomi. Every night I went to my bed in the same room with my sister. Much later, Uncle Sigvard would wake me up and carry me to his bed. Usually, in the morning, I'd wake up in my own bed.*

Meanwhile, my uncle treated me more and more to sweets and to the cinema. He let me light his cigarettes and have as many puffs as I liked. "This will always be our little secret." ....

My three deer spend whole afternoons beneath the Arbutus. No longer able to reach the raspberry canes, they're content to nibble grass along the bank and doze in the shade. They did chomp off all my tulips although they don't bother with the daffodils and I'm happy to see they don't eat my Western Sword Fern which look rather like the tops of palm trees in tight dark green bunches. I found those beautiful plants when collecting my rocks just past Halfmoon Bay. They require a daily watering and love the shade of the Arbutus.

.... Night after night, like a clam in a muddy river bed, I clasped my eyes shut and curled up as small as I could. I dreaded the night time awakenings, and the prodding, prying fingers and the sour breath. I hated my uncle's bed.

I never told my sister. As I grew more sullen and distant, she and I drifted apart. [4]

Before long, we were sent to another boarding school. .....

This year, the lilac bush has given me the best blooms ever with glorious perfumed purple flowers which I present in bunches with clippings of pink and white clematis when I go to entertain my friends at Evergreen and Totem Lodge. In fall, I'll do the same with hydrangea flowers which bloom in great blue bunches. They were growing wild among the evergreens when I moved in. They love the acid soil and dappled shade.

From my trellis, I snip pink roses for another elderly shut-in who mourns the loss of her husband after sixty-five years of marriage and beautiful gardens. Then I arrange treasures from my garden in ceramic pitchers and small blue glasses. At Christmas, my son makes wreaths from home-grown cedar and holly, and winds grapevine about them. I put lavender in paper bags and scatter it about the house. Not only does it smell wonderfully, it offers insurance against moths, year after year.

..... We were staying at "L'Ecole d'Hotèlerie" in St. Paul l'Hermite the summer before we moved to Strathmore. Naomi and I used to explore together. This time I was on my own. A man beckoned me to a small storage shed. I went to see. The man slammed the door shut, seized me, yanked down my pants, and threw me over a greasy table. He spat on his finger and rammed it up my rectum. Then he raped me. Just like Uncle Sigvard had done. .....

Even in fall and winter, this garden is beautiful, and I know death will be followed by nature's promise, a promise forever kept. The goldfish disappear among the pots at the bottom of their pond, They'll come back to life on the first warm days of spring and eat the mosquito larvae to keep my evening garden almost free of those pests. I'll not remove the dead lily pads until the spring but add a log or two to keep the top from freezing solid in the coldest weather. I'll also leave fallen leaves and many dead plants in my garden beds to protect fragile roots and dormant insects from the heaviest frosts of

January. In spring, after the snowdrops and crocuses have dropped their petals, I'll carefully rake the debris to expose new growth. Only then will I weed and dig over the vegetable patch in readiness for the few greens I love to harvest fresh for summer salads.

> ..... *The pain was the same. Though I tightened my body to the roughness, I didn't struggle or cry out. Old wounds ripped open.*
> *After the rapist ejaculated inside me, he slapped my face, twisted my arm until I thought he would break it, and growled something in French I didn't understand. I knew what he meant: My life depended on my silence.*
> *Then he left.*
> *I cried for a long time. I didn't dare leave. It was dark when I finally exited the shed. My whole body throbbed with pain. I felt sick. Too terrified to say anything, I ended up spending time in bed "from something I must have eaten". .....* [5]

Though I try to keep my herb garden contained, the plants run wild. Their roots crawl beneath stone barriers. They spread at will among the irises. They even find their way into the goldfish pond. The worst of these horticultural wanderers is mint. Oregano also gives me a run for my money. As does lavender. So, should these tasty herbs be classed as weeds just because they run at will? I too believe in freedom. Welcome friends. There'll be no harsh discrimination here.

> ..... *My nights were filled with nightmares of little men with slobbering lips and sharp, pointed teeth. Their breath smelled of sour milk. I flew, but never high enough; my pursuers grabbed my feet and pulled me down.*
> *I dreamed other, not-so-horrific dreams, too. In one, I sat naked on a toilet in the middle of a large room. I tried to hide but little men jumped out from hiding places and grabbed me. In another, I sat in my classroom and felt I had to pee. I left the room but couldn't find the toilet. Suddenly, I stood by the blackboard and started to pee. All the other boys pointed and laughed. Humiliation made me "wake up" and walk to the bathroom.*
> *Part way through, I realized I was still in bed, dreaming. .....*

On the high terrace, bamboo sprouts through patio rocks and beneath the greenhouse floor. And English ivy thrusts its way through greenhouse walls to smother shelves and cover windows. If I fail to remain ever vigilant, the jungle will obliterate all signs of civilization.

Maybe that's the way God intended things to be.

.....Sometimes I got up several times, only to find I was still in bed, having another dream. I wondered if I'd ever wake up, or if I would continue dreaming until I died.
Whenever I wet the bed, I lay there shivering, afraid to get up. Bogeymen waited in every dark corner, ready to do terrible, painful things to me. I dared not move. .....

One day I sat in the garden feeling sorry for myself. All about me the birds sang: "Pull yourself together. You can do anything you set your mind to."

I looked up and saw a squirrel jump from one high tree to another. He aimed for a limb so far out of reach that the leap looked like suicide. Though he missed, he landed safe and unconcerned on a branch several feet lower. Then he climbed to his goal.

If a squirrel can succeed in this way, I can, too,

In Sechelt, a number of supportive, listening friends helped me with my recovery. I shared my most recent woes with them and listened to theirs. Generally, we didn't try to solve one another's problems, but we felt better about ourselves.

I was invited to join a men's group. Five of us met once every two weeks in members' homes. Those who were married arranged for their wives to absent themselves; in this way, we obtained complete privacy to share our deepest concerns. The rule was that nothing said within the group would ever be repeated or discussed outside the group. We observed that rule faithfully. The chief thing the men's group taught me was that I was a good man. I continued with the group long after I ceased my visits to the psychiatrist.

After my divorce, I resolved to get off antidepressant medications. One day, I unwisely quit "cold turkey". Two days later, while I was visiting friends, I felt cold and clammy. My heart raced and my breathing got difficult. As soon as I lay down, my skin paled and my hands shook.

Naturally, my friends were concerned. When I told them I had taken myself off my medication, one of them gave me an antidepressant. Eventually, my symptoms subsided. I learned through this that it is advisable to discontinue meds. on ones own, but only with a physician's guidance.

Over the course of several weeks, with my doctor's approval, I decreased my dosage to one tablet a day and, later, to one every second day. Sometimes my panic attacks returned. At those times, I had to take an extra pill.

Eventually, I went off antidepressants entirely. My sleeping and appetite improved, I learned to prepare healthy meals, with fresh fruit and vegetables, and I grew less dependent on pastas and cans of stew.

Writing poetry, writing my memoirs, singing, acting, painting in oils, and receiving recognition from the community restored my self-esteem.

Before long, I covered my walls with my own paintings. I bought and refurbished a grand piano and began to take lessons. I got involved in the community. I wrote and produced a monthly bulletin for the Royal Canadian Legion. I wrote weekly articles for the local newspapers. I sang with choruses on the Sunshine Coast. I took part in musical theatre productions.

When I look back, a great many people contributed to my healing. There was my son, who called me almost daily and visited me often when he resided in Vancouver. It was he who convinced me to shout out my anger and frustration on the mountain top! Then there was the men's group and my many good friends on the Sunshine Coast.

Yet I have regrets concerning Chris. While just a teenager, he helped and supported me. Yet, when both he and Heidi needed me, I was busy trying to rescue myself. Since I couldn't support and defend Chris, our relationship evolved into a reversal of what's normal. Fathers are supposed to help their sons, not the other way around.

Here's an important question: Since I was abused, did I in turn become an abuser?

In a strictly literal sense, I didn't become one. Yet in a more subtle sense – my daily relationships with others – I cannot say no

314

to this. For an unbearably long time, like Coleridge's Ancient Mariner, I carried around my poorly concealed albatross of victimization, probably engendering guilt and anger in my intimates, and revulsion in others. In addition, after my abusers "slew" me, they hung the responsibility for their own actions upon me, their victim. Since I believed I somehow had caused everything that happened to me, I believed I deserved the guilt and shame I felt.

Clearly, both Joanne and I carried heavy loads, in some ways remarkably similar loads. Maybe that's part of the reason why, in the end, we could not get along with each other.

In time, I stopped blaming my ex-wife for the breakup of our marriage and recognized fully how I made life unbearable for her.

Who is there who can retain sanity while spending a long, long time in the company of a man who cries morning, noon and night, and who experiences difficulty defending himself and his loved ones? How Joanne managed to remain calm and keep the household going under such circumstances is a credit to her.

My recovery has turned out to be a roller coaster ride. Oftentimes, I'd announce to all and sundry that I was fully healed. Then another memory or incident would pop up to knock me down. This remedy for my overweening pride has frustrated me more often than I can count.

Here's an illustration. In the early fall of 1999, the CBC aired The Sheldon Kennedy Story. Kennedy played for the Boston Bruins of the National Hockey League. After undergoing much agony, he finally exposed his own childhood abuse at the hands of his junior league coach. During the part of the film when Kennedy's beautiful wife, Jana, loved and supported him, I descended into an abyss of sadness, self-pity and jealousy.

I didn't have Kennedy's kind of wife. This made me feel both sad and jealous. Why couldn't Joanne have given me the kind of support Jana had given her husband? Why was I always getting left out and picked on? Like an orphan, with no one to love and understand me, I had nobody to turn to.

I angrily resented my wife. She had abandoned me when I needed her the most.

I spent the majority of my years trying to please important people in my life. People pleasing also motivated me to try teaching in the southeastern United States and to seek heroic sanctity with the Christian Brothers. Then, when I married, I transferred this impulse to Joanne, my wife. Deep down, I thought of her as another mother, someone I had to please.

My mother was abandoned by her mother, just as her mother was abandoned before her. In Joanne, I found a woman who, I felt, would not abandon me. That she did so, sometimes I blame her, but sometimes I don't. Blame, like nearly every other emotion, is not an absolute; it is part of a continuum. Yet all continuums have two sides; they work in dualities and gestalts.

In the past, I assiduously maintained a pit of anger, self-pity and resentment concerning Joanne. I have since acquired the beginnings of some feelings of peace and tolerance. Out of this will flow eventually, if I keep working at it, a new gestalt and, with it, some clear perspective [a product of insight, married with the emotions, as well as healing experiences deriving from healthier relationships].

Infinitely more important, I may even realize forgiveness. That would be quite a gift. Complete forgiveness of self is difficult – as we think we as children could have done more to improve or protect our lives.

While I was a counsellor at boys' camps, we would sometimes sit around a campfire and write out the negative things in our lives on little slips of paper. Then we would throw our troubles into the fire. In doing this, we resolved to get rid of past hurts, to forgive, and to make new friends.

One day, thinking back on this, I tried to put my divorce with all its wrangling and bitterness behind me.

Time to get rid of old files, memories of past hurts, and the rubble and litter of the marriage feast. Time for fresh pages. I needed to make room for positive memories of those early marriage days.

I took down my boxes of documents, manuscripts and assorted junk. Out went old letters, bills paid, examination papers, notes and exercises from courses taken and taught, pamphlets and catalogues, empty cheque books, court documents and dusty folders.

Out went so many sad memories.

For one long evening, I fed the stove. My back ached from hours of bending over boxes and bags. The whole house glowed. The years gazed back at me and laughed.

At last, I had begun to jettison the pain of the past.

My recovery continues. One may never be totally healed, especially from childhood sexual abuse. But one can learn to live with the ghosts.

When I'm on my own, I still eat poorly. Many nights, I still don't sleep well.

But when it comes to facing my problems, I'm doing much better. In this, I will always need the support of patient, loving friends. As time goes on, I hope I can give to them as much as they give to me. In doing this, I'll worry less about myself.

Now that I have stopped living a lie, I have cleansed the poisons and have begun to leave the past behind. I have come to terms with the injustice and pain of my life. By feeling anger, re-experiencing the pain, and mourning the loss of what I might have become, I've been able to forgive myself.

Now I can accept who and what I am. I can experience God's love, and enjoy those positive people in the here and now.

Mother was my "gatekeeper". She ruled on her terms. My wife followed the same pattern.

I now can recognize and depart from my traditional pattern of seeking such personalities in my life.

Much more often nowadays, I feel my mother was just a fellow struggler, as I am, who did the best she could with the hand she got dealt. I deeply miss the opportunities we never truly had to really get to know each other.

The essential difference, I suppose, is that Mother died several years ago. So I've had a chance to acquire more perspective about her – which time helps to give a person. I've also had a chance to toss out my grab bag of angers, persecutions and resentments.

In truth, any reasonable person would view my ex-wife just as I now would have people view my mother: as a complex person with many, many grey areas, just a fellow struggler in the pain and travail of this earth.

Also, any reasonable person would say that I am not – cannot be – sinless and spotless where the breakdown of my marriage and the consequent pain suffered by my children are concerned. On the other hand, how could I have been in control when my abused system was too stressed to be understanding of others all the time.

When I first met Joanne, she was a gorgeous, near-celestial being, the object of my poetic impulses. She was my lover and my friend. Most importantly, she became the mother of my children. The problem is, I put her on a pedestal; I saw her unrealistically right from the get-go. Pedestals are difficult spots for women to stand upon for long. Most women want their mates to see and accept them as they are, warts and all. It is on the basis of such emotional honesty that they build up feelings of intimacy toward their loved ones.

* * * * * * * *

[1]   Ecclesiastes 3: 15, in *The Holy Bible* [King James Version]

[2]   see **Thoreau**, Henry David; *Thoreau: Walden and Other Writing*; Krutch, Joseph Wood, ed. (New York: Bantam Books, 1971)

[3]   *Underground stations had bunk beds, three high. Families undressed in public, played cards, chatted, sang, and yelled at their kids to stop chasing up and down the platforms while trains whistled in and out of tunnels. Mothers searched for missing children. Sometimes children, lost, homeless and unhappy, searched station to station for their mothers, grandparents, aunts, uncles.*

4   *I wonder if my sister knew or even suspected what was happening to me. She never said a word. And yet, in view of her close proximity to me, it seems probable that she heard, saw, or felt something or, at least, intuited that all was not right. In such an event, how could Naomi ever talk to me about it? Shame and guilt, after all, are not just felt by the abused. They are felt too, in the form of survivors' trauma, by those in relationship with the abused. Typically, such people grow silent and fearful or angry and resentful or a combination of both. In this way, they add to the victims' trauma. This I can say: Naomi's distancing from me only served to feed my increasing alienation.*

5   *The child who is not supported or protected learns to be isolated and unsupported. He doesn't learn boundaries or how to avoid danger or how to protect himself. In seeking approval, he leaves himself open to ridicule and attack. Those who were supposed to protect me, such as my Uncle Sigvard, abused me. My mother and stepfather had no time for me. Others did not wish to interfere .*

Chapter Twenty-Six

A New Song – May, 2002

> *I have had playmates, I have had companions,*
> *In my days of childhood, in my joyful schooldays-*
> *All, all are gone, the old familiar faces.*
> – Charles Lamb (1775-1834)

Here I am, at last, returning to Finchingfield!

In the past month, since arriving at London's Heathrow Airport, I did a lot of things. In Cornwall, I trudged the country roads between fishing villages. I joined the locals in song and brew. On occasion, I lost my way. And to revisit my Aunt Penny in Cadgwith Cove, I crossed stiles, dared the red-eyed bulls, and walked happily by babbling brooks.

In Dublin, high up on the coastal hills of Ireland, amongst palm trees and giant rhododendrons, I drank my Guinness and sat for tea with Irish cousins in their wee homes.

While hiking the Emerald Isle's coastal roads in sunshine and spring rain, I spent many a night in bed and breakfasts, all toasty warm near peat fires. And many an evening I sat or stood in out-of-the-way pubs, tapping my feet to fiddle and Irish drum and listening attentively to stories of Black and Tan and IRA intrigues.

In total, I hoisted more Guinness than I care to remember.

Now, on this sunny Sunday in mid-May, I walk the nearly two miles from Brook Farm, my bed and breakfast in Wethersfield, Essex, to Finchingfield – where my entire story began, close to seventy years ago.

While I stroll in fields bordered by wild flowers, I stop to contemplate sheep and long-horned cattle. I rejoice in the shrill songs of birds – nightingale, willow tit, bluebird, finch, skylark, and thrush. I haven't heard these since my childhood.

Strangely, maybe not so strangely, I even welcome the aroma of fresh manure!

I stop to relieve myself at the edge of a small wooded area then move on. By a stream, I sit and gaze at tadpoles. Everything brings back moments of a happy childhood. Here, it's so peaceful. Water rushes by in creeks and streams. The breeze blows in the trees and bushes. Disturbed by my presence, grey squirrels scurry away, scolding.

On a stream's surface, a dead bird swirls toward the sea. In reverie, my soul follows this bird to the mighty ocean. There all the pain and filth of my life will be washed away.

As I walk by thatched-roof cottages and ancient churches, my mind flashes back to those wonderful walks, when I rode horseback on my dad's shoulders. A lifetime ago. At last, the upper village of Finchingfield flashes into view. I have returned to an old world, comforting and safe, a world defined by centuries of slow motion. On my left, I read a plaque proclaiming "The Nurse's Cottage". Would she have been the nurse who came to Naomi and me and kept the little people away when we had the measles? Or would she have been the one who started the rumour about German spies? Either way, what a lovely wee cottage!

On this visit, I must take the time to talk to people and to ask questions. Lots of questions. This time I will have no one to hurry me on. I head straight to Willets Cottage where I gaze up at the gable windows. There, at one end, overlooking the common, I see the little window Naomi and I peered through when our mom and dad went out in the evenings to play tennis. Left alone with fairies and little people, how happy we were then.

Suddenly, I miss Naomi.

Throughout the years, we became strangers. If only I could have listened to her long, long ago, shared her pain, recalled the happy days of our early childhood, told her of my love for her.

I mourn this lost opportunity. I shall mourn it for the rest of my life.

Yet, I reminisce, though other things and people had changed – certainly, the war had changed us all – here was Willets Cottage, just like always. Suddenly I notice its roof for the first time. No, it is not thatched; by the looks of it, it never was. So much for birdies in the thatch. They must have nested under the eaves instead. How I teased my little sister about this!

> Beneath the thatch at early light,
> a nest of birdies used to scratch.
> To my delight, they caused some fright!
> My sister screamed with fear
> when I would say: "They're coming here".

I knock at the little door. No answer. Before long, a neighbour ambles over. Agreeably, she answers my questions.

"Ah, yes, there were tennis courts right over there. Removed years ago."

The little gate invites me. We stroll over to look at the back garden. How small everything appears! It was such a big back garden – when I was little. I remember the privy and its mixed smell of excrement and Dettol. Automatically, I hold my breath in disgust although the little shed is long gone with nary a trace. I can't help but reflect on our world today where one flush of the toilet, and it's all gone down into the sewage system.

After the neighbour leaves, I stroll up the little path to the windmill, now fully restored. Even though it's Sunday, the mill is open for visitors, courtesy of one of the many regional restoration societies. I ascend the tall steps and gaze a long time into the mill's interior. Here are the ghosts of villagers with their sacks of grain, of millers and farmers and farmers' children, some busy, some not so busy.

My thoughts flash about everywhere. Are these the shadows of those I knew when children talked with spirits, as though they were part of our every day? All is ancient and all is oh-so-sturdy. If I return tonight, will the children still be dancing with the little people?

From the top story, I peer down upon Willets Cottage. It looks so close I feel I can reach out and touch my past. Here are the fields, once wide open for boyhood ramblings, now crowded with tall hedges, scrub, and houses, houses, houses everywhere, in places where naught but grass and dreams once grew.

Where is the hill Naomi and I rolled down on afternoon picnics? I long to touch that part of my past that lived hermetically sealed, beyond tears. I walk away.

Soon I stand before the little lane that led to Duck End, nearly opposite Willets. I recall the bully who lived there. My memory shuts out his name. I speculate: I dared not remember it then; therefore, I cannot remember it now.

Could that boy now be the old man shaking his cane at the little barking dog? I want to think so. I feel the bully twisting my arm behind my back. "Swear to Jesus ..." I wouldn't swear. I wouldn't swear.

The crack of a breaking twig brings me back to the present. For a moment, I don't know where I am. Then I remember. This place is where I once played. The grove of trees was populated with imaginary tribes. I was Robinson Crusoe. I made a den with a secret entrance that only I could find and crawl through.

Tears come to my eyes.

A tap on my shoulder brings me back to the present. Unhappily, I see only a tangled mass of thorn bushes and brambles.

"Are you all right?"

"Thank you, I'm fine. Just reminiscing."

I smile at the young lady. Such a gentle face!

After what seems a few moments – but really an hour or more – I walk over to the village. The pump? Where is it? It's no longer there. I inquire. An old-timer tells me, "Yes, there were pumps. Two of them. Gone now." I feel cheated, robbed of another tangible. I remember my dad walking home with two three-gallon cans, one for us and one for the old lady across.

I stroll past the butcher shop – once the village workhouse, now a private home – and over the foot bridge, past the post office, and toward Swan House, the place of mixed memories, the place I wanted to explore when my father refused to go farther. There it is! Looking just as I remembered it; even the garage is unchanged. There, under the leaning roof, old Bessie, the family car, sits on blocks. I blink. No. Old Bessie has vanished, a mirage generated by my overheated brain.

I pluck up my courage and ring the doorbell. "Hello. My name is Ben Nuttall-Smith. I'm visiting from Vancouver, Canada. I lived in this house more than sixty years ago." My last words fade off in a wave of emotion and my voice catches.

Michael and Lynn Bethell prove to be delightful. Yet I wonder. How can people so young live in this house? And the house ... It looks even younger than they, recently renovated, in fact.

The back garden has diminished in size. It is much smaller than the field where Nellie and Joyce once grazed. The apple tree has moved to the same magical memory realm as the barn – the one that, decades ago, was destroyed by an incendiary bomb.

For a moment, I see the flash of bursting bombs above my head. I hear the strange, humming, whining sound, like a swarm of bees.

I shake myself back to the present.

My only reminder of years gone by turns out to be the horse equipment hanging on the garage wall, lonely and tattered. All of a sudden, I feel lonely and tattered too. I sense an unlucky ... what? Omen? It was here, certainly, that my world began to change so drastically.

I philosophize a little. If I had known what lay ahead, would I have been able to go on? Probably not. For this reason, it may be God's special gift that most of us cannot see into our own futures. If we could, the results could be devastating; in fact, most of us likely would go stark, raving mad.

I ask to see the little cellar window, the one that plagued so many of my nightmares. I look around the back and side walls. And see no window. Am I mistaken? Is this the right house? Then Lynn Bethel shows me, partly covered in the sun room, the old cellar window.

Finally, I see it clearly.

It seems so ordinary. So unthreatening. So incapable of admitting a host of demonic creatures.

A tidal wave of relief drowns my momentary panic. All the vampires, with their razor-sharp teeth, disappear in the cataclysm. They will invade my sleeping hours, to suck my blood in endless nightmares, no more.

It doesn't take long to see all I need to see. I thank my hosts and carry on, instinctively, towards the anti-aircraft placement up on the hill.

I walk up a minor incline along lanes between country houses. Though I think I know where my destination must be, I turn out to be wrong. Eventually, when I give up trusting my own memory, I encounter a middle-aged lady out in her back garden, with apron and gloves, cutting stalks of rhubarb.

"You must mean the wartime machine gun post, which used to be in Wincey Chase. Just a moment. I'll fetch my husband. Maybe he can help you."

A very pleasant chap, Ron Hawkins reminds me of a retired military officer, just like the people one sees in country gardening magazines. He welcomes me into his garden and introduces himself as president of the Finchingfield Heritage Society.

Together, we set out on a short walk. "There, where that small mound is. That's where the gun sat. It only got removed a short while ago. It's being restored."

All that remains is a small, grassy mound. To ease my disappointment, Betty Hawkins invites me in for a slice of fresh rhubarb pie and coffee.

Indeed, Ron remembers "The Witch of Finchingfield". He even remembers the kindly old lady who lived opposite Willets Cottage. He tells me that, after Miss. Timms' fiancé was killed in the Great War, she found no one to replace him. So she remained a spinster until her death. When she got old, the children made up stories about her as "the witch".

When I mention the German parachutists, Ron Hawkins offers the most significant information. "Ah, yes. One landed on the war memorial, and the second got tangled in a tree in a farmer's field. The third came down some distance away. He was frog-marched into the village at the end of a pitchfork. The local first aid people looked after them all until the Home Guard took them away."

Excitedly, I tell Ron of my mother's involvement as a first aid person and translator. I also tell him that my sister and I met the German pilot who spoke fluent English, that my mother spoke to him in German, and that, as a result, our maid refused to join us for tea.[1]

I soon form the opinion that everyone knows everyone else in Finchingfield. Furthermore, the people have a keen interest in British history, especially in Finchingfield's role in it. Ron, for example, had researched much of what went on during World War Two. One of his stories, about the very raid I remembered, already had been published in the village newsletter.

After coffee, Ron drives me three quarters of a mile to look at Spains Hall, an Elizabethan manor house where, if memory serves, my father played cricket. Its owner during those days was Sir Archibald Ruggles-Brise, a Member of Parliament. Its gardens had been beautiful, its trees tall and shady. In fact, the Manor of Spains Hall had been mentioned in the "Domesday Survey".[2]

Sadly, on this visit, I only get to see the Manor from a distance. Therefore, I must continue relying on vague memories of events past.

After saying farewell to Ron and Betty, I visit the Guildhall, built in the late 15th Century. Here I'm shown a commemoration embroidery of the German parachutes coming down from the sky, following England's first air raid. I feel a sense of history now – I'm truly a part of it. Yet I feel a little, niggling ... something. Where, on that illustration, is the little boy climbing down from his apple tree?

On my way back down the hill, I rediscover Mrs. Turner's greengrocer shop – now a craft shop, closed on Sundays. I stroll through the yard of the Church of St. John the Baptist, with its large Norman tower. The building was constructed mainly in the 14th Century. Like so many Christian churches in England nowadays, it is locked shut. I would have loved to explore its interior. Still, I'm not all that disappointed; I never dared venture inside as a child. So no memories are present, urging me on.

The sun is warm as I search amongst the gravestones – many indecipherable – and lean for a while against a chest-high tomb dedicated to the memory of someone who died in 1742. A tomb nearby features a skull and crossbones and anchor. I wonder if this old sailor could have been a pirate?

In a quiet spot beneath the trees, I contemplate a stanza from Thomas Gray's <u>Elegy Written In a Country Church Yard</u>:

Perhaps in this neglected spot is laid
Some heart once pregnant with celestial fire;
Hands that the rod of empire might have swayed,
Or waked to ecstasy the living lyre.

There's still more to see. I walk back down to the pond, across the road bridge and past "The Fox" – now undergoing flood repairs – to the United Reformed Church, built in 1799. Next door is the old schoolroom, presently owned by an architect and remodeled as a private house.

Was it here that Naomi and I went to school for a while? I can't recall! So many memories flood my mind. I only remember a big room, divided by a windowed partition, and classes taught by two matrons. Was it from here that I got sent home in disgrace having

326

dared to add a penis to the horse I had been commissioned to draw?

Yes, here's the school yard. But it was so, so long ago. My cloudy memories easily could be wrong. How I want to connect. Here is my past; here were my happy days. If only I could step back in time! But could I undo the pain and just keep the happiness? If I could perform such a miracle, who would I have become? And would I like this person any better than I like myself as I am now? Who knows? Is pain God's way of moulding us into better, more loving people? If so, why would I wish to avoid it?

Up beyond the church on the hill, I see another old school. Is this the one I attended? If only my father had come with me to answer my questions, twenty years earlier. For the fact that I can never know the whole story, I feel angry and disappointed. On the green, I stop at the War Memorial. Twenty-seven men from the village – I count them – perished in the Great War. Six in World War Two. Many of their descendants still live in the village.

Down by the village pond, I stand on the footbridge and gaze at the River Pant, now a mere trickle. The river had flooded the previous year and caused considerable damage to houses and shops.

I remember this very spot from so many years before.

'Neath the bridge in Finchingfield,
in the waters of that river,
dwelt a fish of huge proportion.
I have seen him finning there.

When as yet a barefoot angler,
bobbed my line beneath the shadow.
felt a tug, then flashed the monster
from the deep and snapped my line.
Hook and cork were gone forever.
still, I must not tell a lie:
even though he's surely hiding
still the greatest anywhere.

Four weeks after my visit with him and his wife, Ron Hawkins reaches me by e-mail.

Dear Ben,
After asking around the village, I found two people who remember you: your sister and your mother. Firstly, Flo Hardy. She

helped your mother in the First Aid Centre. She remembers her as a fine, upright woman with blonde hair down to her shoulders. Flo remembers the name of your dog; not only that, she recalls Paul Robeson walking around the village. Her husband remembers your old Morris car.

The second woman who vividly remembers you and your family is Floss Halls, who used to 'do' for your mother sixty-four years ago. I met her in the post office the other day. After saying, "Of course I remember the Nuttall-Smiths", she immediately recalled your name, Bendt, as well as your sister's name. She, too, remembers your dog, a springer spaniel named Buller.

In April, 2000, I wrote a story for 'The Villager', which I called "The Germans Have Landed". It was based upon reminiscences, told to me by Chris and Flo Hardy, about a 'dogfight' (aerial combat between two aircraft) that resulted in a German Dornier bomber of the No. 7 Staffel Bomber Group getting shot down by a pilot of the Royal Canadian Air Force. As a result, four German airmen had to parachute into Finchingfield.

Unfortunately, following the encounter, the Canadian lost his life when his aircraft crash-landed in Little Hydes, Little Bardfield. Much of my data about the RCAF pilot [Flying Officer Robert Leonard Edwards of No. 1 Squadron] has been taken from official RAF records. Edwards arrived in England on June 20th, 1940. His craft was a Hurricane Mark 1 [serial number P3874]. His body is buried at Brookwood Military Cemetery.

One of the German parachutists injured himself, ironically, on the War Memorial itself! Alice Nuttall-Smith, Cecilia Ruggles-Brice, and the Rev. Paul Walde, who all possessed language skills, interviewed the four Germans, firstly in Swan House, then later in the first aid centre. The first aid centre, located in Spring Mead, is now the home of Pam and Michael Shaw.

On Friday the 31st, I spoke to Mrs. Kemp. She remembers the "witch woman". Her name was Miss. Timms, a lady bent double with advanced age. Mrs. Kemp also remembers you. She also recalls your sister, who occasionally visited her home to play with her daughter.

I called upon Rhoda Cornell [née Hardy], who lives in one of the cottages opposite Willets. She told me that Mrs. Timms was one of three sisters. Another was Rhoda's grandmother. During the early part of the 1900's, all the sisters moved to Canada. When Rhoda's grandmother died, her grandfather, and Mrs. Timms moved back to Finchingfield, leaving the other sister in Canada.

Rhoda remembers Mrs. Timms as having an abrupt and abrasive manner. Could this be why the children thought her to be a witch? Mrs. Timms died in early 1942.

Rhoda also remembers that your mother gave Mrs. Timms "some small wooden figures".

About two years ago, I interviewed Rhoda about her life, etc. At that time she mentioned "a foreign lady who lived on the causeway and gave some figures to Mrs. Timms". I know now that we were talking about your mother.

The more I speak to older residents of Finchingfield, the more I'm surprised concerning how many remember your family. In fact, I only have to mention 'Nuttall-Smith', and they remember both yours and your sister's names.
– Ron Hawkins, Finchingfield Heritage

* * * * * * * *

[1]   *Ron assures me that he had already confirmed all this with the villagers, who still remember us from long, long ago.*

[2]   *The "Domesday Survey" was ordered by William the Conqueror approximately twenty years after the Norman invasion. The purpose of the survey was to find out who owned what and the value of each holding for tax purposes. It was called the "Domesday Book" by the landowners because it was the final authoritative register of rightful possession. Its judgment was as final as that of "Domesday", or Doomsday.*

Epilogue

"You cannot prevent the birds of sorrow
from flying over your head,
but you can prevent them
from building nests in your hair."
– Chinese proverb [apocryphal]

While I carried emotions from my past, I hid them like soiled underwear, all tucked away. I went through much of my life in fear that the shame of my youth would be found out. I repressed traumatic memories until they resurfaced, to cause depression, chronic fatigue, and even thoughts of suicide. I sought means of not remembering in all manner of distraction.

As a child, I often lived an imaginary life to escape the trauma of my abuse. Fantasy was more comfortable for me than reality. Fortunately, as an adult, I managed to escape two of the most common consequences of a dysfunctional childhood: alcoholism and drug addiction. But I did not escape workaholism, an even more common consequence.

In seeking emotional ways to escape the lack of love I felt as a child, I used avoidance and denial. In codependent relationships, I confused suffering with love. In my mind, love became associated with pain, even punishment. I still remember the terror of facing my abuser – who happened to be the same person I wanted so desperately to please and gain approval from.

Sigmund Freud describes what he calls "the repetition compulsion", where people repeat the patterns of their parents and the torments of their past. For example, children raised by depressed parents will be more likely to grow up depressed unless, that is, they have healthy outside influences and activities which distract them and bring them much-needed fulfillment and self-esteem.

It is so easy to be a victim, to wallow in self-pity, to decline to face reality, and to become adaptive and compliant. It is so much harder for the victim to face reality; this, after all, involves facing down one's victimizer. One has to become assertive about one's legal and moral rights. Such assertiveness is not to be confused with selfish aggressiveness.

Here I speak about the difficult work of defiance and rebellion.

Camus discusses this concept best. In his seminal work, <u>The Rebel</u>,[1] he states that the true rebel lives under strict imperatives, to see events clearly, to differentiate between what is truly right and what is truly wrong according to long-standing moral and ethical principles, and to struggle, no matter the odds, for what is truly right – and, if necessary, to sacrifice himself. The rebel, then, may be the bravest of all people. He may operate in as large a context as the world and as small a context as the family. According to Camus [a quasi-atheist], Jesus was a rebel.

Cycles, once recognized and understood – awareness is the key to it all – can be broken. Though raised in an atmosphere of shame, hostility and intimidation, I have faced, dealt with, and even forgiven my tormentors. I feel no need to continue submitting to those who attempt to victimize me, in order, selfishly, to release their own inner demons.

I have been able, with professional help, to make peace with my past. In humility, with God's help, I face it now. I can survive and thrive!

In January, 2003, I sold my home in Sechelt, got rid of most of my belongings, sold or gave away most of my paintings, and bought a condominium in Vancouver.

Then I met my new love, and my life started over. Together, we attend concerts and symphonies, plays, art galleries and museums. Together, we travel and enjoy our golden years. She is an accomplished artist. With her encouragement, I continue to paint, better than ever before. We are very open with and respectful of each other.

Most important of all, I have learned to forgive my mother and my ex-wife as I have had to forgive myself. In forgiving, I have found true love – healthy love!

My life has come full circle.

Finchingfield, where my memories began almost seventy years ago, sits in the same peaceful part of England, grown up-to-date yet essentially unchanged. Here the older people live on with their memories, and all are connected.

In Finchingfield, I rediscover and confirm the love of a father, the love which has sustained me through a lifetime. In rediscovering this love, I rediscover my stolen identity.[2]

In Finchingfield, the name Nuttall-Smith is remembered with fondness. This is the source and confirmation of my art. Here, in my childhood, I know the love and joy of music. Here is beauty and spirit, regeneration and connectedness. All the things I tried to pass on to Heidi and Chris.

Here also is sadness revisited, and anger, rage even. How could a mother deliberately keep a son away from his father? How could she even tell her son that his father is dead? Yet now I know the answer: Mother had her own way to deal with her difficult life.

How did I – better: how do I, despite the many years – survive the abuse I suffered? In a different context, Sir Winston Churchill said it best:

"If you are going through hell, keep going."

To the many victims, afraid to speak up because they still fear that someone might accuse them of the same unspeakable crime, I offer only this: Eventually, one has to speak up. Or else forever suffer unspeakable shame. In revelation is redemption.

I'd like to say my shame is gone. But, I still must remind myself that I am clean, whole and innocent. I always will have to remind myself of this. Old habits die hard.

When I was a child, I lost my sense of innocence and beauty. This resulted from the actions of my uncle, and the man in Saint Paul l'Hermite [who pushed me into a shed and raped me], and myriad other bullies.

I washed and washed; yet I couldn't rid myself of the filth I felt inside. Dirtiness is lost beauty. Loss of an inner sense of goodness and purity [self-esteem] is lost innocence.

My love of children represents, at least partially, my need to regain my own beauty and innocence, vicariously.

My scrupulous, lifelong desire for cleanliness, especially in the bathroom and kitchen, is a continuation of my need to regain externally that which I've lost internally – my inner beauty.

In this wondrous world of ours, flowers and birds and beasts love easily and naturally. And they teach me to do the same. Thus, my love of nature and animals.

I'm healed of the sickness that plagued me – the anger, the shame, the bitterness, the pain. ...

On a beautiful Sunday evening, (only weeks before sending this manuscript for publication), my dearest friend and I were enjoying the nostalgia of some long-play recordings. One was of themes and commercial jingles from radio programs of the 1940's which I recalled so vividly from my first years in Canada and which took my friend back to her happy days with her parents and grandmother. The second recording was titled *George Formby Souvenir*. [3] My friend hummed happily along.

Without warning, I grew painfully uncomfortable and felt increasingly agitated until I wanted to scream "Shut up! Shut the f... up!" George Formby's high-pitched voice irritated me beyond belief. My friend's happy humming made me angry. My reaction embarrassed me. I could see no reason for it. Fortunately, she noticed my discomfort and turned the music off.

We sat silently reading but I was unable to concentrate. My chest grew heavy, my breathing laboured. I closed my book. She reached for my hand, and the tears began to trickle down my face.

Only then did I remember. George Formby movies had been my reward for "being good". My Uncle Siegvard took me to see the singer with the ukulele to help ensure my silence in those darkest days of my life. Now, I was feeling the anger and the unspeakable revulsion that I had been unable to express for most of my life.

Fortunately, I was now with a person who not only understood, but also was not fearful or distancing. Instead, she was able to support me in that moment. She reaffirmed my goodness and I recovered quickly.

One may never be totally healed, especially from childhood sexual abuse. But one can learn to live with the ghosts.

* * * * * * *

[1]   see **Camus**, Albert, 1913-1960, *The rebel : an essay on man in revolt* / Albert Camus; with a foreword by Sir Herbert Read; a revised and complete translation of L'homme Révolté by Anthony Bower. (New York: Alfred A. Knopf, 1967).

[2]   *A man's identity is passed on through his father. It's fair to say that the best of a man – and the worst – is deeded him by his father. If a man doesn't find his father, deep within himself, he will flounder through life, unmotivated in any true sense – and directionless*

[3]   *George Formby Souvenir*, Ace of Clubs, London ACL 7906

Lord, thank you for the many gifts You have giv'n to me.
Thank you for what you have chosen to take away.
Lord, thank you for what you have permitted me to keep.
– Thomas More

Life is a dream, a confusion of memories.
Sorting out the bits of truth can be like sorting through a garbage dump, looking for small treasures here and there.

The human spirit is strong. One can survive.
I am a survivor. I not only survived, I conquered. I'm a free man! But the battle continues.

– Ben Nuttall-Smith, March, 2007

334

Also from Trafford Publishing

WORD PAINTING

**Fifty pages of poems and vignettes
by the same author**

The chameleon illustration by Ben Nuttall-Smith
is purely imaginary and not intended to represent
a particular species.

Printed in the United States
123936LV00007B/16/A

9 781412 068628